Prayer Book Studies
Volume Five

Trial-use Baptism, Calendar and Ordination,
Issues 18-20

Edited by
Derek A. Olsen

Copyright © 2026 The Domestic and Foreign Missionary Society of the Protestant Episcopal Church in the United States of America

The English text of the liturgies presented in this book is in the public domain and is freely available for quotation without restriction.

Unless otherwise noted, Scripture quotations are from The New Revised Standard Version Bible, copyright © 1989 National Council of the Churches of Christ in the United States of America. Used by permission. All rights reserved worldwide.

Seabury Books
19 East 34th Street
New York, NY 10016
www.churchpublishing.org

Seabury Books is an imprint of Church Publishing Incorporated.

Cover design by Newgen
Typeset by Integra Software Services Pvt. Ltd.

ISBN 978-1-64065-933-9 (paperback)
ISBN 978-1-64065-934-6 (hardback)
ISBN 978-1-64065-935-3 (eBook)

Library of Congress Control Number: 2025945262

CONTENTS

Introduction vii

Prayer Book Studies 18: On Baptism and Confirmation

Preface 3

Holy Baptism with the Laying-on-of-Hands and Holy Communion

Introduction 7
  1. Baptism 7
  2. Confirmation 9
  3. Unifying the Rite 11
  4. The Rite 12
  5. Special Circumstances 14

Bibliography 15
  Christian Initiation 15
  General Works on Liturgy and Sacramentalism . . . 16

The Proposed Rite 17
  Concerning the Service 17
  At the Ministry of the Word 18
  The Presentation and Affirmations 18
  The Blessing of the Water 20
  The Blessing of Oil 21
  The Baptism and Laying-on-of-Hands 21
  Additional Directions and Suggestions 22
  Conditional Baptism 24
  The Ministration of Baptism by Deacons 24

Emergency Baptism 24

Admission to Holy Communion 25

Appendix: Texts of Scripture Passages 26

Prayer Book Studies 19: The Church Year
The Calendar and the Proper of the Sundays and Other Holy Days Throughout The Church Year

Preface 31

THE CHURCH YEAR:
PART I

The Calendar 34
  1. Calendars in General 34
  2. Religious Calendars 35
  3. Radical Proposals 36
  4. The Meaning of the Church Year 38
  5. Present Proposals 41

Sundays, Seasons, and Holy Days 45
  1. Sundays 45
  2. Seasons 47
  3. Fixed Holy Days 52
  4. Special Occasions 56

The Proper 57
  1. The Collect 58
  2. The Psalms 60
  3. The Lessons 62
  4. Proper Prefaces 67

Tables 67
Rules for Finding the Date of Easter Day 67
A Table to Find Easter Day 70
A Table to Find Movable Feasts and Holy Days 72

Appendices 74

Appendix I: The Calendar 74
  1. Changes of Dates in the Calendar 74
  2. New Roman Calendar Dates not Adopted 76
  3. New Entries in the Calendar 78

Appendix II: The Collects 82
  1. Sources of the Collects 82
  2. Prayer Book Collects Omitted in Present Proposals or Superseded by New Collects 88

Appendix III: Index of Psalms 89

Appendix IV: Index of Scripture Lessons 98

Appendix V: Bibliography 124
   Episcopal Church 124
   Other Anglican Churches 124
   Roman Catholic Church 125
   Other Churches and Groups 125
   Anthologies of Prayers 126
   Selected Modern Works 126

PART II
THE CALENDAR OF THE CHURCH YEAR

Observed in This Church 128
   1. Sundays 129
   2. Holy Days 129
   3. Days of Special Devotion 130
   4. Days of Optional Observance 130

The Titles of the Seasons Sundays and Major Holy Days 143
   Observed in this Church Throughout the Year 143

PART III
THE PROPER

General Directions 147

The Nativity of our Lord Jesus Christ or Christmas Day 151

The Epiphany, or the Manifestation of Christ to the
Gentiles 155

Lenten Season 162

Holy Week 170

Easter Season 182

The Common of Saints 241

Special Occasions 247

Prayer Book Studies 20: The Ordination of Bishops, Priests, and Deacons

Preface 271

Introduction to the Proposed Rites 275
1. The Three Sacred Orders 275
2. An Historical Survey 278
3. Recent Revisions 283
4. The Present Proposed Rites 286
5. Trial Use of These Rites of Ordination 293

Select Bibliography of Works on Ordination Rites and
Related Topics 294
1. Translations into English of Ancient Rites of Ordination 294
2. Recently Compiled or Revised Rites of Ordination 294
3. Critical and Historical Studies 295

The Ordination of Bishops, Priests, and Deacons

The Ordination of a Bishop 297

The Ordination of a Priest 305

The Ordination of a Deacon 311

A Litany for the Ministry 318

The Litany Noted for Chant 320

INTRODUCTION

The Series as a Whole

The *Prayer Book Studies* (PBS) series documents the 26-year process of study and conversation that led to the adoption of the American 1979 Book of Common Prayer. It falls broadly into two parts, distinguished by the use of Roman numerals and Arabic numerals. PBS I-XVII were published by the members of the Standing Liturgical Commission between 1950 and 1966 to communicate research and draft liturgies leading toward a revision process; PBS 18-29 were published by the various drafting committees between 1970 and 1976 once the revision process was formally begun and the earlier drafts were being transformed into new usable liturgies, leading up to the adoption of the new prayer book in 1979. Finally, PBS 30 and its commentary were added in 1989 to discuss inclusive and expansive language for God for further liturgical efforts.

Context of these Studies

These three studies begin the second series of *Prayer Book Studies*, those using Arabic numerals for their numbering (PBS 18-29), and that followed the kickoff of a formal revision process with the 1967 General Convention. Within these eleven studies, the first seven (PBS 18-24), containing the most critical materials for public worship and pastoral use, were all published in 1970. The rites within these studies, shorn of their exposition, would be printed as *Services for Trial Use*, also known as "the Green Book." The next four (with two supplements) were published in 1973. These would be collected with the preceding materials into *Authorized Services 1973*, also known as "the Zebra Book" for its striped cover. The final study in this second series (PBS 29) is the sole publication in 1976, introducing the complete set of new rites to The Episcopal Church.

In contrast with the first series, a wide range of voices are brought into the conversation as both drafters and readers. The preface to the first of the new studies, PBS 18, describes the processes followed by the Standing Liturgical Commission, the drafting committees, reader-consultants, and the Editorial Committee, and should be consulted for full details.

At the same time, the timeline for completing these studies and their liturgies was greatly compressed. While some work on the first series had been ongoing since the publication of the 1928 Book of Common Prayer, all of the work here—building on and informed by the work of the First Series—had to occur at lightning speed.

One telltale sign of the haste and subsequent disorganization present within this period is the wide range of formatting choices between the studies issued in this period. The choices of fonts for text and headings, the formatting of headings, and the presence or absence of color are entirely inconsistent between studies, leading to an impression of speed and chaos across the material.

Finally—and contributing even more to the pressure on the committees—all of the rites appear in contemporary language (now known as Rite II), rather than the Elizabethan/Jacobean idiom that had been used for all of the preceding liturgical work. Several rites, of course, appear in both (Rites I and II).

These Studies

PBS 18

As noted above, the preface to this study gives invaluable details on the back-and-forth processes between the Standing Liturgical Commission, the drafting committees, the reader-consultants, and the Editorial Committee, and deserves study to grasp the complexity of the process and the large number of moving parts—all completed without computers, email, or smartphones!

Rather than a full historical survey, the initial material describes the basic theological intention of baptism, then confirmation, and then moves to a section titled "Unifying the Rite" that explains that the basic principle of the proposed rite is to combine baptism, confirmation, and First Communion into a single continuous service. The rite then proceeds to do just that, with a few supplementary rites included after for conditional baptism, emergency baptism, and an "admission to communion" for officially receiving into The Episcopal Church a person baptized in another Christian church.

PBS 19

The second study returns once again to the Church Year but takes up a whole new body of work. Since PBS II and its revision of the Eucharistic Lectionary, all of the calendar work had focused on lesser feasts and fasts—the sanctoral calendar in particular. This study, incorporating the reforms of Vatican II wholeheartedly, follows that revision by abolishing the pre-Lenten season, elevating the Easter Vigil to the principal liturgy of Easter, revamping the collects for each Sunday as well as offering them in both contemporary and traditional language, and adopting a 3-year Gospel lectionary—introducing into it not only an Old

Testament lesson but also two psalms for each temporal occasion (the first for the entrance rite, the second placed between the Old and New Testament lessons). Needless to say, it is the longest study of this volume by quite a lot, more than doubling the word count of the other two studies combined.

PBS 20

The third study contains the Ordinal and makes extensive changes to the earlier contents of PBS VIII. One of the central causes for caution in the earlier work had been its relationship to the Roman rites of ordination, but these had just been renovated by the work of Vatican II. This revision addresses head-on the classical conundrum that the seven ordained ranks of the medieval West concluded with "priest," leaving "bishop" in some nebulous ecclesiastical state; accordingly, there are now three parallel rites for the ordination of bishops, priests, and deacons.

PRAYER BOOK STUDIES 18: ON BAPTISM AND CONFIRMATION

The Study and the Order of Service in the following pages were prepared by the Standing Liturgical Commission of The Episcopal Church as part of the program of Prayer Book Revision authorised by the General Convention of 1967.

1970

PREFACE

THE GENERAL CONVENTION of 1967 approved a Plan for Prayer Book Revision submitted, at the Convention's request, by the Standing Liturgical Commission. Under the terms of the Plan, the Commission itself rather than a specially appointed body was designated as the instrument of revision. The Plan provided for the appointment of a large body of Consultants to assist the Commission in its task. The Commission was requested to present drafts of revised portions of the Prayer Book to the General Convention of 1970 for trial use.

In implementation of this Plan, the Standing Liturgical Commission nominated, and the Presiding Bishop and the President of the House of Deputies appointed, some 250 Consultants. They are a representative cross-section of the whole Church, including Bishops, priests and lay persons. There are among them poets and writers, scholars of unquestioned distinction and eminence, young people, parish priests and retired priests, businessmen, executives, housewives, lawyers, doctors, and teachers.

Under the Revision Plan, the Consultants are divided into two main groups. The members of one group serve on fourteen drafting committees established by the Standing Liturgical Commission. To ensure close and constant liaison between the drafting committees and the Commission, each committee is under the chairmanship of a member of the Commission.

The members of the other group serve as Reader-Consultants, acting mainly through correspondence. They receive all the materials prepared by the drafting committees at all stages of the work, and they submit comments, criticisms, and suggestions. These are channeled to the drafting committees concerned and are carefully studied and taken into account. In this way the knowledge, experience, and judgment of a large and representative group of Churchmen is an ever-present factor in the work of the drafting committees and of the Standing Liturgical Commission itself.

The Commission also invited a group of fourteen distinguished members of other Communions to serve as Reader-Consultants, thus giving the Commission the benefit of an ecumenical perspective.

Co-ordination among the various participants in the work, reproduction and distribution of working papers and documents, and channeling of comments from Consultants, was entrusted to a Co-ordinator, appointed on the nomination of the Standing Liturgical Commission.

At a later stage of the work, the Commission found it desirable to include in its program of Church-wide consultation the Chairmen of diocesan liturgical commissions or committees. Experience with the evaluation of the trial use of The Liturgy of the Lord's Supper (*Prayer Book Studies XVII*) demonstrated the competence, keen interest, and efficiency of diocesan liturgical bodies. They have a direct concern in the work of the national Commission, especially as the General Convention approves for trial use all or parts of the several revised rites. The diocesan bodies, through their Chairmen, add a still further, somewhat more practical, dimension to the work of Prayer Book revision.

As the drafts of the various sections of the Prayer Book began to take shape, the Commission decided that it would be more helpful to the Church if some, at least, of the revised rites were published separately as Prayer Book Studies, rather than held back until all the sections were completed. Separate publication of revised rites would make it possible for each section to be considered carefully on its own merits, uninfluenced by reactions, whether favorable or otherwise, to other parts of the same book. Separate publication would also make it possible to include with each revised rite an informative introduction and rationale. Finally, it would make it possible to subject each rite to separate trial use, should this be authorized by the General Convention. This in turn would facilitate adjustments and corrections in the several parts before they are brought together in a single, more-or-less definitive, volume.

The present study on Baptism and Confirmation is the first to be completed under the 1967 Plan of Revision. It was prepared by the Drafting Committee on Christian Initiation, constituted as follows:

> The Reverend Bonnell Spencer, O.H.C., member of the Standing Liturgical Commission and Chairman of the Drafting Committee
> The Right Reverend George W. Barrett
> Mrs. Howard O. Bingley
> The Reverend Reuel L. Howe* [Dr. Howe was able to attend only the first meeting.]
> The Reverend James F. Madison
> Dr. Margaret Mead
> The Reverend Leonel L. Mitchell
> The Reverend William S. Spilman

The following persons also helped with the drafting: the Reverend Hugh McCandless, Mrs. Richard L. Harbour, the Reverend Canon Louis Weil, and Captain Howard Galley of the Church Army.

To illustrate the procedures followed under the Revision Plan of 1967, it may be useful to give a brief chronological account of the stages in the development of this Study.

The Drafting Committee held two meetings to determine the principles of revision (May 2-3 and September 19-20, 1968). At its third meeting (December 16-17, 1968), the Committee drew up a first draft of the rite. The Standing Liturgical Commission considered this draft in January 1969. The Committee revised the rite at its fourth meeting (April 21-22, 1969) in the light of the Commission's comments, and drafted the introduction.

The Commission reviewed both the revised rite and the introduction in June 1969, and made some further corrections. This material was then referred to the Editorial Committee, under the Chairmanship of the Reverend Robert Estill, which edited both the introduction and the rite in July 1969. In September 1969, the Commission gave a final reading to the introduction and the rite and authorized the publication of *Prayer Book Studies 18*.

At each stage, the Reader-Consultants received reports on the Drafting Committee's work and made comments and suggestions. In addition, the Commission decided to circulate the texts of both the introduction and the rite as they emerged from the Editorial Committee, to all the Bishops of the Church and to the Chairmen of diocesan liturgical commissions and committees. Following the final reading in September 1969, a document containing the changes made by the Commission was circulated to all who had received the edited introduction and rite.

The Standing Liturgical Commission wishes to record its appreciation to all who had a share in the production of this Study: to the members of the Drafting Committee on Christian Initiation in the first place, to others who assisted in the work of drafting, and to the Editorial Committee. It is impossible to list by name all the Reader-Consultants who studied the work-in-progress and made valuable comments, criticisms, and suggestions.

The incoming correspondence from the Consultants alone fills four large files. Their contribution represents an extraordinary fund of knowledge and experience. Without their constant attention, both to the substance and the wording of the introduction and the rite, the result would not have been as satisfactory as the Commission hopes the Church will find it.

The Commission also desires to express its gratitude to the Bishops of the Church who have offered comments, and to the Chairmen of diocesan liturgical commissions and committees. Finally, the Commission would like to record its gratitude to the Dean and Faculty of the General Theological Seminary in New York, who provided meetings rooms for the Drafting Committee, and extended hospitality to its members.

The process of consultation does not end with the publication of *Prayer Book Studies 18*; on the contrary, its area and scope are widened. Now the Commission invites all who may see this booklet, whether clergyman or lay persons, whether members of the Episcopal Church or of another Communion, to contribute to this consulation by sending comments to the Standing Liturgical Commission,

815 Second Avenue, New York, N.Y. 10017. All correspondence will be acknowledged and all comments will be given serious consideration.

To those who may respond to this invitation, the Commission expresses in advance its sincere thanks.

THE STANDING LITURGICAL COMMISSION

Chilton Powell, *Chairman*
John W. Ashton
Dupuy Bateman, Jr.
James D. Dunning
Robert W. Estill
William C. Frey
Charles M. Guilbert, *Secretary*
Mrs. Richard Harbour
J. Joseph Harte
Louis B. Keiter
H. Boone Porter, Jr.
Charles P. Price
Massey H. Shepherd, Jr., *Vice Chairman*
Jonathan G. Sherman
Charles W. F. Smith
Bonnell Spencer, O.H.C.
Albert R. Stuart
Leo Malania, *Co-ordinator*

HOLY BAPTISM WITH THE LAYING-ON-OF-HANDS AND HOLY COMMUNION

Introduction

1. Baptism

BAPTISM is the sacrament in which we accept salvation from sin and reconciliation with God by participation in the death and resurrection of Jesus Christ. By the Holy Spirit a person is born anew into the fellowship which, because it is responsive in faith, is used by Christ as his Body through which he continues to work and serve in the world. In Baptism, as in all the sacraments, the principal action is God's. He accepts the candidate as his own child by incorporating him into the Son, and raises him to newness of life. He gives him the power of the Holy Spirit to fulfill his vocation in this world and to reign with Christ in his eternal kingdom.

But because God is love and always seeks with man a relationship of love, our free and willing acceptance of his benefits is necessary. Acceptance involves faith in what God has done in Christ to achieve our salvation, and commitment to follow him in the way of worship and service.

The necessity for the response of faith has given rise to the controversy whether infants are fit subjects for Baptism. For several centuries there have been those who have maintained that since the infant is unable to make an act of faith, he is incapable of being baptized. Today some members of Churches that have always advocated infant Baptism are expressing misgivings about this practice. A baptismal liturgy, therefore, which may be used for infants must confront this problem of faith.

The problem has been particularly acute in the past four centuries because of a prevailing individualism. Faith has been conceived of by many as exclusively an individual act. In this sense an infant cannot make an act of faith. But to what extent can an adult? The difference between infant Baptism and believers' Baptism is easily exaggerated. Although in the latter the candidate can declare his faith, it may or may not reflect a true commitment. Far more important is the response of faith of the Church into which one is sacramentally incorporated by Baptism. This is true both for an adult and for an infant.

Faith and commitment remain voluntary throughout a Christian's life. The capacity for them, as well as the willingness to exercise them, varies considerably. They do not always increase with age. Indeed, open and childlike acceptance is often succeeded by a period of doubt. Even the committed adult finds from time to time difficulty in reconciling his knowledge of the universe, of human nature, and of society, with Christianity as he understands it. Today many earnest seekers after God and dedicated servants of humanity cannot in conscience follow Christ as he was portrayed to them in their childhood.

The likelihood of fluctuations in faith and commitment underlines the need for continuous instruction geared to a person's intellectual growth and experience, and for continuous emphasis on the call to commitment. It is possible that continuity in both these areas has been seriously disrupted by the practice of Confirmation as the Episcopal Church has received it in the western tradition of Christianity.

Before we turn to Confirmation, however, we should take note of another argument for infant Baptism. Psychologists have helped us to see that there is a level of human understanding—vital for growth into maturity—that is non-verbal and non-rational. We now know that this unconscious level responds to reality as it is conveyed by means of symbolic forms and actions. We know that such an unconscious response begins at birth, if not earlier.

The truth about God and his relation to man is received by our unconscious mental processes through many channels. Long before a child can be reached in verbal and rational ways, his life-style is already being permanently shaped.

In the liturgy, the symbols, figures, and actions awaken the depths of the human psyche to a genuine relationship with God. The Baptism of infants, followed by participation in the Eucharist, corresponds to the natural basic patterns of human growth. Sacramental living beginning in infancy, is a solid witness to the psychological and religious fact that explicit verbal communication and conscious individual decisions, important though they are, do not by any means constitute the whole of life.[1]

But this corporate and liturgical influence on the growing child presupposes not only that he is a regular participant in the worship of the local congregation (instead of being relegated to a Sunday School "worship service"), but also that the local congregation is a loving fellowship in the Body of Christ. It has the obligation of being a true family of God, with a personal concern on the part of all its members for the nurture of its children and the full development of their individual characters. It will, therefore, include the children in terms of their growing capacities both in its eucharistic worship and in its mission to the community, and will give them the best possible instruction in the foundation, significance, and responsibilities of the life in Christ.

---

1. Macquarrie, John, *Principles of Christian Theology* (Scribners, 1966), page 412; also pages 407-416. Cf. Cope, Gilbert, *Symbolism in the Bible and the Church* (SCM, 1959), especially chapter III, though the whole work is an excellent study of sacramental symbolism.

2. Confirmation

IN THE EARLY CHURCH the Bishop was the normal president at Baptism as he was at the Eucharist. When it became impossible for him to be present at every Baptism in person, one of two adjustments was made. Almost everywhere the parish priest replaced the Bishop as the minister of the entire rite, as he had earlier replaced him as the usual celebrant of the Eucharist. However, in Rome and those parts of Italy under the direct supervision of the Pope, the final anointing and Laying-on-of-hands were reserved to the Bishop alone, and so became separated from the rest of the rite on those occasions when no Bishop was present at the administration of Baptism. During the Middle Ages, this local Roman usage spread throughout Western Europe.[2]

This separated episcopal action has developed into what we know as Confirmation. In the course of the centuries, three other practices have become associated with it: before Confirmation the candidate is instructed in the Christian Faith and practice; he commits himself to it by a renewal of his baptismal vows; and Confirmation is normally required as a preliminary to the reception of Holy Communion. It should be emphasized that these three practices associated with Confirmation as we know it are medieval or Reformation additions.[3]

People today commonly deplore the alleged inadequacy of confirmation instruction. As a matter of fact, many priests work hard at the preparation of children for Confirmation. That the result is less than satisfactory is due not so much to their lack of effort, as to other factors inherent in the situation. One of the reasons

---

2. It is not possible here to deal adequately with the apostolic visit to the Samaritans in Acts 8:14-17. The use of this passage in the American Prayer Book Confirmation Service gives most Episcopalians the impression that the practice of Confirmation is referred to in it and required by it. A large proportion of biblical scholars, however, question or flatly deny that interpretation. Discussion of the problem, and other possible interpretations, will be found in Lampe, G. W. H., *The Seal of the Spirit* (Longmans, Green, 1951), pages 64-81; and Beasley-Murray, G. R., *Baptism in the New Testament* (Macmillan, 1963), pages 104-125. The difficulty of finding in Acts 8:14-17 the justification for separating Confirmation from Baptism is that there is no other passage in the New Testament which indicates such a separation, and no evidence for such separation anywhere in the early Church until the third century. Therefore the episode in Acts, whatever its significance, would seem to be an exception rather than the norm.

3. Fisher, J. C. D., *Christian Initiation: Baptism in the Medieval West* (SPCK, 1965), gives the details of how these features came to be added. Instruction prior to Confirmation or first Communion was obviously impossible so long as these were administered to infants, a practice which obtained in England as late as 1536. Queen Elizabeth I, for example, was baptized and confirmed three days after her birth. The *Sarum Manuale* expected candidates for Confirmation to be able to say the Lord's Prayer, the Hail Mary, and the Apostles' Creed. The requirement that candidates be of "years of discretion" and learn the Catechism dates from the Prayer Book of 1549. The ratification of the baptismal vows did not appear until 1662. The practice is apparently based on the view of Calvin (*Institutes*, IV.19.4) that this was the primitive custom, although it clearly was not. (See Fisher, *op. cit.*, pages 134-140.) The requirement that no one be admitted to Communion unless he had been confirmed, or reasonably prevented, dates from the Council of Lambeth under Archbishop Peckam in 1281. Its purpose was to combat what it described as "damnable negligence" in the reception of Confirmation (*ibid.*, page 124).

for the endless dispute about the right age for Confirmation is that none of the usual ages is suitable for the instruction. From ages six to eleven, children are too young for the conceptual form of teaching in which the Faith and much of the practice are expressed. At about age twelve there begins a process of questioning the religion they have accepted as children. This is a necessary part of their thinking things through for themselves, but it makes it a difficult time to review the Faith and practice.

Great damage, moreover, is done to the normal pattern of Christian education. The confirmation instructor, faced with the urgency of ensuring that the child knows all that is thought necessary to be known before he is confirmed, and recognizing that some of the children (because of faulty teaching, poor attention, or irregular attendance), have learned little in their previous instruction, is tempted to try to get the whole Christian religion into a single brief course. To the extent that he yields to this temptation, he breaks the continuity of Christian education. It is not surprising that many confirmands, after a condensed survey of the whole Faith and practice, feel that their education is complete and that they have now "graduated from Sunday School", if not from the Church itself.

In the same way, the continuity of Christian commitment is broken by the once-for-all renewal of baptismal vows which is demanded in Confirmation. On the one hand, a child, as soon as he is able to make self-determined choices, should strive to carry out his baptismal commitment to follow Christ. On the other hand, even in the mid-teens, a young person living at home, or in a Church school, is still under pressures that hinder his making a fully independent commitment. Although he may at the time be entirely sincere, he is likely to repudiate it a few years later, if for any reason, good or bad, he is unable or unwilling to participate in the Church's life.

One who in infancy has been incorporated into the household of faith needs, of course, to affirm personally his baptismal commitment. But affirmation best takes the form of commitment now, regularly renewed at frequent intervals. The intent of the liturgy here proposed is that it shall be celebrated as the main Sunday service several times a year, with the whole congregation joining in the baptismal promises. It is designed to express the corporate faith with which the candidates for Baptism are being united, and to allow every person present, explicitly to renew his own commitment, and to enable the fellowship to recognize its responsibility to the candidates. And since Baptism is here associated directly with the Holy Communion, that sacrament will come to be understood, even on other occasions, as an opportunity for personal and corporate commitment, self-oblation, and re-consecration to Christ.

Finally, Confirmation as currently practiced disrupts the connection between Baptism and the Holy Communion. Those who have been made members of the family of God have the right to be fed at the Lord's table. Those who have been incorporated into Christ should be able to complete their eucharistic self-oblation in worship and love by receiving him. Those who are admitted by Baptism into the Communion of Saints should be allowed to partake of the Holy Communion.

Instead, at present we exclude baptized Christians from Communion until they reach the age at which their parish custom permits them to be confirmed. It is not surprising that some of them think of Communion as a reward for having attended the confirmation instructions and for renewing their baptismal vows, rather than as an offering of themselves to Christ in worship and love.

3. Unifying the Rite

THE BASIC PRINCIPLE of this proposal is the reunion of Baptism, Confirmation, and Communion into a single continuous service, as it was in the primitive Church. Thus, the entire liturgy will be recognized as the full reception of the candidate into the family of God by the power of the Holy Spirit: beginning with the acceptance, through faith, of forgiveness of sins and redemption in Christ—of burial with Christ in the water in order that we may rise in him to newness of life; followed by the conferring of the gifts of the Spirit by the Laying-on-of-hands; and ending with participation in the holy meal at which the entire family is united, nourished, and sanctified.

This proposed rite avoids both the practical disadvantages of delaying Confirmation, and the theological problem of attributing to Confirmation separately, some necessary aspects of Christian initiation that belong to the very beginning of our Christian life. It will make possible a proper understanding of the priesthood of all believers, which the baptized are to exercise in the worship of God and the service of man.[4]

The proposed liturgy will also strengthen the personal contact between the Bishop and his flock. It is intended that when the Bishop visits a parish, he will officiate at the administration of Baptism, the Laying-on-of-hands and the Eucharist. This will demonstrate that he is the chief sacramental minister of the Diocese, the clergy of the parish joining with him as fellow ministers. By making provision for the Bishop to take the leading role in the whole sequence of initiatory rites, this proposed liturgy expresses more clearly the true relationships among the Bishop, the priest, the deacon, and the people, than the present practice of reserving to the Bishop only one small section of the action of Christian initiation. This might help to correct the impression of many laymen today that the only function a Bishop performs, apart from administrative duties, is to confirm. When, because of unavoidable circumstances, the Bishop cannot be present,

---

4. "The laity is the fundamental Holy Order in the Church, and all of us are made laymen in our Baptism. We must rid ourselves of all the common parlance that suggests that Confirmation is the so-called 'ordination of the laity.' Baptism is the layman's ordination.... The first step, therefore, in the reconstruction of the initiation liturgy, would seem to me one that restores to the Bishop his presidency and office in the total initiation of the Christian, and not just in that part we call Confirmation. Indeed, I should go so far as to say that there is more meaning in the episcopal office, succeeding from the apostles, when it is viewed as a mission to preach and baptize than when it is restricted to a duty to visit and confirm.' Shepherd, M. H., *Liturgy and Education* (Seabury, 1965) page 106.

the unified rite provides that the priest be empowered to act as his deputy and to perform the Laying-on-of-hands. There are ample historical precedents for the delegation to the priest of the complete sequence of initiatory rites. This will, of course, mean that personal contact with the Bishop will not be required at every service of initiation. But far from eliminating the Bishop from the life and thought of the average layman, the intention of this proposed liturgy, as indicated above, is quite the contrary.

Baptism with the Laying-on-of-hands followed by regular Communion from an early age should strengthen the continuity and effectiveness of Christian education. The child can be led step by step to a deeper understanding of the Faith and practice, each year's teaching being geared to his capacities, and all against the background of full sacramental participation in the Church's life.

The age at which a child is admitted to Communion on a regular basis is a pastoral problem which will require sensitive handling. There will, of course, be those who object to a young child's receiving Communion on the grounds that he does not understand what he is doing. Again, the question might be asked, How much does an adult understand? A small child often has a natural recognition of the Sacrament; but even when there is little evidence of such recognition, early admission to the Altar has this great value: Communion becomes an integral part of the child's Christian experience from the beginning. He can never remember when he was not fed at the table of the Lord.

But in the course of history we have made admission to the Lord's table conditional upon one portion of the rite isolated from its context. We have made of it a separate rite, called Confirmation, and have thereby obscured the intimate relationship between the two sacraments ordained by Christ himself.

Those who were baptized as infants, and therefore have no conscious memory of the event, think of Confirmation as the great moment of Christian initiation, the time when one "joins the Church" or when one "becomes an Episcopalian." The result of giving such importance to Confirmation is to depreciate the full significance of Baptism and to make Confirmation alone, rather than Baptism, the sacrament that leads to the Altar. This, in turn, may be the reason why many of us regard ourselves primarily as having joined a denomination, rather than as being "members incorporate in the mystical Body of Christ."

To emphasize the essential unity of Christian initiation, the Standing Liturgical Commission proposes to bring together the separated acts of the sacramental drama of salvation, by placing Baptism with the Laying-on-of-hands within the context of a celebration of the Holy Communion.

4. The Rite

THE OPENING VERSICLES of this liturgy emphasize the unity of the holy catholic Church into which the candidates are to be baptized. The Collect prays that we may lay hold on our baptismal privilege of living in the power of Christ's resurrection. Lessons from the Old and New Testaments have been chosen that bring out the various aspects of Baptism. They should not, however, be allowed to interrupt the continuity of the three-year cycle of Readings now being worked out for the Sunday Eucharist.

The presentation of the candidates at the font by their sponsors follows naturally upon the Ministry of the Word and introduces the baptismal action. Its relationship to the Offertory of the Eucharist is obvious.

A rubric requires that sponsors be instructed beforehand in the responsibilities they are undertaking, and that they agree to assume them. This seems more realistic than the formality of an exhortation and assent in the service itself. Instead, the sponsors join with the congregation in renewing their faith and commitment to Christ, thus showing that the candidates are being enveloped in the Faith of the whole Church, and that the sponsors are representatives of the congregation in ministering to them its loving concern and fellowship. The congregation then prays for the candidates in a Litany which stresses the benefits and responsibilities of their new status.

To place Baptism in the biblical perspective of the history of salvation, the prayer for the Blessing of the Water includes references to the Old Testament antecedents. The new creation, like the old, is effected by water and the Spirit. As Israel rescued from the bondage of Egypt passed through the sea to become the people of God under the Old Covenant, so the new Israel rescued from sin and death passes through Baptism into the New Covenant in Christ.

A prayer for the blessing of oil, technically known as Chrism, follows. The use of oil is appropriate because by Baptism we are incorporated into Christ, and "Christ" is a title meaning the Anointed One, as "Chrism" means anointing (First John 2:20, 27). This title was given to Jesus because he fulfilled the work of both priest and king, who in the Old Testament were consecrated by anointing with oil.[5] Chrism has been associated with Baptism at least since the second century, it was used universally until the sixteenth century, and it is still used today by the majority of Christians. This long historical association of Chrismation with Baptism is reflected in our familiar term Christening.

---

5. Exodus 29:1-7, 21, 29 ff.
   Leviticus 8:12, 30
   First Samuel 9:16, 10:1, 16:13
   Second Samuel 2:4 and 5:3
   First Kings 1:39 and 19:16
   Psalms 2:2 and 84:9

See also spiritual interpretations:

   Isaiah 61:1
   Luke 4:18
   Acts 10:38
   Second Corinthians 1:21-22
   First John 2:20, 27

The use of Chrism provides a vivid reminder that Baptism is the ordination of the laity into the servant ministry of the Lord—a birth into the covenanted community which serves the world in the name of Christ. When used by a priest in the absence of a Bishop, Chrism is a visible physical link with the Bishop who had blessed it.[6]

The baptismal formula has been left unchanged, despite some suggestions that it be put into the passive voice.

Between the baptizing of the candidates and their reception into the congregation, there have been inserted in this rite, a revised form of the traditional prayer for the Gifts of the Spirit, and the action of the Laying-on-of-hands. The formula of welcome includes the recognition that the candidates have received the priesthood of all believers. The liturgy continues either with the Intercession or with the Offertory of the Eucharist. It is anticipated that Holy Communion will be administered to all who have been baptized at this service: by ancient custom, infants are communicated from a spoon or by intinction.

5. Special Circumstances

Provision has been made for

1. A different ending for occasions when the Eucharist is not celebrated;
2. A form for Emergency Baptism, including the direction that when the person recovers, he shall receive the Laying-on-of-hands at a public service and be welcomed by the congregation; and
3. The Laying-on-of-hands for persons baptized in accordance with the 1928 rite, or any other Baptismal rite that does not include Confirmation.

An optional Admission Service has been provided for those who come from other Communions. It will be noted that this service does not include the Laying-on-of-hands in order to avoid any possible misapprehension that this action is an essential prerequistite for admission to the communion of the Episcopal Church. The Laying-on-of-hands is, of course, available to all such persons who may desire it.

---

6. Chrism is pure olive oil, to which it is customary to add a small amount of an aromatic substance, such as oil of balsam.

Bibliography

Christian Initiation

Aland, K.: *Did the Early Church Baptize Infants?* London: SCM Press, Ltd.; 1963.
Arndt, E. J. F.: *The Font and the Table.* London: Lutterworth Press; 1967.
Bailey, D. S.: *Sponsors at Baptism and Confirmation.* London: S.P.C.K.; 1952.
Baptism and Confirmation (Prayer Book Studies I). New York: Church Pension Fund; 1950.
Baptism and Confirmation (Report of the Church of England Liturgical Commission). London: S.P.C.K.; 1959.
Baptism and Confirmation Today (Report of the Joint Committees on Baptism, Confirmation and the Holy Communion of the Convocations of Canterbury and York). London: S.P.C.K.; 1955.
Barth, K.: *The Teaching of the Church regarding Baptism.* London: SCM Press, Ltd.; 1948.
Beasley-Murray, G. R.: *Baptism in the New Testament.* London: Macmillan and Co., Ltd.; 1963.
Bohen, M.: *The Mystery of Confirmation.* New York: Herder and Herder; 1963.
Bouyer, L.: *Christian Initiation.* London: Burns & Oates; 1960.
Bromiley, G. W.: *Baptism and the Anglican Reformers.* London: Lutterworth Press; 1953.
Carr, W.: *Baptism: The Clue & Conscience for the Church.* New York: Holt, Rinehart & Winston, Inc.; 1963.
Commission On Education Of The Lutheran World Federation: *Confirmation, a Study Document* (Orig.); tr. by Walter G. Tillmanns. Minneapolis: Augsburg Publishing House; 1964.
Confirmation Crisis. New York: The Seabury Press; 1968.
Crehan, J.: *Early Christian Baptism and the Creed.* Westminster, Md.: The Newman Press; 1950.
Culley, K. B. (ed.): *Confirmation: History, Doctrine, and Practice.* New York: The Seabury Press; 1962.
Cullmann, O.: *Baptism in the New Testament.* London: SCM Press, Ltd.; 1950.
Dix, G.: *Confirmation, or Laying on of Hands?* London: SCM Press, Ltd.; 1936.
―――― *The Theology of Confirmation in Relation to Baptism.* Westminster: Dacre Press; 1946.
Eliade, M.: *Birth and Rebirth.* New York: Harper & Brothers; 1958.
Every, G.: *The Baptismal Sacrifice.* London: SCM Press, Ltd.; 1959.
Fisher, J. D. C.: *Christian Initiation: Baptism in the Medieval West.* London: S.P.C.K.; 1965.
Flemington, W. F.: *The New Testament Doctrine of Baptism.* London: S.P.C.K.; 1948.
Gilmore, A.: *Baptism and Christian Unity.* Philadelphia: American Baptist Publication Society (The Judson Press); London: Lutterworth Press; 1966.
Gilmore, A. (ed.): *Christian Baptism; a fresh attempt to understand the rite in terms of scripture, history and theology.* Philadelphia: American Baptist Publication Society (The Judson Press); London: Lutterworth Press; 1959.
Jeremias, J.: *Infant Baptism in the First Four Centuries.* Philadelphia: The Westminster Press; 1962.
―――― *The Origins of Infant Baptism.* London: SCM Press, Ltd.; 1963.
Lampe, G. W. H.: *The Seal of the Spirit.* Second Edition. London: S.P.C.K.; 1967.

Marty, M. E.: *Baptism* (ed. by Helmut T. Lehmann). Philadelphia: Muhlenberg Press; 1962.
Mason, A. J.: *The Relation of Confirmation to Baptism.* London: Longmans, Green and Co.; 1891.
Mitchell, L. L.: *Baptismal Anointing.* London: S.P.C.K.; 1966. Modern Liturgical Texts. London: S.P.C.K.; 1968.
Moss, B. S. (ed.): *Crisis for Baptism.* New York: Morehouse-Barlow Co.; 1965.
Neunheuser, B.: *Baptism and Confirmation.* New York: Herder and Herder; 1964.
Pocknee, C. E.: *Infant Baptism Yesterday and Today.* London: A. R. Mowbray & Co., Limited; 1966.
_____ *The Rites of Christian Initiation.* London: A. R. Mowbray & Co., Limited; 1962.
_____ *Water and the Spirit.* London: Darton, Longman & Todd; 1967.
Schnackenburg, R.: *Baptism in the Thought of St. Paul.* New York: Herder and Herder; 1964.
The Theology of Christian Initiation (Report of a Theological Commission appointed by the Archbishops of Canterbury and York). London: S.P.C.K.; 1949.
Thornton, L. S.: *Confirmation: Its Place in the Baptismal Mystery.* Westminster: Dacre Press; 1954.
Thurian, M.: *Consecration of the layman; new approaches to the sacrament of confirmation.* Baltimore: Helicon Press; 1963.
Whitaker, E. C.: *The Baptismal Liturgy.* London: The Faith Press; 1965.
_____ *Documents of the Baptismal Liturgy.* London: S.P.C.K.; 1960.
Wirgman, A. T.: *The Doctrine of Confirmation.* London: Longmans, Green and Co.; 1897.

General Works on Liturgy and Sacramentalism

Bouyer, L.: *Rite and Man.* London: Burns & Oates; 1963.
Cope, G.: *Symbolism in the Bible and the Church.* London: SCM Press, Ltd.; 1959.
Danielou, J.: *The Bible and the Liturgy.* Notre Dame, Ind.: University of Notre Dame Press; 1956.
Davies, J. G.: *The Spirit, the Church, and the Sacraments.* London: The Faith Press; 1954.
_____ *Worship and Mission.* New York: Association Press; 1967.
Dillistone, F. W.: *Christianity and Symbolism.* London: Collins; 1955.
_____ (ed.) *Myth and Symbol.* London: S.P.C.K.; 1966.
Eliade, M.: *Images and Symbols.* New York: Sheed & Ward; 1961.
Howe, R. L.: *Man's Need and God's Action.* New York: The Seabury Press; 1953.
James, E. O.: *Sacrifice and Sacrament.* New York: Barnes & Noble; 1962.
Macquarrie, J.: *Principles of Christian Theology.* New York: Charles Scribner's Sons; 1966.
Pittenger, W. N.: *Sacraments, Signs, and Symbols.* Chicago: Wilcox & Follett Co.; 1949.
Quick, O. C.: *The Christian Sacraments.* Fourth Edition. London: Nisbet & Co., Ltd.; 1932.
Shepherd, M. H.: *Liturgy and Education.* New York: The Seabury Press; 1965.
Spencer, B.: *The Sacrifice of Thanksgiving.* West Park, N.Y.: Holy Cross Publications; 1965.

The Proposed Rite

HOLY BAPTISM
WITH THE
LAYING-ON-OF-HANDS

Concerning the Service

NORMALLY, the Bishop will be the chief Minister at this Service; but a Priest may act for him in his absence.

It is appropriate that the chief Minister be assisted by other priests and deacons, if any are present, and by lay persons.

When the Bishop is present, he shall officiate at the Presentation of the Candidates, shall bless the water (and the oil), and shall say the Prayer over the Candidates and lay his hand on the head of each of them.

One or more baptized persons shall serve as Sponsors to present each Candidate. Sponsors are to be instructed about Baptism and their duty to help the Candidate grow in his Christian privileges and responsibilities. Sponsors shall sign the baptismal register as the expression of their assent. Parents may be included among the Sponsors of their own children.

Normally, this Service is to be celebrated as the chief Service on a Sunday or other Feast, and the Proper shall be of the Day. The opening versicles of this Service may always be substituted for the portion of the Liturgy that precedes the Collect of the Day.

Those who have been baptized in this or any other Christian Church, but have not been confirmed, may receive the Laying-on-of-hands at this Service.

NOTE:
Additional Directions and Suggestions will be found on pages 22-23.

HOLY BAPTISM
WITH THE
LAYING-ON-OF-HANDS

A Psalm or Hymn may be sung during the Entrance of the Ministers.

The Bishop or Priest says,

BLESSED BE GOD: Father, Son, and Holy Spirit.
And blessed be his Kingdom, now and forever. Amen.

There is one Body and one Spirit;
There is one hope in God's call to us.

One Lord, one Faith, one Baptism;
One God and Father of all.

> The Lord be with you.
> *And also with you.*
> Let us pray.

The Collect of the Day is then said, or the following Collect:

THE COLLECT

GRANT, O LORD, that we who are baptized into the death of Jesus Christ your Son may also live with him in the power of his resurrection; who lives and reigns with you in the unity of the Holy Spirit, one God, for ever and ever. *Amen.*

At the Ministry of the Word

LESSON	EPISTLE	GOSPEL
	2 Corinthians 5:17-20	Mark 1:9-11
Ezekiel 36:24-28	or, Romans 8:14-17	or, John 3:1-8
	or, Romans 6:3-5	or, Mark 10:13-16

[For convenience, the Scripture passages are printed in full on pages 26-27]

THE SERMON

After the Sermon, the Ministers, the Candidates, and their Sponsors may go to the font.

The Presentation and Affirmations

Each Candidate shall be presented to the chief Minister by his Sponsors, as follows:

I present *Name* to receive the Sacrament of Baptism.

Then, if the Candidate is able to answer for himself the chief Minister asks him,

Do you desire to be baptized?
Answer I do.

When all have been presented, the Minister appointed asks the Candidates, their Sponsors, and the Congregation, the following questions, all standing,

Will you obey and follow Jesus Christ as your Savior and Lord?
People That is my desire.
Will you seek and serve Christ in all men, loving your neighbor as yourself?
People I will, with God's help.
Will you strive for justice, peace, and dignity among all men?
People I will, with God's help.
Do you then renounce evil in all its forms?
People I do.

Minister Do you believe in God the Father?
People
I Believe in God, the Father almighty,
    creator of heaven and earth.

Minister Do you believe in Jesus Christ, the Son of God?
People
I believe in Jesus Christ, his only Son, our Lord.
    He was conceived by the power of the Holy Spirit
        and born of the Virgin Mary.
    He suffered under Pontius Pilate,
        was crucified, died, and was buried.
    He descended to the dead.
    On the third day he rose again.
    He ascended into heaven,
        and is seated at the right hand of the Father.
    He will come again to judge the living and the dead.

Minister Do you believe in God the Holy Spirit?
People
I believe in the Holy Spirit,
    the holy catholic Church,
    the communion of saints,
    the forgiveness of sins,
    the resurrection of the body,
    and the life everlasting.

[The version of the Creed which appears here is the common text recommended by the International Consultation on English Texts in October 1969.]

The Minister then says,
Let us pray for *these persons* who *are* to receive the sacrament of new birth.

A person appointed leads the following Litany:
Redeem *them*, O Lord, from all evil, and rescue *them* from the way of sin and death.
Lord, hear our prayer.
Open *their* hearts to your grace and truth.
Lord, hear our prayer.
Keep *them* in the faith and communion of your holy Church.
Lord, hear our prayer.
Teach *them* to love others in the power of the Spirit.
Lord, hear our prayer.
Send *them* into the world in witness to your love.
Lord, hear our prayer.
Bring *them* to the fullness of your peace and glory.
Lord, hear our prayer.

The Blessing of the Water

Then the Bishop, or in his absence the Priest, shall bless the Water, first addressing the People, and then facing the font.

> The Lord be with you.
> *And also with you.*
> Let us pray.

WE THANK YOU, HEAVENLY FATHER, for the gift of water. Over it the Holy Spirit moved in the beginning of creation. Through it you led the children of Israel out of the bondage of Egypt into the land of promise. In it your Son Jesus received the Baptism of John and was anointed by the Holy Spirit as the Messiah, the Christ who would lead us by his death and resurrection from the bondage of sin into everlasting life.

We thank you, heavenly Father, for the water of Baptism, in which we are buried with Christ in his death that we may share in his resurrection, and through which we are renewed by the Holy Spirit. In joyful obedience, therefore, to your Son, we make disciples of all nations and baptize them in the Name of the Father, and of the Son, and of the Holy Spirit.

Now sanctify this water, we pray you, *[Here he is to touch the water with his hand]* by the power of your Holy Spirit, that those who here are cleansed from sin may be born again, and continue for ever in the risen live of Jesus Christ our Savior;

To him, to you, and to the Holy Spirit, be all honor and glory, now and for ever. *Amen.*

The Blessing of Oil

When Oil of Chrism is to be blessed, the Bishop now says,

Let us pray.

ETERNAL FATHER, whose Son Jesus Christ was anointed by the Holy Spirit to be the servant of all men, [*Here he is to lay his hand on the vessel of oil.*] we pray you to consecrate this oil, that those who are sealed with it may have a share in the ministry of our great High Priest and King; who lives and reigns with you and the Holy Spirit, one God, for ever and ever. *Amen.*

When there are many Candidates, the People may be seated.

The Baptism and Laying-on-of-Hands

One of the Ministers shall dip each Candidate in the water, or pour water on his head, saying,

Name, I BAPTIZE YOU IN THE NAME OF THE FATHER, AND OF THE SON, AND OF THE HOLY SPIRIT. AMEN.

Then, the People standing, the Bishop, or in his absence the Priest, shall say the following prayer over the newly-baptized and other candidates for Confirmation.

Let us pray.

HEAVENLY FATHER, we thank you that by water and the Holy Spirit you have bestowed upon these your servants the forgiveness of sins, and have raised them to the new life of grace. Strengthen and confirm them, O Lord, with the riches of your Holy Spirit: an inquiring and discerning spirit, a spirit of purpose and of perseverance, a spirit to know and to love you, and a spirit of joy and wonder in all your works. *Amen.*

The People may be seated.

Here the Bishop, or in his absence the Priest, shall lay his hand on the head of each of them, making on the forehead the sign of the Cross (using Chrism if desired), and saying the following words to each one:

Name, YOU ARE SEALED BY THE HOLY SPIRIT.

When all have been sealed, the Ministers and People, standing, say to them,

We receive you into the Household of God, that you may confess the faith of Christ crucified, and share with us in his eternal priesthood. May the Lord arm you with his heavenly grace, that you may daily increase in his favor all the days of your life. Amen.

Then the Ministers and People exchange the Peace:

The peace of the Lord be always with you.
And with your spirit.

The chief Minister continues either with the Intercession or with the Offertory of the Eucharist. Those who have now been christened may receive Holy Communion.

The following Proper Preface may be used when no other preface is provided:

Because in Jesus Christ our Lord you have received us as your children, made us citizens of your kingdom, and given us the Holy Spirit to guide us into all truth: Therefore, etc.

If for sufficient reason there is no Communion, the Service continues with

THE LORD'S PRAYER

The Minister then says,

All praise and thanks to you, most merciful Father, for receiving us as your own children and incorporating us into your holy Church, and for making us worthy to share in the inheritance of the Saints in light; through Jesus Christ your Son our Lord, who lives and reigns with you and the Holy Spirit, one God, for ever and ever. *Amen.*

Alms may be received and presented in the usual manner, and the Minister may add other prayers, concluding with this blessing:

Almighty God, the Father of our Lord Jesus Christ, from whom all fatherhood in heaven and earth is named, grant you to be strengthened with might by his Spirit. May Christ dwell in your hearts by faith, that you may be filled with the presence and the power of God. *Amen.*

Additional Directions and Suggestions

THE FONT is to be filled with clean water, either before the Service, or immediately before the Blessing of the Water.

When this Service is not the main Service on a Sunday, the Scripture readings cited in the text may be used; SUBJECT, however, to the rules of precedence governing the observance of the Church Year.

The Lesson from the Old Testament may be read in addition to the Epistle or instead of it. Lay persons shall normally be assigned this function. It may be appropriate for Sponsors to act as readers. The Gospel shall be read by a Deacon or Priest. The Nicene Creed is not used at this Service.

Hymns, Psalms, or Canticles may be used after the Old Testament Lesson and after the Epistle; particularly suitable are Psalms 15, 27, 42, 84, 87, or 122; and Te Deum, Jubilate, Benedictus, and Magnificat.

It is fitting that the Minister who officiates at the Baptismal Affirmations (pages 18-19) be one who has direct pastoral responsibility for the Candidates, whether this minister be Priest, Deacon, Deaconess, or Lay Reader.

The Presentation of the Candidates and the Affirmations shall normally take place at the font. But if, because of the arrangement of the church building, the congregation find it difficult to see the Ministers or to participate in the Affirmations, this part of the Service may take place in the chancel. Thereafter, the Ministers, Candidates, and Sponsors go to the font for the Blessing of the Water.

If the movement to the font is a formal procession, a suitable Psalm, such as Psalm 42, or a Hymn may be sung; alternatively, they may go to the font while the Litany for the Candidates (page 20) is being said or sung.

It is desirable that this Litany be led by a person who is not a Sponsor, from his place in the church.

The Blessing of the Water is the prerogative of the Bishop as the chief sacramental Minister of the Diocese. In his absence, it will normally be done by the Rector or Priest-in-Charge.

The Blessing of Chrism is reserved to the Bishop alone. It is desirable that this be done in the presence of the congregation. Oil blessed by the Bishop for this purpose is left in the church to be used by the Priest when the Bishop is not present.

Any Bishop, Priest, Deacon or Deaconess present may be appointed to assist in administering the Baptism of the Candidates.

It is desirable, especially when a large congregation is present, that the Prayer over the Newly-Baptized (page 21) and the Laying-on-of-hands take place near the Holy Table. If the font is located some distance away, a suitable Psalm, such as Psalm 23, or a Hymn may be sung while the Ministers, Candidates, and Sponsors go to the chancel.

In the absence of the Bishop, the Rector or Priest-in-Charge is the normal officiant at the prayer over the Newly-Baptized and the Laying-on-of-hands.

The Bishop, when present, should be the principal celebrant at the baptismal Eucharist. For reasonable cause, however, he may delegate this privilege to the Rector or Priest-in-Charge.

It is appropriate that the oblations of bread and wine be brought forward by Sponsors. It is also fitting that the Sponsors accompany the newly-christened persons at the reception of Holy Communion.

Conditional Baptism

If there is reasonable doubt that a person has been baptized with water *In the Name of the Father, and of the Son, and of the Holy Spirit*, the person shall be baptized in the usual manner, but the form of words shall be,

> IF YOU ARE NOT ALREADY BAPTIZED, *Name*, I BAPTIZE YOU IN THE NAME OF THE FATHER, AND OF THE SON, AND OF THE HOLY SPIRIT. AMEN

The Ministration of Baptism by Deacons

There are times when, in the absence of a Priest, serious pastoral reasons make it necessary for a Deacon or Deaconess to officiate at public Baptism.

It is not appropriate, however, to the Office of Deacon, to bless the water, or to say the Prayer over the Newly-Baptized, or to perform the Laying-on-of-hands.

WHEN OFFICIATING, let a Deacon follow this order:

Begin the Service (page 17) in the usual way, and do and say everything assigned to the Minister as far as the end of the Litany on page 20;

THEN, baptize the Candidate, using the form for Emergency Baptism.

Emergency Baptism

In case of emergency, the following form shall be used.

A baptized lay person may administer Baptism according to this form in the absence of a clergyman.

> POUR WATER *on the head of the one to be baptized.*
> ADDRESS HIM *by his first name.*
> THEN SAY,

> I BAPTIZE YOU IN THE NAME OF THE FATHER, AND OF THE SON, AND OF THE HOLY SPIRIT. AMEN.

Then make the sign of the Cross on his forehead with your thumb, and say the Lord's Prayer.

OUR FATHER, who art in heaven, Hallowed be thy Name. Thy kingdom come. Thy will be done, On earth as it is in heaven. Give us this day our daily bread. And forgive us our trespasses, As we forgive those who trespass against us. And lead us not into temptation; But deliver us from evil.
For thine is the kingdom, and the power, and the glory, for ever and ever. Amen.

Other prayers, such as the following, may be added.

Heavenly Father, we thank you that by water and the Holy Spirit you have bestowed upon this your servant the forgiveness of sins and have raised him to the new life of grace. Strengthen him, O Lord, with your presence; enfold him in the arms of your mercy, and keep him safe for ever. *Amen.*

A person so baptized may receive Holy Communion. He shall, when able (preferably at a public service), make the Baptismal Affirmations and receive the Laying-on-of-hands.

Admission to Holy Communion

Any person who in another Christian Church has been baptized with water In the Name of the Father, and of the Son, and of the Holy Spirit, *may be officially received into The Episcopal Church in the following manner:*

At a celebration of the Holy Communion, before the Peace, the person shall be presented to the Priest by a member of the congregation who will say,

I present *Name* to be received into the communion of this Church.

The Priest then asks,

Have you been baptized with water In the Name of the Father, and of the Son, and of the Holy Spirit?
Answer I have.

Do you wish to be a member of this Fellowship within the one holy catholic and apostolic Church?
Answer I do.

Do you accept the discipline of membership in The Episcopal Church, its teaching of the Faith, its ways of worship, and its mission in the world?
Answer I do.

The Priest then says,

We receive you into the communion of this Church, and we welcome you into this congregation of the Family of God; In the Name of the Father, and of the Son, and of the Holy Spirit. *Amen.*
The peace of the Lord be always with you.
Answer And with your spirit.

Pursuant to the Canon, persons so received shall be enrolled in the Parish Register as baptized members of the Congregation.

To receive the Laying-on-of-hands, persons so admitted to Holy Communion shall present themselves at a public service of Baptism.

Appendix: Texts of Scripture Passages

The following passages are provided for those occasions when the Bible readings proper to the Day are not used.

[The passages quoted here are from the Revised Standard Version, copyright 1946 and 1952 by the Division of Christian Education of the National Council of the Churches of Christ in the U.S.A. It is to be understood, however, that these passages may be read from any of the versions of the Holy Scriptures authorized by Canon 20.]

Ezekiel 36:24-28

I will take you from the nations, and gather you from all the countries, and bring you into your own land. I will sprinkle clean water upon you, and you shall be clean from all your uncleannesses, and from all your idols I will cleanse you. A new heart I will give you, and a new spirit I will put within you; and I will take out of your flesh the heart of stone and give you a heart of flesh. And I will put my spirit within you, and cause you to walk in my statutes and be careful to observe my ordinances. You shall dwell in the land which I gave to your fathers; and you shall be my people, and I will be your God.

2 Corinthians 5:17-20

If any one is in Christ, he is a new creation; the old has passed away, behold, the new has come. All this is from God, who through Christ reconciled us to himself and gave us the ministry of reconciliation; that is, God was in Christ reconciling the world to himself, not counting their trespasses against them, and entrusting to us the message of reconciliation. So we are ambassadors for Christ, God making his appeal through us. We beseech you on behalf of Christ, be reconciled to God.

Romans 8: 14-17

All who are led by the Spirit of God are sons of God. For you did not receive the spirit of slavery to fall back into fear, but you have received the spirit of sonship. When we cry, "Abba! Father!" it is the Spirit himself bearing witness with our spirit that we are children of God, and if children, then heirs, heirs of God and fellow heirs with Christ, provided we suffer with him in order that we may also be glorified with him.

Romans 6:3-5

Do you not know that all of us who have been baptized into Christ Jesus were baptized into his death? We were buried therefore with him by baptism into death, so that as Christ was raised from the dead by the glory of the Father, we too might walk in newness of life. For if we have been united with him in a death like his, we shall certainly be united with him in a resurrection like his.

St. Mark 1:9-11

In those days Jesus came from Nazareth of Galilee and was baptized by John in the Jordan. And when he came up out of the water, immediately he saw the heavens opened and the Spirit descending upon him like a dove; and a voice came from heaven, "Thou art my beloved Son; with thee I am well pleased."

St. John 3:1-8

There was a man of the Pharisees, named Nicodemus, a ruler of the Jews. This man came to Jesus by night and said to him, "Rabbi, we know that you are a teacher come from God; for no one can do these signs that you do, unless God is with him." Jesus answered him, "Truly, truly, I say to you, unless one is born anew, he cannot see the kingdom of God." Nicodemus said to him, "How can a man be born when he is old? Can he enter a second time into his mother's womb and be born?" Jesus answered, "Truly, truly, I say to you, unless one is born of water and the Spirit, he cannot enter the kingdom of God. That which is born of the flesh is flesh, and that which is born of the Spirit is spirit. Do not marvel that I said to you, 'You must be born anew.' The wind blows where it wills, and you hear the sound of it, but you do not know whence it comes or whither it goes; so it is with every one who is born of the Spirit."

St. Mark 10:13-16

They were bringing children to him, that he might touch them; and the disciples rebuked them. But when Jesus saw it he was indignant; and said to them, "Let the children come to me, do not hinder them; for to such belongs the kingdom of God. Truly, I say to you, whoever does not receive the kingdom of God like a child shall not enter it." And he took them in his arms and blessed them, laying his hands upon them.

PRAYER BOOK STUDIES 19: THE CHURCH YEAR THE CALENDAR AND THE PROPER OF THE SUNDAYS AND OTHER HOLY DAYS THROUGHOUT THE CHURCH YEAR

1970

PREFACE

SINCE the launching of Prayer Book Studies in 1950, the Standing Liturgical Commission has given much attention to the problems of calendar and lectionary reform. Five of its volumes have been devoted to this concern: *Prayer Book Studies* II, IX, XII, Supplement to XII, and XVI. The first stage in the trial use of these materials came with the authorization by the General Convention of 1964 of the calendar and proper for the lesser feasts and fasts and for special occasions, proposed in *Prayer Book Studies* XVI. With minor modifications, this authorization for trial use was repeated by the General Convention of 1967.

In the same year the General Convention entrusted the Standing Liturgical Commission with the task of preparing a revision of The Book of Common Prayer. The present Study is one of several prepared in compliance with this decision.

Meanwhile interest in calendar and lectionary revision has taken on an ecumenical dimension through consultations that have involved inter-Anglican, Roman Catholic, and Protestant groups. Representatives of the Standing Liturgical Commission have participated actively in these conferences. As a result of these deliberations, there has emerged a general consensus regarding major changes in the Church Year, but as yet no overall agreement with respect to the eucharistic lectionary. However, it has been agreed that in a period of experimentation several lectionary systems might well be tried, and later assessed as to their particular merits. Our Commission has unanimously voted to propose for trial use the new three-year lectionary cycle of the Roman Catholic Church approved in 1969 and now in experimental use in that Church. We have nonetheless made a number of changes in the specific lections of the Roman Catholic cycle; and we have made other adjustments and adaptations in the lections of Sundays where we have differed from the Roman Catholic arrangement of the Church Year. These differences will be explained in the ensuing Study.

If approved for trial use by the General Convention of 1970, the proposed reform of the Church Year and of the eucharistic lectionary will presumably go into effect in Advent 1970, beginning with year C of the Roman three-year cycle, so as to accord with the schedule of experiment now under way in the Roman Catholic Church.

The preparation of this Study has been in charge of a Drafting Committee on the Calendar, Eucharistic Lectionary, and Collects. This is one of several

Drafting Committees established by the Standing Liturgical Commission under the terms of the Revision Plan of 1967 to prepare drafts of portions of a Revised Book of Common Prayer. The Drafting Committee was constituted as follows:

> The Reverend Massey H. Shepherd, Jr., Vice-Chairman of The Standing Liturgical Commission and Chairman of the Drafting Committee
> Miss Emma Lou Benignus
> The Reverend Canon James R. Brown
> The Reverend Reginald H. Fuller
> The Reverend Donald L. Garfield

The Committee held its first meeting in January, 1968, in the rectory of the Church of St. Mary the Virgin, New York. Subsequent meetings were held at the Episcopal Church Center, New York, and the final meeting was held in a hotel in Chicago. Thereafter, the Committee's business was conducted by correspondence. Eleven progress reports were circulated to the Commission and its 260 Consultants appointed under the Revision Plan of 1967. The Standing Liturgical Commission considered these proposals and approved them. The Drafting Committee continues to work on a revision of "Lesser Feasts and Fasts," as a supplement to, and enrichment of these proposals.

The Standing Liturgical Commission wishes to place on record its deep gratitude to its Consultants, and also to the many others of the clergy and laity who have greatly assisted the Drafting Committee and the Commission by their suggestions and criticisms of the Committee's progress reports. The Commission appreciates the hospitality of the Reverend Donald L. Garfield, Rector of the Church of St. Mary the Virgin and member of the Committee, and the assistance rendered by the staff of the Episcopal Church Center, New York.

Needless to say, the preparation of this Study has greatly benefited from the published works of scholars in many Christian communions: the Bibliography is a small token of the Commission's indebtedness. The value of the fruitful exchanges in the ecumenical consultations referred to above cannot be overestimated.

THE STANDING LITURGICAL COMMISSION

> Chilton Powell, *Chairman*
> John W. Ashton
> Dupuy Bateman, Jr.
> James D. Dunning
> Robert W. Estill
> William C. Frey
> Charles M. Guilbert, *Secretary*
> Mrs. Richard Harbour

Joseph M. Harte
Louis B. Keiter
H. Boone Porter, Jr.
Charles P. Price
Massey H. Shepherd, Jr., *Vice Chairman*
Jonathan G. Sherman
Charles W. F. Smith
Bonnell Spencer, O.H.C.
Albert R. Stuart
Leo Malania, *Co-ordinator*

THE CHURCH YEAR
PART I

The Calendar

1. Calendars in General

WE LIVE TODAY by many calendars. Their inter-related schedules vary according to our personal, social, civic, seasonal, and religious circumstances and commitments. Unifying them all is the civil calendar that hangs on our walls or lies on our desks.

From the ancient Hebrews we received the seven-day week. From the Romans we inherited the year of 365 days and 12 months, beginning with January 1st. By this calendar we mark our business commitments, our social engagements, our correspondence. Its universality and regularity are a great convenience, and, in the complexities of modern life, a remarkable simplification. Yet for many of us, it is not the only calendar by which we really live.

Each one of us has an individual calendar of remembrances that remind us of our growth and insight into the meaning of life: birthdays, wedding anniversaries, and the passing of loved ones. We think of our life-years in terms of such annual commemorations, or of work-projects accomplished, changes of job or residence, or unusual events that have affected us.

A primary division of our lives is made by the four seasons of spring, summer, autumn, and winter, for they determine the kind of work we do and the leisure we enjoy. Though equinox dates mark the lengthening or shortening of days and nights, these seasons vary, depending upon our geographical location. In New England the spring is short and the Indian summer of autumn is long; but in the South and Southwest the winter is short and the summer is long. Hawaii has no winter at all, and California has in reality only two seasons, rainy and dry.

Technology has mitigated, for all but the poor, unnecessary exposure to extremes of heat and cold, through heating and air-cooling devices. A husband may still follow the custom of sending wife and children to the seashore or the mountains in summer to escape the city heat, but he lives and works in their absence in the comfort of air-conditioned house and office. For agricultural workers the seasons determine the times of seeding and harvest: but many enjoy the food they wish at any time of the year from well-stocked super-markets and from deepfreezes at home.

Technology has also changed the work-week for thousands of manual laborers, office and professional personnel. The injunction of the fourth commandment. "Six days shalt thou labor and do all that thou hast to do," no longer applies.

The "long week-end" promises to become longer, with respites also in midweek. Added leisure does not mean that all work ceases on weekends or at specified daytime hours. Necessary work has to be staggered to take care of all hours of every week in certain industries, communication, transportation, and service agencies, hospitals, and welfare institutions, and public agencies, such as the police and fire departments. But the invention of electricity dissolved the boundaries of day and night, whether for work or for play. We must not forget, however, the thirty million and more in our country who live in poverty or on the edge of it, and enjoy little or none of these advantages.

For many families with sons and daughters of school and college age, the important calendar is the school year from September to June, with its intermittent holidays and summer vacation. This pattern of time affects more than academic activities. It also affects business cycles, recreation and travel, and life its the home. But an increasing number of summer educational programs engage more and more students of all ages; and greater leisure and affluence provide adults with new opportunities for vacation trips at any time of the year.

2. Religious Calendars

PERSONS of religious commitment observe other calendars. Civil law protects them from interference with their devotions on days of festival or fast. The Jewish Sabbath and the Christian Sunday are acknowledged as days of rest and recreation by many who care little for their religious significance. Christmas Day is an acknowledged civil holiday; Thanksgiving Day is an unusual combination of religious and national festival.

This accommodation of secular society to religious observance is largely formal, since it is left to individual conscience how each one celebrates the holy days of faith, whether Sabbath or Sunday, Christmas or Thanksgiving Day, or other days of religious feast or fast. Devout people find themselves under many pressures to turn holy days into holidays.

For social and business purposes, the Christmas season now begins not on Christmas Day, but on the day after Thankgiving Day. The "twelve days of Christmas" lead to an Epiphany anticlimax. In many churches Christmas is celebrated on the Fourth Sunday in Advent, not on the First Sunday after Christmas; and churches that observe liturgically the season of Advent often include Christmas carol services within that season.

Easter Day is as yet less corroded by advance commercialization—possibly because it is more difficult to reach it without passing through Lent and Holy Week. Always a Sunday, Easter Day benefits from the "long week-end," and often from school vacations. Unlike the Christmas season, the social events of Eastertide do not generally begin before Easter Day itself. The increasing pressures from secular and religious groups for a fixed date of Easter gather together many diverse interests.[1]

Secular pressures are also affecting the observance of Sundays. This is due not so much to the gradual removal of restrictive "blue laws" that go back to Constantine's edict of 321, which made Sunday a day of rest after the pattern of the Jewish Sabbath, but rather to the "long week-end" which takes so many away on vacation to places where religious services may not be easily available. Decline in attendance at Sunday worship may be due in part to a breakdown of spiritual discipline; but it may also be due to the failure of the Church to follow people where they are on Sundays.[2]

3. Radical Proposals

MOST PARISHES of the Episcopal Church gear their working calendar for church school, parish organizations, and every-member canvass to the school year from September to June, since this affects so many families. Though summer is no longer the "dead season" that it used to be in many congregations, there is nonetheless a notable pick-up of activity after Labor Day, which maintains its vigor until early June.

Several attempts, some more explicit than others, have been made to adjust the traditional Church Year to this circumstance. In 1966 a committee of the Diocese of Central New York produced a two-year lectionary for Sunday Morning Prayer, beginning in early September ("when the pace of parish life changes"), with provision for eight Sundays in a "Season of God the Father," and four Sundays for "All Saints' Tide," before moving into Advent.[3]

---

1. Since the turn of this century many business and professional groups have sought through international agencies the adoption of a fixed world calendar, including a fixed date for Easter. A declaration appended to the Constitution on the Sorted Liturgy of the Second Vatican Council records the willingness of the Roman Catholic Church to adopt a fixed date, provided that no world calendar interferes with the regular sequence of the seven-day week. The World Council of Churches is canvassing its member bodies for an opinion: and the Faster message of the Patriarch of Constantinople in 1969 has called on Eastern and Western Churches to agree on a common date of Easter. The date most commonly proposed is the second Sunday in April.

In all fairness it should be said that a fixed date of Easter would simply dissociate the feast from the spring full moon, in a way similar to the long-standing dissociation of Christmas from the winter solstice. The imagery of spring survives in many Easter hymns (and sermons), though this is rather alssurd for Christians living in the southern hemisphere-and even in some places of the northern hemisphere where the coming of spring is late. Nonetheless, the motivation for a fixed date of Easter (apart from ecumenical considerations) is primarily secular.

2. The Roman Catholic Church, traditionally very severe about the obligation of Sunday worship, has recognized the sociological change by introducing afternoon and evening masses on Sundays. Recent indults given to bishops allow Saturday evening masses also to serve as fulfillment of the Sunday obligation. See *Newsletter* of the Bishops' Committee on the Liturgy, June-July 1960, published by the Secretariat. 1312 Massachusetts Ave., N.W. Washington, D.C. 20005.

3. *A Suggested Lectionary 1966, With Lessons, Introductions and 1967 Supplement*. In addition to this "green book," there is a "white book" entitled "The Suggested Lectionary and the Holy Communion,

For many years Methodists in America have divided the Pentecost season in two, the latter half entitled "Kingdomtide." The most recent edition of *The Book of Worship for Church and Home* (1964) appoints eleven to sixteen Sundays after Pentecost, and thirteen or fourteen Sundays, beginning with the last Sunday in August to Kingdomtide. The aids to worship provided for the latter season suggest that the Kingdom is conceived not so much in eschatological terms, as in terms of the "social gospel."[4]

An ecumenical Joint Liturgical Group in Britain, meeting since October 1963, has produced a restructure of the Church Year based upon the three major feasts of Christmas, Easter, and Pentecost, with a two-year lectionary for both Eucharist and Daily Office, and Collects for Sundays and major holy days. The scheme is as follows:

Nine Sundays before Christmas

Six Sundays after Christmas

Nine Sundays before Easter

Six Sundays after Easter

Twenty-one Sundays after Pentecost[5]

In recent proposals for experimental use, the Liturgical Commission of the Church of England has adopted this scheme, with only minor revisions.[6]

This restructure is justified primarily by the need for a longer preparation for Christmas than the Advent season provides, so that the lectionary does justice to the Old Testament background of the Incarnation. Three lections are provided for each Sunday, and the Gospel lesson is required; but the principal lesson establishing the theme is the Old Testament lesson on the Sundays before Christmas, the Gospel lesson from Christmas Day to Pentecost, and the Epistle on the Sundays after Pentecost.[7]

With an appraisal of the Sunday Collects, Epistles and Gospels."

4. The season of Kingdomtide stems from a pamphlet, *The Christian Year* (1957), prepared by Fred Winslow Adams for the Commission on Worship of the Federal Council of Churches. A rationale for the season will be found in *The Celebration of the Gospel*, by H. Grady Flanlin. Joseph D. Quinlan, Jr.. and James F. White (New York-Nashville: Abingdon Press, 1964) pp. 87-88.

5. To date four volumes of essays by members of the Group have been published, all of them edited by Canon Ronald C. D. Jasper: *The Renewal of Worship, A Book of Essays* (Oxford, 1965); *The Calendar and Lectionary, A Reconsideration* (Oxford, 1967); *The Daily Office* (S.P.C.K.—Epworth Press, 1968); *An Additional Lectionary, for use at a Second Sunday Service* (S.P.C.K.—Epworth Press. 1969).

6. *The Calendar and Lessons for the Church's Year* (S.P.C.K., 5959). The scheme provides for eight Sundays after Christmas, and twenty-three after Pentecost, with the used holy days of the Prayer Book.

7. The lectionary provides topical themes, doctrinal or ethical, for each Sunday in sequences related to history or catechesis. Thus the pre-Christmas season has topics such as the Creation, the Fall, Noah, Abraham, Moses. The older Pre-Lenten Sundays (Ninth to Seventh before Easter) have Christ the Teacher, Christ the Healer, Christ the Worker of Miracles. This is highly artificial, but the aim is obviously pedagogical.

A novel rearrangement of the traditional Church Year appears in a volume of *Eucharistic Liturgies*, prepared by the Woodstock Center for Religion and Worship.[8] It divides the year into four seasons: 1) The Season of Promise, from Septuagesima through Palm Sunday; 2) the Season of Fulfillment, from Maundy Thursday through the Day of Pentecost; 3) the Time of the Church, or the Sundays after Pentecost; and 4) the Future Promise, from Advent through Epiphany season, with the Last Sunday after Epiphany as the festival of the Presentation. In effect, this scheme transfers to Pre-Lent and Lent the traditional theme of Advent, and makes of the Advent, Christmas, and Epiphany seasons times of primarily eschatological expectation.[9]

4. The Meaning of the Church Year

HOWEVER laudable the aims of these recent proposals for restructure of the Church Year, they are open to serious objections, which are not merely due to an attachment to ancient tradition. The inherent fallacy in these reconstructions is their approach to the Christian Year on a pedagogical rather than a kerygmatic basis. The Church Year is a Christian Year, an epitome of the Christian era, the "time of Christ" between his two advents. It proclaims at all times the *mysterium Christi*. It is neither a chronological review of the whole of salvation-history, nor a comprehensive course in all the doctrines of the faith. Its basic framework is the recurrence of Sunday, the day of the Resurrection; and its primary, original season is the great fifty days from Easter to Pentecost, that divides the year roughly into two coordinate periods: the one presents Christ in his earthly life and mission; the other presents him in his reigning life through the Spirit in his Church until his coming again.[10]

---

8. The Woodstock Center for Religion and Worship is an ecumenical undertaking to study the character of the American religious experience, and to develop forms of worship which reflect this experience. With office and studio in the Interchurch Center in Morningside Heights, New York, in the midst of Union, Jewish, and Woodstock Theological faculties, Columbia School of the Arts, Manhattan School of Music and the National Council of Churches, it is currently bringing together artists, musicians, poets, and theologians for an investigation of the processes that bring art into being in order to develop new insights into the dynamics of ritual.

9. *Eucharistic Liturgies, Studies in American Pastoral Liturgy*, edited by John Gallen, S.J. (New York: Newman Press. 1969). The treatment of Advent, Christmas, and Epiphany is a reversal of the traditional emphasis of these seasons upon the first advent of Christ (see below, Chapter II); and it is difficult to see how the Feast of the Presentation can be made the climax of the Church Year without considerable allegorical interpretation. One wonders if there is a strange relic of the old monastic office that began the year's lectionary with Genesis on Septuagesima (see below, n. 11).

10. One cannot improve upon the definition of the Church Year in the *Constitution on the Sacred Liturgy* (v. 102) of the Second Vatican Council: "Within the cycle of a year, [the Church] unfolds the whole mystery of Christ, not only from his incarnation and birth until his ascension, but also as reflected in the day of Pentecost, and the expectation of a blessed, hoped-for return of the Lord. Recalling thus the mysteries of redemption, the Church opens to the faithful the riches of her Lord's powers

It may be true that the majority of our congregations still operate in their parochial structures and activities upon the secular pattern of the school or work year. But will this always be so? We have already noted that the natural seasons no longer have a predominant impact upon our ordinary work and leisure, and that the summer season is by no means as dead in church life as it was in times past. The increasing mobility of our people at all seasons does not mean that they do not attend worship when they are not in their own parishes. In vacation centers, some congregations are larger in the summer, others in the winter, depending upon their geographical location. There are few parishes that do not welcome visitors from other congregations almost every Sunday of the year. Even so, we question whether the Church Year should be geared to the interests of seasonal parochial organizations.

We question also the psychological value of the more radical British scheme in lengthening the pre-Christmas and pre-Easter seasons. These two high points of the Church Year are better served by shorter and more intensive times of preparation, not by longer and more diffuse ones. The elimination of an Epiphany season in favor of a prolonged post-Christmas season is not realistic. Granted that Epiphany is not as exciting a feast as Christmas, it does mark nonetheless the psychological end of Christmas celebration. The Epiphany season provides a different emphasis and rhythm that bridge the Incarnation and the Passion themes.

The Church Year developed as a frame for the Sunday eucharistic worship of the Church, with its two foci of celebration: the Gospel lesson and the Gospel Sacrament. Saints' days have the same character, since they are commemorations of the death and resurrection of Christ in his members. The primary lectionary scheme of the Church Year is the Gospel lesson. Old Testament lessons and Epistles are but background and commentary upon the Gospel, and not vice versa. The conformity of the Daily Office to the Church Year was a gradual development, and was never completely carried out.[11]

---

and mercies, so that these are in some way made present at all times, and the faithful are enabled to lay hold of them and become filled with saving grace." (Translation by Walter M. Abbott, S.J.)

11. The Daily Office is founded upon a course reading of the Psalms and other Biblical books, developed first in private devotion and later by monastic communities. The earliest descriptions of monastic worship point to special lessons and customs on Sundays and in Eastertide. Only later were they enriched with seasonal antiphons, responsories, and collects. In the ancient Roman office, the entire Psalter was recited each week, and the lectionary was a course reading that began with Genesis at Septuagesima, interrupted only by assignment of Acts and Revelation to Eastertide, and of Isaiah to Advent.

The first Prayer Books ordered the Psalter in a monthly course, and began the course reading of Scripture in January. Only a few holy days had appropriate lessons. But the Elizabethan Prayer Book of 1559 extended proper lessons to Sundays and major holy days—a trend continued in later Prayer Books, along with proper Psalms. The American Book of 1892 provided proper lessons for 109 days, but otherwise ordered the office lectionary according to the civil year. Only in the 1920's was the office lectionary ordered according to the Church Year: and the American lectionary of 1943 completely reordered the Psalter away from the older rigid monthly course. The American Book also

The seasons of the Church Year are all Christ's seasons, including Pentecost. This has been obscured for us by the late medieval custom of dating half of the Sundays after the feast of the Trinity, instead of after Pentecost.[12] We have consequently lost the meaning of Advent as a linking of the two advents of Christ in an annual cycle that epitomizes the historical era of Christ—*Anno Domini*, in the year of our Lord. One result of this misunderstanding has been a certain pedagogical scheme that divides the Church Year into a twofold pattern of 1) the life of Christ, and 2) the teaching of Christ. Yet every Gospel of every Sunday reveals both his life and his teaching.[13]

Since the Church Year is "Christ's Year"—the year of the Lord—it points us to what Christ has done and is doing now in the time of our history. The theme of every eucharistic celebration is how the eternal God "came down from heaven" in the person of his Son Jesus Christ, who continues to live among us by his Holy Spirit, until "he shall come again to judge the living and the dead." Every specific celebration of this kerygma or proclamation is made present now—in this time, in our time—and thus realizes now the eternal verities of God and his Kingdom. It is a mistake, therefore, to organize the Church Year by a credal or pedagogical scheme based on a trinitarian division of times of God the Father, God the Son, and God the Holy Spirit. For every liturgy is offered to God the Holy Trinity in its doxologies and hymns and prayers—but offered always through Jesus Christ, who reveals to us Him "who was, and is, and is to come."[14]

Like all religious calendars, the Church Year is rooted in tradition. The calendars of primitive religions were response to astronomical and seasonal changes. Hebrew religion, building upon this foundation, transformed the cycle of festival and fast by reference to divine revelation in history. The Christian Year has

---

added in 1928 seasonal antiphons to the *Venite*. A few recent Anglican revisions suggest the inappropriateness of the *Te Deum* in penitential seasons (Advent, Pre-Lent, Lent: the 1549 Book forbade its use only in Lent). See B. H. Jones, *The American Lectionary* (New York: Morehouse-Gorham Co., 1944). pp. 13-16, 37-38.

12. The custom, never adopted at Rome, was characteristic of churches in England and northern Europe, and survives in Anglican and Lutheran rites, and those of a few religious Orders.

13. The absurdity is evident from any examination of the Prayer Book Gospels. They exhibit teaching on Advent 2 and 3, Epiphany 5 and 6, Septuagesima, Sexagesima, Lent 3 and 5. Easter 2 and 5, Sunday after Ascension, and Pentecost. Narratives of his life occur in the Gospels of Trinity 5, 7, 12, 14, 16, 19, 21, 24, and the Sunday next before Advent.

14. The Methodists' season of Kingdomtide is subject to similar objections, in that the Kingdom of Cod is an eternal reality and also an eschatological reality that is now breaking into history as a consequence of Christ's revelation and resurrection. Every season of the Church Year points to the Kingdom-whenever and wherever God is obeyed in acknowledgment of Christ as Lord. No season can celebrate the Kingdom as an accomplished fact in history, except in so far as it celebrates its accomplishment in the life and death and resurrection of Christ and the earnest of his Spirit.

Similarly, the proposal of an "All Saints' Tide" by the Central New York committee ignores the fact that All Saints' is the festival of the Church as the Body of Christ within the season after Pentecost. In one sense, the season after Pentecost is the season of the Church between the two advents of Christ.

developed this insight, as it concentrates upon a particular moment of history—a moment that illuminates all history and all historical revelation, in the coming of Jesus Christ into our life and in his resurrection from the dead.

The Church Year still bears the marks of its pre-Christian history. But it is not tied to natural phenomena, and it is not a divinely revealed law of observance. It is evangelical in the truest sense, for it is the result of ecclesiastical regulation for purposes of commemoration and edification based upon the one and final revelation of Christ. It is therefore possible for the Church to revise and re-order it at any time, if it deems this necessary for pastoral reasons. In this sense, the radical reconstructions being proposed are not out of order in so far as they attempt to meet particular needs of edification. But our critical evaluation of them refers to a principle: namely, the revelation in time of the "mystery of Christ," and, more particularly, of all that is implicit in the Paschal mystery. "For salvation is nearer to us now than when we believed; the night is far gone, the day is at hand."[15]

5. Present Proposals

THE PROPOSALS for reform of the Church Year herewith offered by the Standing Liturgical Commission are conservative. They are rooted in sound tradition, and are designed to restore the integrity of the year without novel or adventitious embellishments. Our principal inspiration has been the great work of our Roman Catholic brothers in reforms that are responsive to the directives of the Second Vatican Council. We are in complete accord with the Council's objectives in the reform of the Church Year:[16]

1. The primary importance of Sunday, the Lord's Day.
   "The Lord's Day is the original feast day.... Other celebrations, unless they be truly of overriding importance, must not have precedence over this day, which is the foundation and nucleus of the whole liturgical year."
2. The greater importance of the Proper of Time.
   "The minds of the faithful must be directed primarily toward the feasts of the Lord in which the mysteries of salvation are celebrated in the course of the year. Therefore, the Proper of Time shall be given preference which is its due over the feasts of the saints, so that the entire cycle of the mysteries of salvation can be suitably recalled."
3. The subordinate place of the Proper of Saints.
   "Lest the feasts of the saints, however, take precedence over the feasts which commemorate the very mysteries of salvation, many of them should be left

---

15. Romans 13:11-12. from the Epistle on the First Sunday in Advent.
16. *Constitution on the Sacred Liturgy*, v, 106-111.

to be celebrated by a particular Church or nation or religious community; only those should be extended to the universal Church which commemorate saints who are truly of universal significance."

The agency responsible for this reform in the Roman Catholic Church has been the Council for Implementation of the Constitution on the Sacred Liturgy (*Consilium ad exsequendam Constitutionem de Sacra Liturgia*).[17] In 1966 the Consilium admitted to its deliberations and consultations six Observers from the non-Roman Catholic Churches, including two representatives of the Anglican Communion appointed by the Archbishop of Canterbury.[18] The Consilium has now completed its work of revision of the Calendar and a three-year cycle of lections and graduals for the Mass. These went into effect on an experimental basis beginning in Advent 1969.[19] The Consilium held its last plenary session in April 1970; hereafter the work will be in the charge of the new Congregation for Divine Worship.

Meanwhile consultations in other Churches on calendar revision have been moving in similar directions. Following the Lambeth Conference of 1968, a Liturgical Consultation was held at Westminster by representatives of all the Anglican provinces. With regard to the Calendar, it was agreed to drop the season of Pre-Lent and to name Sundays after Pentecost in place of the long-standing Anglican custom of naming them after Trinity.[20] The Inter-Lutheran Commission on Worship, representing the major Lutheran bodies of the United States and Canada, have also agreed to similar changes. Its proposed liturgy is due to be published in 1970. Likewise, the Commission on Worship of the Consultation on Church Union has recommended the observance of the following seasons: Advent, Christmas, Epiphany, Lent (with Holy Week), Easter (including

---

17. The Consilium is the continuation of the Vatican Council's Commission on the Liturgy, and meets biennially. It is an international body of some 50 cardinals, archbishops and bishops, assisted by about 200 counsellors and consultants. Subject to papal approval, decisions of the Consilium are embodied in formal decrees and instructions by the Sacred Congregation for Divine Worship (*Sacra Congregatio pro Cultu Divino*), formerly the Sacred Congregation of Rites. These documents and other pertinent matters, with explanatory papers, are published in the monthly periodical *Notitiae*. These are admirably summarized in the monthly *Newsletter* of The Bishops' Committee on the Liturgy (U.S.A.), and often in the pages of the periodical *Worship*, published by St. John's Abbey, Collegeville, Minnesota.

18. The Anglican Observers are the Reverend Canon Ronald C. D. Jasper and the Reverend Massey H. Shepherd, Jr. The Observers have no voice or vote in plenary sessions, but are free to offer their opinions in writing, and frequently discuss the issues in informal meetings with members and consultants.

19. See the *Calendarium Romanum* and the *Ordo Lectionum Missae*, both published by the Vatican Press in 1969, following promulgation by Pope Paul VI on February 14 and April 3, respectively.

20. The minutes of this consultation have not been published, but have been circulated to all liturgical commissions of the several Anglican Churches.

Ascension Day), and Pentecost.[21] This is in line with recent liturgical revisions being prepared in new service books of the Presbyterians and the United Church of Christ.[22]

During the past two decades, the Standing Liturgical Commission has published several studies of the Calendar and the Proper for Holy Days. The General Convention of 1964 approved the optional and experimental use of a revised Calendar, with proper collects and lessons for "The Lesser Feasts and Fasts and for Special Occasions." With minor modifications, this revised Calendar and Proper were approved for another triennium by the General Convention of 1967. In addition, General Convention has authorized for optional use *The Book of Offices*, which includes a section entitled "Benedictions for Certain Occasions in the Church Year."[23] These publications, reviewed in the light of recent ecumenical discussions as outlined above, form the basis for the present proposals presented to the Church for trial use, subject to approval by the General Convention of 1970.[24]

In the prefatory material of the Prayer Book, a major recasting has been made of the "Tables and Rules for the Movable and Immovable Feasts," which have had only minor modifications since 1789. The new Table has been placed before the Calendar and given a new heading: "The Calendar of the Church Year Observed in this Church." These rules give basic directives for the respective rank of holy days, and adjustments that must be made when fixed ones coincide with movable ones.

---

21. See *An Order of Worship for The Proclamation of the Word of Cod and The Celebration of the Lord's Supper* (Cincinnati: Forward Movement Publications, 1968), pp. 77-79. The use of this liturgy under specified conditions was approved by Special General Convention II, at South Bend, Indiana, in September 1969.

22. *The Directory of Worship*, revised and approved in 1961 by the United Presbyterian Church U.S.A. and the Presbyterian Church in the U.S., distinctly recommends the observance of the chief seasons (chap. 4. sec 4).

23. In the series of *Prayer Book Studies* (New York: The Church Pension Fund) see the following volumes: II *The Liturgical Lectionary* (1950); IX. *The Calendar* (1957); XII. *The Propers for the Minor Holy Days* (1958); XII. *Supplement. The Collects, Epistles and Gospels for the Lesser Feasts and Fasts* (1960); XVI. *The Calendar and the Collects, Epistles and Gospels for the Lesser Feasts and Fasts*, A Supplementary Revision of Prayer Book Studies IX and XII (1965).

The second half of Study XVI was published separately by The Church Pension Fund in 1963: *The Calendar and the Collects, Epistles, and Gospels for the Lesser Feasts and Fasts and for Special Occasions*. It was this publication that received approval from the General Convention of 1964, and was approved again for a further triennium by the General Convention of 1967.

24. *The Book of Offices*, Services (or Certain Occasions not provided in the Book of Common Prayer (Third Edition: New York: The Church Pension Fund, sg60). The General Convention of 1958 approved this new edition, subject to approval by the House of Bishops. This was given at its meeting October 17-2a, 1959.

Certain reference tables for finding the date of Easter and other movable feasts have also been revised, and we recommend that these be placed in an appendix and not in the prefatory section of the Book.[25]

The principal features of the new rules are as follows:

1. The peculiar privilege of Sundays as feasts of our Lord, so that no other commemoration may take precedence of them, except a few major festivals of Christ, and certain occasional observances of primary significance in the life of a congregation.
2. The elimination of octaves,[26] though maintaining the privilege of Holy Week and Easter Week from the intrusion of other holy days.
3. The addition of seven new major feasts ("Red Letter Days"), all of them of New Testament events or persons, except Holy Cross Day. One of these is a new feast: the others are drawn from "Lesser Feasts and Fasts."[27]
4. The exclusion from the days marked for fasting and self-denial of Fridays in the Easter season and of major feasts that may fall on other Fridays or on the weekdays of Lent.
5. Optional observances of additional saints' days and special occasions (as is now the case in "Lesser Feasts and Fasts"), but with the proviso that none may usurp the place of Sundays and major holy days. Days of absolute privilege are Christmas Day, Ash Wednesday, the last three days of Holy Week, Easter Day, Ascension Day, and the Day of Pentecost.
6. A placing here of the two general rubrics that regulate the use of the Sunday proper on weekdays (cf. Prayer Book, page 90).

The Calendar is printed on twelve pages, one for each month, and includes the full listing of both the major fixed feasts ("Red Letter Days") and the minor or optional holy days ("Black Letter Days"). as in "Lesser Feasts and Fasts." Several dates have been changed from the listing in previous authorized calendars, and several new entries have been added.[28] We do not propose, however, to include in

---

25. These are: 1) A Table to Find Easter Day, from A.D. 1900 to A.D. 2089 (cf. Prayer Book, pp. liii-liv): 2) A Table to Find Movable Feasts and Holy Days (cf. Prayer Book, p. lv); and 3) Rules for Finding the Date of Easter Day (cf. Prayer Book, pp. lii and lvi). This third table has been rewritten in more simplified language to aid in calculating the Golden Numbers and the Sunday letters.

26. In Roman use no feast is now observed with an octave.

27. The new feast is the Confession of St. Peter on Jan. 18. The others, from LFF, are: St. Joseph, the Visitation, St. Mary Magdalene, St. Mary the Virgin, Holy Cross Day, and St. James the Brother of our Lord. The feast of the Circumcision is now called The Holy Name of our Lord Jesus Christ.

28. Of major feasts: the Visitation (May 31), as in the new Roman Calendar, for it belongs chronologically between the Annunciation and the Nativity of St. John Baptist. New entries, in addition to the major feast of the Confession of St. Peter (Jan. 18), are: Beech (Apr. 2); Mireki (June 18); Neale (Aug. 7); DuBose (Aug. 18); Martyrs of New Guinea (Sept. 2); Grosseteste (Oct. 9); Commemoration of All Faithful Departed (Nov. 2); and Ferrar (Dec. 1). The Commission has adhered to its

the Prayer Book the proper of the lesser or optional days, but only the Common of Saints and the proper for Special Occasions. These latter propers include due provision for the traditional Ember and Rogation Days, though allowing their observance at any appropriate time.[29]

Sundays, Seasons, and Holy Days

THE ORDER of the Church Year is laid out in three major sections—a plan that has been followed in Western service books since the Gelasian Sacramentary of the eighth century. These are:

1. The Proper of Time (Temporale), which includes the Sundays and other movable feasts of the Church Year, and three fixed days in the Incarnation cycle: Christmas, Holy Name, and Epiphany.[30]
2. The Proper of Saints (Sanctorale), or the fixed holy days listed in the Calendar, except the three feasts of the Incarnation cycle. It also includes the Common of Saints.
3. Special Occasions (Votives), which may be observed at appropriate times for the purpose of particular devotion and intercession.[31]

1. Sundays

BASIC to the whole reform of the Church Year is the restoration of Sunday as a privileged feast of our Lord. Sunday is more than an extension of Easter; it is an epitome of all the fundamental mysteries of our faith. It recalls specifically the resurrection of our Lord on the first day of the week, and the gift of the Holy Spirit on the Day of Pentecost. Sunday is the day of the "new creation," which ties

---

principle that no new entries should be admitted until at least fifty years after the death of the person to be commemorated. The one exception to this rule is the Martyrs of New Guinea.

29. The re-ordering of material will necessitate a new edition of the "Lesser Feasts and Fasts," which, it is hoped, may be authorized on a permanent basis, similar to *The Book of Offices*, (1960). As now projected, the new edition would include propers for the weekdays of Lent, and for the lesser holy days; and, for convenience, the Common of Saints.

30. The feasts of St. Stephen, St. John, and Holy Innocents, which have traditionally been included in the Proper of Time are now shifted to the Proper of Saints, since they are not to take precedence over the First Sunday after Christmas. The new Roman Calendar also has this rearrangement.

31. The new Roman reforms classify Votives in three categories: 1) *Rituales*, those propers used in connection with the celebration of various rites, such as baptism, marriage, burial: 2) *Ad diversa*, associated with special times of intercession, such as unity, peace, labor, the sick: and 3) *Votivae*, in association with devotions to the Holy Trinity, the Holy Cross, the Name of Jesus, etc.

together the first day of creation (Genesis 1:1-5) and the final day of consummation, the "day of the Lord" (Revelation 1:4–10)[32]

There is no evidence that the ancient Church interrupted the Sunday observance with special commemorations, though it was customary, within the Sunday celebration, to consecrate bishops.[33] The oldest Roman Sacramentaries do not provide a proper for all Sundays, but only when there was a papal "stational mass." Later Sacramentaries, designed for priests in parish churches, filled in the gap with a complete set of propers for every Sunday. Thus from the ninth century there was established a tradition that certain Sundays, generally those of the papal stational mass, were more privileged than others; and hence saints' days and other feasts were allowed to take precedence over Sundays of lesser rank.

The Prayer Book continued this medieval custom. Sundays after the Epiphany and after Pentecost, and even several Sundays after Easter could be supplanted by fixed feasts. In the modern Roman Catholic Church, this substitution of other propers for that of the Sunday reached enormous proportions, until a reverse trend was set in motion by Pope Pius X in 1911, and later accelerated by Pope John XXIII in the first comprehensive reform of the Calendar since the sixteenth century. Pope John's Calendar of 1960 has now been superseded by the Calendar of 1969, which conforms to the directives of the Second Vatican Council, The new Calendar gives absolute privilege to all Sundays in Advent, Lent, and Eastertide. In other seasons Sunday may be superseded only by feasts of the highest rank (*Solemnitas*) or by a major feast of Christ (*Festum*).[34]

The Eastern Church has maintained the privilege of Sunday more consistently than the Churches of the West. Only a few festivals have been admitted on Sundays—all of them connected with the "mysteries of Christ" in his Church. Christmas or the Epiphany has precedence, of course, when it falls on a Sunday.[35] Churches of the "free" tradition of worship have always kept Sunday as their holy day, for it is the "Lord's Day" of the New Testament. Most of them observe Easter and Pentecost on their appropriate Sundays; but commonly celebrate other feasts of Christ, such as Christmas, the Epiphany, and Ascension on the Sundays

---

32. H. B. Porter, *The Day of Light: The Biblical and Liturgical Meaning of Sunday* (Greenwich: Seabury Press, 1960). For the origin and early development of Sunday, see Willy Rordorf, *Sunday* (Philadelphia: Westminster Press, 1968).

33. Hippolytus, *Apostolic Tradition* 2; *Apostolic Constitutions*, viii. 4.

34. Of the fourteen days noted as *Solemnitas*, four are always on Sunday: Easter Day, Pentecost, Trinity (1 Pentecost) and Christ the King (Last Sunday after Pentecost). Six may take precedence: Christmas Day, Epiphany, Nativity of St. John Baptist, SS. Peter and Paul, Assumption of the Blessed Virgin Mary, and All Saints'. Two feasts of our Lord (of the class called *Festum*) are assigned to Sundays: Holy Family (1 Christmas) and the Baptism of Christ (1 Epiphany).

35. Orthodoxy Sunday (1 Lent), which commemorates the end of the iconoclastic controversy and the restoration of reverence for holy images; the Holy Fathers of the Council of Nicaea (7 Easter); and All Saints (1 Pentecost).

near their date. Often, however, their Sundays have been given over to special observances, which in more traditional terms would be called Votives.[36]

Objections have been raised to the new rule of giving privilege to the Sunday Proper over that of any saint's day or fixed holy day (other than the six feasts of our Lord)[37] on the ground that occasional occurrence of a saint's day on a "lesser" Sunday has devotional and pedagogical value. In answer it may be said that the present Prayer Book excludes certain major holy days from Sunday observance in the seasons of Advent, Pre-Lent, Lent and part of Eastertide.[38] The new three-year cycle of lections will greatly increase the number of Epistles and Gospels assigned to Sundays, which hitherto have been assigned only to fixed holy days.[39] The sequential reading of the Synoptic Gospels on the Epiphany and post-Pentecost Sundays, the readings from John scattered throughout the year, and the lessons from Acts in the Easter season, should provide ample opportunity for preachers to develop themes related to the New Testament apostles and evangelists. The preacher may also use a saint's day collect at the beginning or close of his sermon, if he thinks it appropriate; and the insertion of special commemorations may be made in the prayers.

2. Seasons

ADVENT. This season with its four Sundays has not been materially altered. The old Gallican rites, from whence the season comes, had a longer period of six weeks or "forty days." It was essentially penitential in character and emphasized the eschatological second advent. The revision of the season at Rome in the late sixth century reduced the period, and suffused into it more joyful theme of of the Nativity. Traces of the longer period survived in medieval usages, and one trace comes to us by way of the Sarum Use in the Sunday next before Advent, whose proper has really an Advent character.

---

36. For example, Race Relations Sunday (second in February); Rural Life Sunday (5 Easter-Rogation Sunday); Christian Home Sunday (Mother's Day, second in May); Labor Sunday (first in September); Reformation Sunday (last in October), etc. For a defense of these observances, see Clarence Seidenspinner, *Great Protestant Festivals* (New York: Henry Schuman, 1952).

37. These are Christmas Day, Holy Name, Epiphany, Presentation, Transfiguration, and All Saints' Day—the last named a celebration of Christ in his Body the Church, which may always be observed on a Sunday in addition to the feast day.

38. Always excluded are St. Andrew, St. Thomas, and Annunciation; and frequently excluded are the Conversion of St. Paul, Presentation, St. Matthias, St. Mark, and occasionally SS. Philip and James, and St. Barnabas.

39. Present Gospel lessons for fixed holy days included in the proposed three year cycle for Sundays are: Andrew, 3 Epiphany A; Annunciation, 4 Advent B; Confession of St. Peter, 14 Pentecost A; Conversion of St. Paul, 16 Pentecost C; Matthew, 3 Pentecost A; James, 22 Pentecost B (the Markan parallel); James of Jerusalem, 3 Pentecost B; Matthias, 5 Easter B; Michaelmas, 2 Epiphany B; Philip and James, 5 Easter A; Simon and Jude, 6 Easter C; Thomas, 2 Easter; Transfiguration, Last Epiphany.

The present revision, in line with the recent Roman schedule, develops the eschatological theme in the last Sundays after Pentecost, with a climax on the First Sunday of Advent—thus linking the two halves of the Church Year. The Second and Third Sundays are devoted to John the Baptist, the story of whose ministry and teaching serve, not only as the heralding of the coming Incarnation, but also as the foretelling of the Judgment to come. The Fourth Sunday emphasizes the Annunciation as an immediate prelude to Christmas.[40]

The peculiar emphasis given to the Second Sunday by the Collect of the 1549 Prayer Book, so that it has come to be known popularly as "Bible Sunday," is now transferred to the Fourth Sunday after the Epiphany, where it is more suitably placed and set forth in a proper that recalls the Lord's ministry and teaching as the fulfillment of the Scriptures.

CHRISTMAS. Though the season of twelve days is not changed in length, considerable reworking of its arrangements and propers has been done. Christmas Day itself has been assigned three sets of propers, to accord with ancient tradition in the West and to meet the needs of parishes with several celebrations of the feast. The First Sunday after Christmas is given privilege over the three saints' days that follow Christmas Day—these being reduced in rank to those of comparable holy days. The theme of Christmas Day is therefore continued on the Sunday following. In the new Roman Calendar this Sunday is the feast of the Holy Family. But we have transferred this theme to the Second Sunday (which occurs in four out of every seven years), by combining the themes of our present Second Sunday after Christmas and the First Sunday after the Epiphany.

The eighth day after Christmas, or New Year's Day, is to be called "The Holy Name of our Lord Jesus Christ," for this is the basic theme of the proper.[41] It is also a more fitting title than the older emphasis on the Circumcision for what is in popular celebration a feast of the New Year, since it is in "the Name of Jesus" that all men find their salvation (cf. Acts 4:10-12). The Roman Church has returned to its ancient tradition of celebrating this day as a feast of St. Mary the Mother of God.[42]

---

40. The theme of the Annunciation on this Sunday has much precedent in the ancient Sacramentaries, and also in the custom of many Eastern Churches from which it probably derived. Because the Sundays in Lent and of Easter, and the Days of Holy Week and Easter Week are privileged, the Annunciation is never celebrated on a Sunday. The new arrangement also removes the anomaly of the Gospel of the "annunciation to Joseph" on the First Sunday after Christmas.

41. Desire to change the title is also evident in recent Anglican proposals. The Canadian Prayer Book of 1962 gives as the major title: "The Octave of Christmas." The proposed Calendars of the Church of England (1969) and of the Church of Ireland (1969) call it "The Naming of Jesus."

42. The rationale given in the new Roman Calendar is simply that of ancient tradition. But it may also be due to pragmatic considerations—a festival near Christmas that celebrates the place of Mary in the economy of salvation, and that devotes the New Year to her honor. This day has always been a holy day of obligation for Roman Catholic. It makes more sense, therefore, to have such a day devoted to Mary than to the Circumcision.

EPIPHANY. The feast of the Epiphany retains its traditional Western theme of the Magi, but the Sunday after the Epiphany is a new festival of the Baptism of Christ. The Baptism theme, of course, has always been primary in the Epiphany celebration of the Eastern Churches, and the Roman Calendar has observed it on the octave of the Epiphany. Our American Prayer Book revision of 1928 introduced the Baptism on the Second Sunday after the Epiphany. By transferring the Holy Family theme to the Second Sunday after Christmas, we are able to join the Roman Catholics with this new feast on the First Sunday and keep the traditional celebration of the first miracle at Cana on the Second Sunday, as has been customary in the Roman and Anglican tradition.

The elimination of the Pre-Lenten season (see below) makes it possible to lengthen and enrich the Epiphany season with three more Sundays, and thus more adequately set forth the beginnings of our Lord's ministry, when he openly manifested himself, by his teaching and his deeds, as the Redeemer of the world.

The Last Sunday after the Epiphany—regardless of how many Sundays there may be[43]—will always be devoted to the Transfiguration, which serves as a significant link between the revelation of the Lord's glory in his Incarnation and in his Passion. It is thus made both a climax of "epiphany" and a preparation for his "exodus." An appropriate Collect, other than the one for the feast on August 6, has therefore been provided.[44]

PRE-LENT. This season has been suppressed in the new Roman Calendar, and there has been general agreement in the Anglican and Lutheran Churches to eliminate it in future revisions of the liturgy. It originated in the sixth century in Rome with stational Sunday masses at the principal papal basilicas, at a time of special supplication for God's defense and protection in the midst of Italy's desolation from war, pestilence, and famine. Though some scholars attribute its adoption at Rome, especially in monastic circles, to the influence of the Eastern Churches, with their longer season of Lent, Pre-Lent has never been actually included in the Lenten discipline. It is a shadowy season of neither festival nor fast, and the original purpose no longer seems particularly significant. It would seem more advantageous today to add its three Sundays to the Epiphany season.[45]

---

43. Because of the movable date of Easter there may be from four to nine Sundays. But the minimum of four Sundays is rare—only when Easter falls as early as March 22-24, which will not occur within the next century except in A.D. 2008.

44. The Roman lectionary continues to observe the Transfiguration on 2 Lent. But the new Lutheran liturgy supports our scheme of observing the Transfiguration on the Sunday before Lent; cf. *Service Book and Hymnal of the Lutheran Church in America* (1958), p. 80.

45. The proposed Calendar of the British Liturgical Group has, however, incorporated the three Sundays into its season of Nine Sundays before Easter, though it preserves the traditional beginning of Lent on Ash Wednesday. This does not seem to us as helpful a solution as the Roman one of giving these Sundays to the post-Epiphany season. Psychologically, it is difficult to begin the preparation for Easter so many weeks ahead of the feast. See above, pp. 37, 39.

LENT. The forty days of Lent retain their primary character of preparation for Easter, with the traditional themes of penitence, discipline, and learning, admirably summarized in the Invitation of the new Penitential Order for Ash Wednesday, which has been adapted from the Canadian Prayer Book. The re-ordering of the proper of the season returns to the ancient emphasis upon a synopsis of the history of salvation in the Old Testament, and the signs in Jesus' ministry that point to his death and resurrection. These are all gathered together in the great Vigil Service of Easter Eve.

The subsidiary period known as "Passiontide" has been shifted, in order to concentrate the theme in Holy Week, which has been given its own proper title. The true "Passion Sunday" is Palm Sunday, marked by the reading of the gospel passion narratives.[46] The liturgy of this Sunday has been enriched with suitable forms for the Blessing of Palms and the Procession, now almost universal in our churches;[47] and similarly, the Good Friday liturgy has been outlined in full and, following the reading of the St. John Passion, has been provided with the solemn intercessions that have been characteristic of the day from the most ancient times.

A distinction has been made between Holy Saturday and Easter Eve. In the ancient liturgies, Easter celebration began with the solemn Vigil on Saturday evening which marked the conclusion of Lent. No liturgical offices, other than the daily choir offices, were observed on that day before the Vigil. The First Prayer Book introduced a proper for the Communion on Saturday (called "Easter Even"), contrary to the devotional instinct of the early Christians that no celebration of the Eucharistic feast is appropriate during the time when "the bridegroom is taken away" (cf. Mark 2:20). We have therefore provided for only a "Ministry of the Word" on Holy Saturday.

EASTER. The restoration of the concept of the "great fifty days" is one of the principal features of the present revision. The season begins with the dramatic ceremonies of the Lighting of the Paschal Candle and the Vigil, which have become increasingly popular in our churches.[48] These observances are optional,

---

46. The *Gregorian Sacramentary* entitles the Fifth Sunday of Lent as "Sunday of the Passion," and this title passed into some editions of the Sarum Missal. But "Passiontide" became a common term in Anglicanism only in the 19th century, and first appears in Anglican Prayer Book revisions of the 1920's, including the American 1928. Our proposals are in accord with the new Roman Calendar.

47. For the Blessing of Palms and Procession, cf. *The Book of Offices* (3rd ed., 1960), pp. 96-99; Indian Prayer Book Supplement, 1960, pp. 91-93. Several Anglican Prayer Books provide for a Gospel of the "Triumphal Entry" at an extra celebration on Palm Sunday—English 1928, Scottish, South African, and Indian. For the Good Friday rite, cf. *Holy Week Offices*, edited by Massey H. Shepherd, Jr., for the Associated Parishes, Inc. (Seabury Press, 1958). pp. 74-86.

48. The Easter Vigil is common to both Eastern and Western Churches, but its observance in the Roman Church was revised and restored to the nighttime by Pius XII in 1950. Since that date its popularity has spread to other Churches. Cf. *The Book of Offices*, 3rd ed., 1960, pp. 99-102; Shepherd, *Holy Week Offices*, pp. 87-106.

however, and not mandatory. The privileged character of all the days of Easter Week is marked by an individual proper for each day of the week. But the octave has been eliminated by dating the Sundays according to the season and not after Easter Day itself. Hence, what was formerly the First Sunday after Easter is now the Second Sunday of Easter, and so on. The principal resurrection narratives have been spread over the first three Sundays, and the traditional "Good Shepherd Sunday" is now the Fourth of the season. The rest of the Sundays take up the Gospels from the Johannine discourse, with the "high-priestly" prayer of our Lord on the Seventh Sunday. The Day of Pentecost is now included within the season as its proper (and ancient) climax.[49]

Ascension Day remains as a major feast, but it is more definitely a part of the total Paschal celebration, without an octave or the mark of a new season called Ascensiontide. For the redemptive acts of resurrection, ascension, and gift of the Spirit belong together—each one implying the others.

The Rogation Days are provided in the section of "Special Occasions," with option to use their propers at any convenient time, since the days of "seeding and ploughing" vary in different geographical areas according to the climate. It is hoped that the freeing of these days from a fixed place in the Calendar before Ascension Day will make them more popular, especially since the propers have been enriched by themes of stewardship in work and in the use of natural resources.

AFTER PENTECOST. The second half of the Church Year is coordinate with the first, since it celebrates the continuing work of Christ in his Church by the Spirit,[50] between his first and second advents. For this reason, it has seemed wise to return to the more ancient custom of naming the Sundays as after Pentecost, rather than after the special feast of the Holy Trinity on the First Sunday of the season. This proposal was actually made by the revision commission of our 1928 Prayer Book, but was rejected at the time because other Anglican Churches were not prepared to make the change. Today, consultations with other Anglican liturgical commissions and with the Lutherans reveal a strong desire to abandon the datings after Trinity and return to a post-Pentecost season. The new calendars and lectionaries of the Church of England and the Church of Ireland already have made the change.

The new three-year lectionary cycle provides a rich store of Biblical materials, with particular course reading in the Gospels and Epistles. Towards the end of the season the emphasis becomes eschatological, thus leading into Advent. The Roman feast of Christ the King has been shifted to the Last Sunday of the

---

49. The early Christians generally used the word "Pascha" to refer to the mysteries of Easter Eve and Easter Day; "Pentecost" was the common term for the whole fifty days. Cf. Tertullian, *On Baptism* 19 and *On the Crown* 3; Origen, *Against Celsus* viii. 22; Council of Nicaea, 325, can. 20.

50. See above, pp. 40–41.

season; and though we have not adopted the name, we have provided the same proper for this final Sunday. The celebration of Christ's universal lordship is a fitting conclusion to a year that began with the advent of Christ as our Savior and our Judge.

3. Fixed Holy Days

THE First Prayer Book of 1549 drastically reduced the number of fixed holy days for liturgical observance to major feasts of our Lord, commemorations of the apostles and evangelists, one feast of the angels, and All Saints' Day. The purpose was not merely to simplify the overloaded calendar of the late Middle Ages, but also to concentrate on the primary authority of Scripture, since no saint's name was admitted later than the New Testament period.

The Second Prayer Book of 1552, however, added certain calendrical notes and a few additional names of saints, probably for the convenience of schools, courts, and trade, after the manner of an almanac calendar. The new Calendar issued by Elizabeth I in 1561 included a much larger listing of saints, but all these "Black Letter Days" were excluded from any liturgical commemoration. The Prayer Book of 1662 (still standard in the Church of England) continued the list, with a few additions; but only the "Red Letter Days" were provided with a proper for regular observance.

A new turn was taken in the revisions of Anglican Prayer Books in the 1920's. Additional feasts of New Testament saints, drawn from tradition, were provided, along with "Commons" that might be used for saints listed among the "Black Letter Days," or for patronal saints. The Prayer Books of Ireland and Scotland raised to "Red Letter Days" the feasts of their national patron saints; and the American Book included the celebration of Independence as a "Red Letter Day."[51] The American revisers also proposed a list of "Black Letter Days" for the 1928 Book; and although this was rejected, the Book contained a common for "A Saint's Day," without further direction as to what saint may be commemorated.

The desire for a richer Calendar and proper has continued in Anglicanism from a variety of motives. It has been felt that the seeming restriction of "sanctity" to the figures of the New Testament has been a distorted view not only of history, but also of the witness of the Holy Spirit in the life of the Church in all ages. The great increase in the number of weekday celebrations of the Eucharist has raised the practical problem of the devotional value of monotonous repetition of Sunday propels through the week, except on the few days for which "Red Letter" provisions have been made. An enriched Calendar and proper would open to

---

51. For the history of this development, see W. K. Lowther Clarke's essay "The Calendar," in *Liturgy and Worship*, edited by Clarke and Charles Harris (London: S.P.C.K., 1932), pp. 215 ff: and *Prayer Book Studies IX, The Calendar* (1957), Vol. 2, pp. 150-171.

the Church a larger treasure of material for its edification, both from the Bible and from the history of its witness among many peoples its every age and land. Thus in the renewed work of revision of Anglican Prayer Books in the past two decades, Calendars have been markedly enlarged by fresh commemorations, and congregations have been encouraged to keep them.[52]

The Standing Liturgical Commission, in line with this development, produced its first Study on the Calendar in 1957, and followed this by proposals for suitable propers in *Prayer Book Studies* XII (1958; with Supplement, 1960) and XVI (1963). The General Convention of 1964, acting under the amended Article X of the Constitution, authorized for optional, experimental use these "Lesser Feasts and Fasts." With a few minor revisions, this authorization was renewed by the General Convention of 1967.

This experiment has been very satisfactory to those who have used the new Calendar and propers. The Commission, therefore, proposes that the full Calendar of "Lesser Feasts and Fasts," revised in the light of further study and experience, be adopted in the Prayer Book. But it also suggests that the observance of the "Black Letter Days" remain optional, and that the propers for these days continue to be contained in a separate book, authorized by General Convention after the manner of *The Book of Offices* (1960). For purposes of convenience, however, the "Common of Saints" would be included both in the Prayer Book and in the revised "Lesser Feasts and Fasts." The rules governing their use provide that no observance of any of the "Black Letter Days" take precedence over a Sunday or major holy day.

The fixed holy days are of three types: 1) those connected with the Incarnation cycle; 2) the commemoration of saints; and 3) the anniversaries of significant events in the life of the Church.

1. *Incarnation cycle*. No major change has been made in the feasts of our Lord that are related primarily to Christmas Day and the Epiphany: namely, Presentation, Annunciation, and the Nativity of St. John Baptist. Two new major feasts of this cycle have been added: the Visitation on May 31, providing a link between the Annunciation and St. John Baptist;[53] and a festival of the Baptism of Christ on the First Sunday after the Epiphany. The feast of the Circumcision on January 1 has been named, as in "Lesser Feasts and Fasts," the Holy Name of our Lord Jesus Christ. The Transfiguration feast

---

52. The subject was the occasion of a special report prepared for the Lambeth Conference of 1958: *The Commemoration of Saints and Heroes of the Faith in the Anglican Communion*. The Report of a CommissionAppointed by the Archbishop of Canterbury (London: S.P.C.K.. top). The reactions of the Conference are reported in *The Lambeth Conference 1958* (S.P.C.K. and Scabury Press, 1958). pp. 2.94-2.98.

53. We follow the change in the new Roman Calendar, from the date of July it to this new date, to make it chronologically more suitable. Cf. the Gospels for these feasts. This is one of the few feasts taken from "Lesser Feasts and Fasts" and elevated to a major holy day or "Red Letter Day."

on August 6 is retained, but its theme is also linked into the cycle on the Last Sunday after the Epiphany.*

2. *Commemoration of Saints.* The feasts of apostles and evangelists on their customary dates are all retained. Four feasts of New Testament saints are taken from "Lesser Feasts and Fasts" and given rank as "Red Letter Days": St. Joseph (March 19); St. Mary Magdalene (July 22); St. Mary the Virgin (August 15); and St. James of Jerusalem, the Brother of the Lord (October 23). Of these, St. Mary Magdalene is a "Red Letter Day" in most modern Anglican Prayer Books—from the precedent of the First Book of 1549. The others occur among the "Black Letter Days" of recent Anglican Calendars.[54] We believe, given the Prayer Book tradition of emphasis upon the New Testament story of salvation in its ordering of major feasts, that these four should rank with the feasts of apostles and evangelists.

A new feast, not hitherto celebrated in any liturgy, has been assigned to January 18: The Confession of St. Peter. The combination of SS. Peter and Paul on the traditional date of their martyrdom (June 29) has overcome the anomaly of having no special observance of St. Paul's death but only of his conversion (January 25). We believe that the confession of our Lord by St. Peter is of sufficient significance in the New Testament to warrant giving the chief of the apostles an extra day, similar to that accorded to St. Paul. The date chosen is that of an ancient Gallican feast of the Chair of Peter, as St. Paul's Conversion also comes from the Gallican tradition. By a happy coincidence, this new feast is assigned to the opening day of the Octave of Prayer for the Unity of Christians now observed in all Churches, as the feast of St. Paul's Conversion marks its close.

Among the "Black Letter Days" all the entries in "Lesser Feasts and Fasts" have been retained, although the dates of several of them have been changed; and eight new listings have been added (see Appendix I). With the exception of the Martyrs of New Guinea (September 2), all new entries have been kept within our rule of excluding the commemoration of those who have died within the past fifty years, so that a sufficient time may be given for reflection upon their wide influence and achievement. This is also in line with the recommendations of the Lambeth Conference of 1958.[55]

---

* See above, page 49.

54. St. Joseph and St. Mary the Virgin are listed in the calendar of the Scottish, Canadian, Indian, and South African Prayer Book, and the new Calendar of the Church in Wales. St. James of Jerusalem appears in the Prayer Books of India and South Africa. The fears of some that the feast of St. Mary the Virgin on August is would lead to devotion to her "Assumption" have not been justified.

55. Cf. *The Lambeth Conference 1958*, p. 2.97. *Prayer Book Studies XVI* had no entry dated later than 1910. The latest date in our proposed Calendar is 1918.

Many requests have been received by the Liturgical Commission to include All Souls' Day on November 2. The reluctance of the Commission to accede to this popular memorial has been due to the fact that in the Prayer Book tradition All Saints' Day is essentially the celebration of Christ in his whole Mystical Body—the "elect" and the "saints" in the New Testament sense of these terms. On the other hand, popular piety has felt a real need for distinguishing between those saints who have been distinguished, and those who, while belonging no less to the body of the redeemed, are unknown in the wider fellowship of the faithful, but remembered in the more intimate circles of family and friends. We have therefore introduced on November 2 the entry "Commemoration of All Faithful Departed" as an extension of the feast of All Saints, with provision for the observance of All Saints on a Sunday following November 1, in addition to the celebration on the fixed date.[56]

3. *Anniversaries of Events.* Many of the feasts in the Proper of Time relate to events in our Lord's life, and in the Proper of Saints to such incidents as the Confession of St. Peter and the Conversion of St. Paul. In these events the Church acknowledges peculiar manifestations of God's plan for the salvation of the world, and of his actions in the growth of the Church's mission and witness. Consequently, later calendars of the churches introduced memorials of the consecration of bishops, the dedication of new churches, the transferral of relics to new shrines of pilgrimage. Actually, some of the saints' days in our Calendar go back to such occasions, which seemed at the time of institution more important than their known or unknown dates of death.[57]

The Prayer Books of the Anglican Communion have been very sparing in such dates, and have usually confined themselves to national events such as the Accession of the Sovereign (in the English Books), or Dominion Day (Canadian), and Independence Day (American). The "Lesser Feasts and Fasts" Calendar introduced two such dates: The First Prayer Book of 1549 on June 10, and the Consecration of Samuel Seabury, the first American Bishop, on November 14.

A feast, which in its origin strictly belongs to this category, is Holy Cross Day on September 14, which we propose to raise to the rank of a "Red Letter Day." On this day in 335 the church and shrine of the Lord's cross and

---

56. All Saints' Day was originally a festival of St. Mary and All Martyrs, later extended to include all Confessors. Thus, in the Roman Church, it is a feast of saints in the more restricted sense. All Souls' Day was instituted in 998 at the famous monastery of Cluny. The new Roman Calendar lists both All Saints and the Commemoration of All Faithful Departed as "Solemnities," but the latter cannot take precedence over a Sunday.

57. The Church has never allowed the liturgical celebration of the birthday in time of any of its saints, since this is a natural event, not a mystical or sacramental one. In addition to the Birthday of Christ on Christmas, it has admitted only feasts of the Nativity of the Virgin Mary and of John the Baptist, as pointers to the mystery of the Incarnation.

tomb were dedicated in Jerusalem, following their supposed discovery in the time of Constantine. Known today as the Church of the Holy Sepulchre, this site has been through the centuries the object of constant devotion and pilgrimage for Christians, as the traditional place of the Lord's triumph in death and resurrection. Despite all the tragedies of history associated with this site, and the disputes of Christians over it, which make of it an unhappy example of Christian disunity, the Church of the Holy Sepulchre may well be a symbol to us of the beginnings of our faith and witness.

In the Eastern Churches, the feast is known as "The Exaltation of the Holy Cross" and is accounted one of the twelve major feasts of the Church. It is also a major feast of the Roman Catholic Church, where the emphasis has always been on a festal celebration of the Cross of Christ. The Prayer Book has always given some indication of it, as the date for determining the autumn Ember Days; the Calendar of the 1662 Prayer Book lists it as "Holy Cross Day"; other Anglican Prayer Books have retained it as a "Black Letter Day," and in the Indian Prayer Book it is a "Red Letter Day." Holy Cross Day is a festival of dedication—to the victorious defeat of sin and death by our Lord, and to the mission of the Church to proclaim his cross as the sign of salvation to all men "at all times and in all places."

4. Special Occasions

WE PROPOSE to add to the Prayer Book the propers for Special Occasions, now included in "Lesser Feasts and Fasts." Known commonly as Votives, these propers have been widely accepted as filling the need for special celebrations of the Eucharist for devotional or intercessory purposes. They include the Prayer Book proper for the anniversary of the Dedication of a Church, and revised propers for the traditional Ember and Rogation Days. The latter are freed from their customary dates and thus made available for observance at other times when local circumstances dictate. We do not include among them the special proper for such occasions as baptism, marriage, ministration to the sick, burial, and ordination—since these are provided elsewhere in revised services for the proposed Prayer Book.

We reproduce here the note on Votives included in the Commission's report to the General Convention of 1967, since it is not widely known:[58]

> The custom of "votive" celebrations of the Eucharist on special occasions, such as weddings, funerals, and memorial anniversaries, goes back to ancient Christian times. In the early Middle Ages, the "intercessory" emphasis was greatly extended to include a variety of concerns in the

---

[58]. *Journal of the General Convention 1967*, Appendix 53.14-55. A reprint was included in the leaflet sent to all clergy by The Church Pension Fund, following the Convention, with the schedule of changes authorized in "Lesser Feasts and Fasts."

life of both individuals and communities; e.g., times of sickness, travel, danger, war and peace, seedtime and harvest, and many others. The list of special needs and circumstances could be greatly expanded. In most cases, however, provision for such intentions can be adequately subsumed (and, indeed, always may be subsumed) within the framework of intercessory prayers in the regular course of Eucharistic celebrations of the day or season.

There are certain concerns that are either pertinent to the life and witness of the entire Church, or so recurrent in the needs of its members, that propers for them are appropriate and useful. In *Lesser Feasts and Fasts*, the Commission has included several additional propers for this type of "votive," to enlarge the scope of those now included in the Prayer Book (At a Marriage, At a Burial, for the Communion of the Sick, as well as the communal observances of Independence Day and Thanksgiving Day).

The early Middle Ages also inaugurated the practice of "votive" Eucharists designed to give emphasis to certain major doctrines of the Church. One of these, the Mass of the Holy Trinity, was ultimately taken up into the "Proper of Time" as a special feast, on the Octave of Pentecost; namely, Trinity Sunday as we now know it in the Prayer Book.

The Commission has, therefore, offered, in *Lesser Feasts and Fasts*, several "votive" propers of this type, which may be particularly useful in connection with teaching missions and conferences—events that become increasingly significant factors in the life of the whole Church at parochial, diocesan, provincial, and interprovincial levels. The rubrics that point to the peculiar appropriateness of certain of these "votives" to particular days of the week arc not intended to be exclusive, but to indicate the major events of the last three days of Holy Week in the same way that Sunday is always a recalling of Easter Day.

The Proper

THE PROPER of the liturgy refers to those variable formularies of antiphon, psalm, prayer, and lesson that are assigned for use on particular Sundays, holy days, and other occasions of the Church Year. The First Prayer Book of 1549 provided at the Eucharist a proper Psalm for an introit, a collect, and Epistle and Gospel lections. The 1552 Book dropped the introit psalm, and since that time Anglican Prayer Books have simply appointed "Collects, Epistles, and Gospels" as the variables at eucharistic celebrations. The Proper Prefaces before the *Sanctus* have been printed in the service of Holy Communion itself, rather than with the proper of collect and lessons.

Twentieth-Century revisions of the Prayer Book have been gradually developing a richer proper for the Eucharist by providing for optional psalmody and hymnody, Old Testament lessons, a larger number of Proper Prefaces, and in some instances variable, seasonal post-communions.[59] The present proposals include a collect, two optional selections from the Psalter, three lessons, and a notation of appropriate Proper Prefaces.

1. The Collect

The form and value of the Collect of the Day have been often described and discussed.[60] It is a peculiar development of the Latin liturgies of the West; and in the better examples, particularly in the ancient Roman Sacramentaries, the Collect is a superb art-form of prayer combining profound theological substance and rhetorical finesse. Its function in the liturgy has been variously assessed, for the meaning of the term Collect is somewhat ambiguous.[61] For those who see the petition of the Collect as its root, the form is essentially a "gathering together" of the people's prayers and intentions. Others view the Collect as a kind of thematic summary of the particular thrust of emphasis in the liturgy of the day or season. In either case, the Collect is a kind of "bridge" or transition that gathers up what has preceded it to cross over to what will follow it.

Those who are most versed in the Latin Collects recognize how difficult they are to translate into modern vernaculars with the precision and rhythm of the originals. The achievement of Archbishop Cranmer in this respect has been universally applauded, and his style and method have served as a classic model both for translating the Collects and for composing new ones on the ancient pattern. The Collect is nonetheless acomplicated sentence of a particular Latin style of rhetoric. Even the best ones require concentrated attention, repetition, and reflection, whether by hearing or by reading, to savor their full meaning and implication.

---

59. These will be noted in the chapter following except for the post-communions. The Scottish Book of 1912 introduced seasonal post-communions for optional use before the Blessing; and they have been taken up and developed in the Indian and South African Prayer Books.

60. See especially the essays in the anthologies of William Bright and John W. Suter, Jr., noted in the Bibliography. For the history of the Collect in the Western rite, see J. A. Jungmann, *The Mass of the Roman Rite: Its Origins and Development*, I (New York: Benziger Brothers, 1950), pp. 359-362, 372-30 [sic--Jungmann's discussion of the Collect spans pages 359-390.].

61. The Roman Sacramentaries generally entitle these prayers *oratio* ("oration," hence the word "orison"), but use on certain occasions the phrase *oratio ad collectam* for the prayer said at the gathering of the people to begin the procession to the stational mass. The Gallican liturgies preferred the word *Collectio* (of which *Collecta* is a variant) for the opening prayer of the liturgy. In the rubrics of medieval service books the terms are used interchangeably. Walafrid Strabo (d. 849) said, "We call them collects because we gather together or conclude in a brief abridgement their necessary petitions."

Cranmer's versions of the ancient Latin Collects are more often paraphrases than strict translations. This is due in part to what Miss Stella Brook calls "broad antithesis between the means available to English and Latin respectively for achieving balance and pattern. Latin finds the means in its capacity for compression, English in its capacity for amplification."[62] Cranmer was not averse to altering the sense of his Latin originals to suit his own doctrinal point of view.[63] Later Prayer Book revisers, in turn, found no scruple in changing many of Cranmer's Collects, both in their literary and in their substantial form and content. Every revision of the Prayer Book has exhibited modifications and refinements of the Collects, if only to bring them more nearly into line with the changing vernacular. The American Prayer Book, particularly, has often altered many "which's" to "who's" and "them that's" to "those who's." It has been less prone to change meaning than the 1661 English revisers.

Modern English, whether spoken or written, is less given to the Latin sentence-form, with its involved relative and result clauses, especially in what is essentially a second person vocative form. The question has therefore been raised regarding the continuing viability of the classic form of the Collect for use by modern congregations, whose ear is trained to a quite different style of address. Roman Catholic translations today tend to break up the Collect into two or three sentences, and thus avoid the subordinate clauses. In particular, they have changed the relative clause of the opening address to a declarative sentence which is, in fact, an acclamation.

The Standing Liturgical Commission, after much discussion and consideration of alternative forms, has decided to propose for this revision that the classic structure of the Collect of the Day be retained, but with an effort to modernize its grammatical forms and vocabulary. Thus, archaic words have been either eliminated or "translated": e.g., "thou" and "thee" to "you"; "vouchsafe" to "give" or "grant"; "beseech" to "pray" (also used frequently by Cranmer and later revisers); "world without end" to "for ever and ever" or similar phrases; and the past tense has been used in relative clauses in preference to the perfect tense, as, for example, "gave" for "didst give," and "revealed" for "hast revealed."

Every Collect of the Prayer Book has been carefully reexamined, both for style and content. Some have been only slightly altered. Others have been changed materially, usually by shortening (since there is always the tendency to clutter Collects with too much subsidiary comment), or by revising the result clauses. Many Collects have been dropped, chiefly because of overmuch repetition of the

---

62. *The Language of The Book of Common Prayer* (New York: Oxford University Press, 1965), p. 128. This book is of fundamental importance for the study of the style of the Prayer Book.

63. A fundamental study comparing the Latin and English Collects remains the series of sermons of E. M. Goulburn, *The Collects of the Day*, 2 vols. (New York: Pott, Young, and Co., 1880). See also James A. Devereux, S.J., "Reformed Doctrine in the Collects of the First Book of Common Prayer," *The Harvard Theological Review*, LVIII (1965), pp. 49-68.

themes, especially of defense and protection. Many new Collects have been provided, drawn from both ancient and modern sources, or newly composed. Some familiar Collects have been shifted from their present places to other Sundays or holy days, in order to relate them more directly to the themes of the new lectionary. A schedule of these changes is provided in Appendix II.

Seasonal Collects or Collects to be said throughout an Octave have been eliminated, in the interest of simplification and to avoid monotony and for unity of theme. In Holy Week and Easter Week, each day has been provided with its own proper Collect. A greater variety of Collects for the weekdays of Lent will be provided in a revised edition of "Lesser Feasts and Fasts." Where a shift in seasonal emphasis is made evident by the occurrence of holy days during the week (such as Christmas, Epiphany, Ash Wednesday, Ascension Day, and All Saints' Day), it is left to the minister's discretion to use whatever proper is fitting on open days in the week following these holy days. For example, the three sets of propers now assigned to Christmas Day should give ample material for use in the week following Christmas Day without resort to the proper for the Fourth Sunday in Advent. Weekdays between the Epiphany and the following Sunday might appropriately have either the Epiphany proper or that of the Second Sunday after Christmas. Similarly, the Friday and Saturday after Ascension Day could be observed either by the proper of the feast or that of the Sixth Sunday of Easter; and the same principle applies to weekdays after All Saints' Day.

In preparing the revised and new Collects of the Day, an attempt has been made to visualize their function in the eucharistic liturgy. They may be viewed as a conclusion of the preparatory or "entrance" section of the liturgy, or as an introduction to the Ministry of the Word. In many of Cranmer's Collects, the wording was often a synopsis of either the Epistle or the Gospel. This is not inappropriate on certain chief festivals or on many saints' days; but it cannot be easily applied to Sundays for which the new three-year cycle of lessons affords a number of different themes. A good Collect should be useful on many other occasions than on one particular day, or even in one particular season.

2. The Psalms

THE EXCLUSION of all psalmody and hymnody from the Prayer Book eucharistic rite was one of the anomalies of the English reformation of worship in the sixteenth century. It was contrary to the long tradition of both the Eastern and Western liturgies, and to the concerns for popular song by the Reformers of the Continent. Cranmer's single experiment of an introit Psalm in the 1549 Book was not followed up. It may be that he considered the Psalms and canticles provided in Morning Prayer which was recited immediately before the celebration of the Communion, sufficient; and in any case, there was at the time no production of English hymnody comparable to that of the continental Reformation.

However, Queen Elizabeth I's Injunctions of 1559 allowed a hymn (probably a metrical psalm) to be sung "in the beginning, or in the end of common prayers, either at morning or evening."

The American Church took the initiative in restoration of song, whether of psalm or hymn, at the Eucharist. The 1789 Prayer Book allowed a hymn to be sung before Communion, and also as a substitute for the *Gloria in excelsis*. The 1892 revision extended this to the use of Hymns or Anthems in the words of Scripture or of the Prayer Book at the Offertory, or before and after any service or sermon. In the 1928 Book such a Hymn or Anthem was permitted also between the Epistle and Gospel. Thus, the American Prayer Book recovered, though it did not require, the use of song at all the ancient places of the Western rite: Introit, Gradual, Offertory, and Communion. The choice of texts, however, whether from the Bible, the Hymnal, or the Prayer Book, was left open.[64]

Nearly all the recent Anglican revisions of the Eucharist have made rubrical provision for psalmody and hymnody in the traditional places. The Indian Prayer Book and its Supplement have a specific set of Introit Psalms, including the schedule of Introit Psalms associated with "A Liturgy for India" (1933), commonly known as the Bombay liturgy. The Canadian Book of 1962 has a list of two Psalms, or selections from Psalms, for optional use as Introits and Graduals. The recent proposed Calendar of the Church of England Liturgical Commission also suggests two Psalm selections with the proper for each Eucharist.

One of the unexpected by-products of trial use of *The Liturgy of the Lord's Supper* (*Prayer Book Studies XVII*), with its explicit rubrics suggesting the use of Psalms as well as Hymns, has been a widespread interest in many parishes in the use of Psalms at the Eucharist. We are therefore proposing with each set of propers two selections from the Psalter, which may be used at any appropriate place. The first selection has been chosen particularly for its advantage as an Introit, the second one for use with the lessons. But they may also be used as Offertories or as Communion anthems.

Each selection consists of about six to ten verses, and, where only a portion of a Psalm is cited, it is quite permissible, when desired, to use a longer passage, or even the entire Psalm. Unlike the use of the Psalter in the Daily Office, the selection of Psalm verses at the Eucharist is not normally followed in a course sequence, but verses particularly appropriate to the theme of the day or season have been selected. We have generally avoided suggesting those verses of the Psalms which are imprecatory, or which denote despair or doubt, as being unsuitable to the eucharistic celebration. Certain Psalms have become associated in Christian tradition with particular feasts or holy days. This tradition has been respected in the selections, but we have not followed any historical model of selection, whether from ancient or contemporary service books.

---

64. An interesting and unofficial attempt to provide suitable anthem texts from Scripture, for use either at the Offices or the Eucharist, was made by Morton C. Stone and Ray F. Brown, *Anthems of the Day*, Scriptural Verses Set to Anglican Chant and Plainsong (New York: Oxford University Press, 1952).

Reference to the Index of Psalms (Appendix III) will show that the selections have been taken from 110 of the 150 Psalms, and that none of them has been assigned to more than two Sundays of the year. An effort has been made, in the Sunday appointments, to see that the most popular Psalms are listed on Sundays that recur every year in the Proper of Time, regardless of the movable date of Easter. Some of the Psalms omitted in this Index will be included in the projected schedules for the weekdays of Lent, in a revised edition of "Lesser Feasts and Fasts."

3. The Lessons

A MAJOR, if not radical, proposal is made for revision of the lessons at the Eucharist. Our Prayer Book schedule descends to us by way of the Sarum Use, from the lectionary of the Roman Church, which was established at the end of the sixth century. There have been modifications in detail, but no overall review of this schedule—whether in the Roman Catholic, or in the Anglican and Lutheran liturgies—until the present time.

The Second Vatican Council in its *Constitution on the Sacred Liturgy* called for a thorough review of this time-honored usage:

> The treasures of the Bible are to be opened up more lavishly, so that richer fare may be provided for the faithful at the table of God's Word. In this way a more representative portion of the holy Scriptures will be read to the people over a set cycle of years. (ii.5.)

To this end, the *Consilium* responsible for implementing the Council's directives has labored long and hard. The result is the new three-year cycle of lessons promulgated by Pope Paul VI in 1969.[65] Our own Liturgical Commission has been in constant touch with the *Consilium's* work. The inherent excellence of the new Roman lectionary, both in principle and in detail, has justified our expectations, and we should welcome the opportunity to test it in trial use with our Roman Catholic brothers in the coming years. We have not, however, taken over this three-year lectionary without careful scrutiny; and our proposals show many modifications of it both in the choice and in the length of lessons (see Appendix IV)[66, 67]

---

65. See above, pp. 41-42.

66. Cf. *Prayer Book Studies XVII*, Vol. 4, p. 241 f. An account of the work on this lectionary is contained in an article of Gaston Fontaine, *Notitiae*, No. 47 (July-August 1969), pp. 259 ff. A translation of this article was circulated to all consultants of the Liturgical Commission; its substance is herewith abridged:

67. A committee of eighteen members was formed from international experts in the fields of liturgy, Bible, catechetics, and pastoral theology.

Their work was first of all a systematic abstract of all Biblical pericopes read in the liturgy, including the Latin liturgies from the 6th to the 12th centuries; some 15 rites in the Eastern books; and lectionaries in use in the churches of the Reformation from the 16th century to the present.

Before analyzing the rationale of this new Roman lectionary, we should call attention to two recent Anglican lectionaries which make similarly new and radical departures from the tradition. One is that of the British Joint Liturgical Group, whose two-year cycle of lections has been approved and proposed by the Liturgical Commission of the Church of England. This lectionary is tied to the reconstruction of the Church Year which we have already analyzed and rejected.[68] It begins the year with the Ninth Sunday before Christmas, and the Old Testament lesson is made the basis of a thematic structure recalling the high points in the history of salvation leading up to the Incarnation. From Christmas to Pentecost the basic lesson is that of the Gospel. In this respect it follows a more or less traditional pattern. The Sundays after Pentecost, however, are again thematically outlined according to primary Christian teachings, with their basis in the Epistle.

A practical feature of this lectionary is its adaptability for use at either the Daily Office or the Holy Communion. If the Holy Communion is the morning service, all three lessons may be read, or the Old Testament lesson, or the Epistle with the Gospel. If Morning Prayer is the chief service, the Old Testament lesson may be coupled with either the Epistle or the Gospel. Another series based on a two-year cycle is provided for a "Second Service," which might be used at either Morning or Evening Prayer. This Second Service provides three lessons in some cases and only two in others.

A somewhat similar scheme was issued by the Lectionary Committee of the Church of Ireland in 1968. It follows the traditional Church Year, and provides a three-year cycle of psalm selection and three lessons, which may be used at either Holy Communion or the Daily Offices. The selection of the lessons is based on topical themes derived either from the seasons, or on the Sundays after Pentecost, from the Collects of the Day in the present Prayer Book.

On first sight, a thematic scheme for the lessons is attractive, as a help to preachers and teachers, and also for personal devotion. But such a construction

---

Some 30 Biblical scholars established a list of pericopes from both the Old and New Testaments, judged to be of major significance for an understanding of the economy of salvation, but also sufficiently easy of comprehension by the faithful. This list was communicated to 100 consultors engaged in catechesis or in pastoral ministry. From this survey 2,500 comments were received regarding choice of texts and possible utilization.

The committee then prepared general studies and provisory projects which were submitted to consideration and vote of the *Consilium* in four separate sessions. In July 1967 a manuscript form of the new lectionary was submitted to review by all of the episcopal conferences, by the first Synod of Bishops, and by 800 experts in Bible, liturgy, catechesis, and pastoralia. On the basis of these responses (some 400 pages of general remarks and 7,000 specific items on the texts) the committee completely revised its first project: suppression of texts judged too difficult, addition of pericopes that had been omitted in previous drafts, adjustments in the length of selected lections, and revision of those appointed for the Sundays of Lent and for certain great feasts.

The most important of these modifications were approved by the *Consilium* in April 1968, and the completed lectionary was sent to press by the end of July 1968.

68. See above, pp. 37-41.

may be in the long run restrictive, in that it does not allow for the many varieties of themes that are possible in combinations of Scriptural passages. A topical pattern may only indicate the passing interests of homiletics and the changing fashions of exegesis. One may test the varieties of thematic structures not only by comparing the English and Irish schedules, but also those contained in the liturgy of the Church of South India and the experimental rite of the Church in the Province of New Zealand. It is difficult to discover whether the thematic structure has controlled the choice of lessons, or whether the lessons have been interpreted to fit predetermined interests in certain topics. Certain broad topics are certainly inherent in the principal festivals and holy days; but a thematic schedule may be very artificial when it comes to the ordinary Sundays of the Epiphany and post-Penetecost seasons.

For these reasons we have preferred the pattern of the new Roman lectionary, since much of it is a return to the ancient custom of course reading, without loss of the special themes appropriate to principal festivals, fasts, and holy days. Where course reading is involved, opportunity is given to the preacher—as also to the devout reader—to develop a solid insight into a given book of Scripture. There are in the Prayer Book some relics of this ancient use of lessons in the Eucharist as well as in the Daily Office—such as the reading of the latter part of Romans in Epiphany, the discourse material in John in Eastertide, and the Pauline Epistles in the post-Trinity Sundays.

The new Roman lectionary for the seasons and Sundays is divided into two major groupings: 1) The Proper of Time for Advent, the Christmas season (through the feast of the Baptism of Christ on the First Sunday after the Epiphany), Lent, and the Easter season (including Ascension Day and the feast of Pentecost); 2) a cycle of thirty-four Sundays per annum ("through the year") that are assigned to Sundays of the Epiphany and post-Pentecost seasons.

The latter cycle involves some complication, since in some years there are thirty-three, in others thirty-four Sundays.[69] And certain Sundays are privileged in this cycle: namely, the Feast of our Lord's Baptism on the First Sunday after the Epiphany, the feast of Pentecost, and the feast of Trinity on the first Sunday after Pentecost. Consequently the rules of this Calendar are as follows:

- a. The Sunday after the Baptism of our Lord is accounted the Second Sunday of the cycle *per annum*—what would be our Second Sunday after the Epiphany. The Sundays then may follow up to nine after the Epiphany.
- b. The week after the feast of Pentecost is the n accounted as the tenth week, and the week after Trinity Sunday as the eleventh. The proper for the Sundays after Pentecost, in the cycle *per annum*, would then pick up at the

---

69. This difference is perhaps most easily explained by the fact that in some years there are two, in others only one Sunday after Christmas.

twelfth on the Second Sunday after Pentecost, and continue through to the Thirty-Fourth Sunday, which is always the feast of Christ the King.

c. In years when there are only thirty-three and not thirty-four Sundays in the cycle *per annum*, the enumeration of the week after the feast of Pentecost is dropped out, so that the schedule always concludes on the thirty-fourth Sunday or feast of Christ the King.

Such a scheme requires, of course, an annual publication of the official Calendar, depending upon the number of Sundays after the Epiphany, and whether there are thirty-three or thirty-four Sundays in the cycle *per annum*.[70]

We have decided not to adopt this complex figuring of the Sundays after the Epiphany and the Sundays after Pentecost, but to continue the Prayer Book custom of dropping any excess Sundays after Epiphany and starting afresh in a sequence after Pentecost. Since we have made the Last Sunday after the Epiphany a required Sunday, with its theme of the Transfiguration, our schedule is related to the new Roman Calendar for Sundays *per annum* as follows:

a. The Second Sunday after the Epiphany begins, as does the Roman, with the proper for Sunday II *per annum*. We follow the Roman scheme through eight Sundays after the Epiphany. The Last Sunday always has its special proper.

b. The Second Sunday after Pentecost picks up regularly with the ninth Sunday in the Roman sequence *per annum*.

c. We have provided for a maximum of twenty-eight Sundays after Pentecost, of which the Last Sunday must always be observed. This means that we have had to add propers for one extra Sunday beyond the Roman list of thirty-four.[71]

Thus we shall always begin the Sundays after Pentecost with a fixed sequence, and not pick up the Sundays left over when the Epiphany season is shorter than nine Sundays. This means that our lessons will accord with the Roman ones in the season after Epiphany. But in the Pentecost season we shall not be always reading the same lessons on the same Sundays, but we shall be following the same sequence during the season.

The heart of the new lectionary is the Gospel lesson. For the major Sundays and seasons—1 Advent through 1 Epiphany, and 1 Lent through Trinity

---

70. *E.g.*, the official Calendar for 1970 shows five Sundays after the Epiphany, and the Second Sunday after Pentecost picks up at the eighth Sunday *per annum*, for in this year there are only thirty-three Sundays in the cycle *per annum*.

71. The Prayer Book provides now for twenty-eight Sundays after Pentecost, if we include Trinity Sunday and the Sunday next before Advent. In the Roman cycle *per annum* only twenty-seven Sundays are a maximum, since its cycle counts the week after the feast of Pentecost as one in its sequence *per annum*.

Sunday—the lessons are selected for thematic purposes; similarly also for the Last Sundays after the Epiphany and after Pentecost. On the other Sundays—from 2 to 8 Epiphany, and 2 to 27 after Pentecost, inclusive—the Gospels are read in course, with Matthew in year A, Mark in year B, and Luke in year C. Since Mark is shorter than the other Synoptic Gospels, there is inserted from 11 through 14 after Pentecost lections from the sixth chapter of John, which fit in properly as an extension of the Markan narrative of the Feeding of the Multitude.

Even in a three-year cycle of Sunday lections it is not possible to include every verse of all four Gospels. Passages selected for the major seasons are not repeated in the Epiphany and post-Pentecost seasons. Where there are parallel narratives or teachings in the Synoptics, choices are made from among them, so that the same pericope is not repeated from Mark if it has been read from Matthew, or from Luke if it has been read from Mark. In this way, the basic substance of the Gospel is covered. However, on certain major feasts the parallels are read successively in years A, B, and C (*e.g.*, on the Sundays of the Baptism, the Transfiguration, Temptation, Resurrection). The Gospel of John is drawn upon at all seasons, but especially in Lent and Easter.

The Epistles are treated like the Gospels, both in thematic selections and in course readings. In the post-Epiphany season, 1 Corinthians is largely covered in the three years, and after Pentecost the rest of the Pauline epistles, Hebrews, and James. During Eastertide the Book of Acts is read in place of the Old Testament, and the Epistles are taken from i Peter, 1 John, and Revelation.

The Old Testament lessons are freely chosen as background or as illustrations of the Gospel lesson—sometimes of the Epistle. They are not read in course, but most of the books of the Old Testament and Apocrypha are represented in the lectionary. Unfortunately many of the interesting narratives of the Old Testament are excluded, or given only in limited scope, since they are often too long to be suitable at the Eucharist. But the principal passages that are significant in the "history of salvation" are included. We have felt free to alter the Old Testament lessons of the new Roman lectionary, since its use of the Old Testament often reveals a typological exegesis, which is at times adroit but unconvincing. Where New Testament lessons specifically quote or refer to the Old Testament, the choice of lessons provides a valuable clue to the unity of the Scriptures.

We have not therefore slavishly followed the new Roman lectionary, as one may note from a study of the Index of Scripture Lessons in Appendix IV. We have re-ordered some of its sequences in the Christmas and Lenten seasons. In the main, however, we have followed its rationale, since we consider that it is faithful to its purpose of opening the treasures of the Bible in ways that are sound by critical standards, appropriate in liturgical use, and stimulating for exposition and devotion. For the proper of the fixed holy days and for special occasions, we have resorted to a number of sources, especially the schedules of the Prayer Book for both the Eucharist and the Daily Offices. Where these conform to the Roman lectionary, it is due to a common tradition which we have received through the Prayer Book itself.

This lectionary might serve on Sundays and holy days for both the Offices and the Eucharist, whether celebrated in the morning or evening. This is a matter for coordination of rubrics concerning the Ministry of the Word. In this practical respect, our lectionary is quite as advantageous as those of the current English and Irish proposals.

Note: The three-year cycle of the new Roman lectionary is ordered so that Year A is used in years which are divisible by 3 (*e.g.*, 1968 and 1971). The lectionary was put into use in Advent 1969, with the sequence of Year B. If the General Convention decides to approve the lectionary for trial use, we should normally begin in Advent 1970 with Year C, in order to be in accord with our Roman Catholic brethren. The sequence of Year A would then follow in Advent 1971.

4. Proper Prefaces

The texts of the Proper Prefaces will be included, as is customary, in the proposed revision of the Eucharist. We have noted with each proper for Sundays and holy days and special occasions when a Preface is appropriate, whether this is prescribed by the rubrics of the Eucharist or is a matter of option for the celebrant. Where a Proper Preface is not prescribed, we have sometimes suggested alternatives which are appropriate, so that the celebrant may have a choice.

Tables

Rules for Finding the Date of Easter Day

EASTER DAY is always the Sunday after the full moon that occurs upon or after the spring equinox on March 21. This full moon may happen upon any day between March 21 and April 18 inclusive. If the full moon occurs on a Sunday, Easter Day is the Sunday following. But Easter Day cannot be earlier than March 22 or later than April 25.

To find the date of Easter Day in any particular year, it is necessary to have two points of reference—the Golden Number and the Sunday Letter for that year:

1. The Golden Number, or date of the full moon on or after the spring equinox of March 21, according to a nineteen-year cycle. These Numbers are prefixed in the Calendar to the days of the months from March 22 to April 18 inclusive. In the present Calendar they are applicable from A.D. 1900 to A.D. 2099, after which they will be changed.

2. The Sunday Letter, or days of the year when Sundays occur. After every day in the Calendar there is noted a letter—from A to g. Thus, if January 1 is a

Sunday, the Sunday Letter for the year is A, and every date in the Calendar marked by A is a Sunday. If January 2 is a Sunday, then every day marked with b is a Sunday, and so on through the seven letters.

In Leap-years, however, the Sunday Letter changes with the first day of March. In such years, when A is the Sunday Letter, this applies only to Sundays in January and February, but g is the Sunday Letter for all Sundays in the rest of the year. Or if d is the Sunday Letter, then c is the Sunday Letter for all Sundays beginning on March 1.

If one has both the Golden Number and the Sunday Letter for any particular year, then the date of Easter Day may be found in the Calendar as follows:

1. The Golden Number prefixed to a day in the month of March or of April in the Calendar will mark the date of the full moon. Easter Day will be the next Sunday after this date.
2. This Sunday will be the next date bearing the Sunday Letter, after the date to which the Golden Number is prefixed. But when the date of the Golden Number and the date of the Sunday Letter are the same, then Easter Day is a week later. [*E.g.*, if the Golden Number is 19 and the Sunday Letter is d, then Easter Day in that year will fall on March 29. If the Golden Number is 10 and the Sunday Letter is A, then Easter Day will fall on April 9. But if the Golden Number is 19 and the Sunday Letter is b, then Easter Day will be a week later, namely April 3; or if the Golden Number is 10 and the Sunday Letter is d, then Easter Day will be April 12.]

To Find the Golden Number

The Golden Number of any year is calculated as follows: Add to the date desired, and then divide the sum by 19. The remainder, if any, is the Golden Number. If nothing remains, then 19 is the Golden Number.

[*E.g.*, to find the Golden Number of the year 1970:

1970 + 1 = 1971. 1971 divided by 19 leaves a remainder of 14. 14 is therefore the Golden Number of the year 1970, and is found prefixed to March 22 in the Calendar.

Or, to find the Golden Number of the year 1975:

1975 + 1 = 1976. 1976 divided by 19 leaves no remainder. 19 is therefore the Golden Number for the year 1975, and is found prefixed to March 27 in the Calendar.]

To Find the Sunday Letter

The following Table provides ready reference to the Sunday Letter of any year between A.D. 1900 and A.D. 2099. It will be found on the line of the hundredth year underneath the column that lists the remaining number of the year. But in Leap-years the Letter under the number marked with an asterisk is the Sunday Letter for January and February, and the Letter under the number not so marked is the Sunday Letter for the rest of the year.

Years in excess of hundreds

	0*	0	1	2	3	4*	4	5
		6	7	8*	8	9	10	11
		12*	12	13	14	15	16*	16
		17	18	19	20*	20	21	22
		23	24*	24	25	26	27	28*
		28	29	30	31	32*	32	33
		34	35	36*	36	37	38	39
		40*	40	41	42	43	44*	44
		45	46	47	48*	48	49	50
		51	52*	52	53	54	55	56*
		56	57	58	59	60*	60	61
		62	63	64*	64	65	66	67
		68*	68	69	70	71	72*	72
		73	74	75	76*	76	77	78
		79	80*	80	81	82	83	84*
		84	85	86	87	88*	88	89
		90	91	92*	92	93	94	95
Hundred Years		96*	96	97	98	99		
1900		G	F	E	D	C	B	A
2000	B	A	G	F	E	D	C	B

A Table to Find Easter Day

Golden Number	Year	Easter Day	Year	Easter Day	Year	Easter Day
1	1900	April 15	1938	April 17	1976*	April 18
2	1901	April 7	1939	April 9	1977	April 10
3	1902	March 30	1940*	March 24	1978	March 26
4	1903	April 12	1941	April 13	1979	April 15
5	1904*	April 3	1942	April 5	1980*	April 6
6	1905	April 23	1943	April 25	1981	April 19
7	1906	April 15	1944*	April 9	1982	April 11
8	1907	March 31	1945	April 1	1983	April 3
9	1908*	April 19	1946	April 21	1984*	April 22
10	1909	April 11	1947	April 6	1985	April 7
11	1910	March 27	1948*	March 28	1986	March 30
12	1911	April 16	1949	April 17	1987	April 19
13	1912*	April 7	1950	April 9	1988*	April 3
14	1913	March 23	1951	March 25	1989	March 26
15	1914	April 12	1952*	April 13	1990	April 15
16	1915	April 4	1953	April 5	1991	March 31
17	1916*	April 23	1954	April 18	1992*	April 19
18	1917	April 8	1955	April 10	1993	April 11
19	1918	March 31	1956*	April 1	1994	April 3
1	1919	April 20	1957	April 21	1995	April 16
2	1920*	April 4	1958	April 6	1996*	April 7
3	1921	March 27	1959	March 29	1997	March 30
4	1922	April 16	1960*	April 17	1998	April 12
5	1923	April 1	1961	April 2	1999	April 4
6	1924*	April 20	1962	April 22	2000*	April 23
7	1925	April 12	1963	April 14	2001	April 15

8	1926	April 4	1964*	March 29	2002	March 31
9	1927	April 17	1965	April 18	2003	April 20
10	1928*	April 8	1966	April to	2004*	April 11
11	1929	March 31	1967	March 26	2005	March 27
12	1930	April 20	1968*	April 14	2006	April 16
13	1931	April 5	1969	April 6	2007	April 8
14	1932*	March 27	1970	March 29	2008*	March 23
15	1933	April 16	1971	April 11	2009	April 12
16	1934	April 1	1972*	April 2	2010	April 4
17	1935	April 21	1973	April 22	2011	April 24
18	1936*	April 12	1974	April 14	2012*	April 8
19	1937	March 28	1975	March 30	2013	March 31

* The years marked with an asterisk are Leap-years.

Golden Number	Year	Easter Day		Year	Easter Day
1	2014	April 20		2052*	April 21
2	2015	April 5		2053	April 6
3	2016*	March 27		2054*	March 29
4	2017	April 16		2055*	April 18
5	2018	April 1		2056*	April 2
6	2019	April 21		2057	April 22
7	2020*	April 12		2058	April 14
8	2021	April 4		2059	March 30
9	2022	April 17		2060*	April 18
10	2023	April 9		2061	April 10
11	2024*	March 31		2062	March 26
12	2025	April 20		2063	April 15
13	2026	April 5		2064*	April 6
14	2027	March 28		2065	March 29
15	2028*	April 16		2066	April 11
16	2029	April 1		2067	April 3
17	2030	April 21		2068*	April 22

18	2031	April 13		2069	April 14
19	2032*	March 28		2070	March 30
1	2033	April 17		2071	April 19
2	2034	April 9		2072*	April 10
3	2035	March 25		2073	March 26
4	2036*	April 13		2074	April 15
5	2037	April 5		2075	April 7
6	2038	April 25		2076*	April 19
7	2039	April 10		2077	April 11
8	2040*	April 1		2078	April 3
9	2041	April 21		2079	April 23
10	2042	April 6		2080*	April 7
11	2043	March 29		2081	March 30
12	2044*	April 17		2082	April 19
13	2045	April 9		2083	April 4
14	2046	March 25		2084*	March 26
15	2047	April 14		2085	April 15
16	2048*	April 5		2086	March 31
17	2049	April 18		2087	April 20
18	2050	April 10		2088*	April 11
19	2051	April 2		2089	April 3

A Table to Find Movable Feasts and Holy Days

Easter Day	Sundays after Epiphany*	Ash Wednesday**	Ascension Day	Pentecost	Sundays after Pentecost	Advent Sunday
March 22	4	Feb. 4	April 30	May 10	28	November 29
March 23	4	Feb. 5	May 1	May 11	28	November 30
March 24	4	Feb. 6	May 2	May 12	28	December 1
March 25	5	Feb. 7	May 3	May 13	28	December 2
March 26	5	Feb. 8	May 4	May 14	28	December 3
March 27	5	Feb. 9	May 5	May 15	27	November 27
March 28	5	Feb. 10	May 6	May 16	27	November 28

March 29	5	Feb. 11	May 7	May 17	27	November 29
March 30	5	Feb. 12	May 8	May 18	27	November 30
March 31	5	Feb. 13	May 9	May 19	27	December 1
April 1	6	Feb. 14	May 10	May 20	27	December 2
April 2	6	Feb. 15	May 11	May 21	27	December 3
April 3	6	Feb. 16	May 12	May 22	26	November 27
April 4	6	Feb. 17	May 13	May 23	26	November 28
April 5	6	Feb. 18	May 14	May 24	26	November 29
April 6	6	Feb. 19	May 15	May 25	26	November 30
April 7	6	Feb. 20	May 16	May 26	26	December 1
April 8	7	Feb. 21	May 17	May 27	26	December 2
April 9	7	Feb. 22	May 18	May 28	26	December 3
April 10	7	Feb. 23	May 19	May 29	25	November 27
April 11	7	Feb. 24	May 20	May 30	25	November 28
April 12	7	Feb. 25	May 21	May 31	25	November 29
April 13	7	Feb. 26	May 22	June 1	25	November 30
April 14	7	Feb. 27	May 23	June 2	25	December 1
April 15	8	Feb. 28	May 24	June 3	25	December 2
April 16	8	March 1	May 25	June 4	25	December 3
April 17	8	March 2	May 26	June 5	24	November 27
April 18	8	March 3	May 27	June 6	24	November 28
April 19	8	March 4	May 28	June 7	24	November 29
April 20	8	March 5	May 29	June 8	24	November 30
April 21	8	March 6	May 30	June 9	24	December 1
April 22	9	March 7	May 31	June 10	24	December 2
April 23	9	March 8	June 1	June 11	24	December 3
April 24	9	March 9	June 2	June 12	23	November 27
April 25	9	March 10	June 3	June 13	23	November 28

* In Leap-years, the number of Sundays after the Epiphany will be the same as if Easter Day were one day later than in the above Table.

** In Leap-years, the date of Ash Wednesday will be one day later in the month of February than in the above Table.

APPENDICES

Appendix I: The Calendar

1. Changes of Dates in the Calendar

January 13. HILARY

> Hilary died on the 13th. Modern Roman Calendars shifted him to the 14th to avoid the octave of Epiphany (cf. LFF). With the elimination of octaves, the new Roman Calendar has restored his date to the 13th, which is also assigned in Anglican Calendars.

January 14. See January 13.
January 24. See January 26.
January 26. TIMOTHY AND TITUS

> The new Roman Calendar combines the two companions of St. Paul on a common date following the feast of the Apostle's Conversion. The removal of Polycarp to February 23 leaves this date open.

January 28. THOMAS AQUINAS

> The new Roman Calendar has shifted Thomas from March 7 (cf. LFF, March 8) to this date, to remove his feast from Lent. This date is that of his translation to Toulouse. The proposed Calendar of the Church of England has also adopted this date.

February 1. See October 17.
February 6. See January 26.
February 14. CYRIL AND METHODIUS

> The new date in the Roman Calendar adopts the death date of Cyril in 869, also commemorated in the Eastern Churches on this day. Methodius died on May 11 (cf. LFF).

February 23. POLYCARP

> His authentic Martyrdom gives this date, which is observed in the Eastern Churches. The new Roman Calendar has shifted it here from January 26 (adopted in the 13th century through confusion with another of this name). The new Church of England Calendar also proposes this date.

March 8. See January 28.
April 4. See December 7.

April 11. See November 10.
April 14. See June 1.
April 29. CATHERINE OF SIENA

This is the new Roman date—the day of her death.

April 30. See April 29.
May 11. See February 14.
May 25. BEDE THE VENERABLE

The new Roman date has restored him to his death day. This is also proposed in the new Church of England Calendar.

May 27. See May 25.
May 31. VISITATION OF THE BLESSED VIRGIN MARY

This has been shifted from July 2 in the new Roman Calendar to place it chronologically between the Annunciation and the Nativity of St. John the Baptist.

June 1. JUSTIN MARTYR

The date of his death is unknown. The new Roman Calendar has placed him here, to accord with the date in Eastern Calendars, and to remove him from occurrence in Easter Week. This also is the date in new Church of England list.

June 3. MARTYRS OF UGANDA

Their date was placed here in the recent canonization by Paul VI (with which the Anglican martyrs were associated). It is separated from Hannington on October 29, since he was martyred at a different time and place.

June 10. EPHREM OF EDESSA

Ephrem died on June 9, and this is the new date in the Roman Calendar. But the 9th is preempted by Columba, hence the transfer to the 10th. The removal from LFF date of June 18 leaves open that date for Bernard Mizeki.

July 2. See May 31.
August 11. CLARE OF ASSISI

This is her death date, and is so transferred in the new Roman Calendar from the 12th.

August 12. See August 11.

October 17. IGNATIUS OF ANTIOCH

> The ancient Syrian Calendar of the fourth century places the martyrdom on this date, and it has thus been transferred in the new Roman Calendar from February 1. The proposed Church of England Calendar also adopts this date. Other Anglican Calendars observe December 17, the supposed date of the translation of his body to Antioch.

October 19. HENRY MARTYN

> Transferred from the 17th, as first open day.

October 29. JAMES HANNINGTON

> The other martyrs of Uganda have been placed on June 3.

November 10. LEO THE GREAT

> This is the date of his death in 461, and the feast is shifted here from April 11 (the Gallican date) in the new Roman Calendar, to avoid possible occurrence in Holy Week or Easter Week.

December 4. JOHN OF DAMASCUS

> The new Roman date, shifted from March 27, to accord with the Eastern date of commemoration. LFF placed him on the 5th.

December 5. CLEMENT OF ALEXANDRIA

> With the change of date of John of Damascus, Clement has been transferred to the 5th (LFF on the 4th). He has been omitted in the new Roman Calendar.

December 7. AMBROSE

> This is the date of his consecration as bishop. His death date is April 4. The new Roman and proposed Church of England Calendars place him here, to avoid occurrence in Holy Week or Easter Week.

2. New Roman Calendar Dates not Adopted

January 2. BASIL THE GREAT AND GREGORY OF NAZIANZUS

> The Eastern Churches commemorate the death of Basil on January 1, and of Gregory of Nazianzus on January 25. The older Roman dates of June 14 and May 9, respectively, are being retained from LFF, in order

to commemorate the two great patristic fathers on separate dates, and to avoid such a feast during the "twelve days" of Christmas.

May 3. PHILIP AND JAMES, Apostles

The ancient Roman date of May 1 was changed in 1955 to May 11, having been displaced by the new feast of St. Joseph the Worker. The new Roman Calendar has moved it back to May 3 (the 2nd being preempted by Athanasius). As with other feasts of the Apostles (e.g., Matthias and Thomas) we are retaining the dates in other Anglican Calendars.

May 14. MATTHIAS, Apostle

The change from February 24 was due to a desire to remove the feast from Lent and place it in the context of the Easter celebration. We retain the February date in line with other Anglican Calendars.

July 3. THOMAS, Apostle

The new Roman date marks the date of translation to Edessa in the Hieronymian Martyrology. It was desirous of removing the feast from Advent (December 21). We retain the December date in line with other Anglican Calendars.

August 7. DOMINIC

Dominic died on August 6. When canonized, his feast was placed on the 4th, which in the new Roman Calendar is now assigned to John Marie Vianney. We retain the traditional date (cf. LFF), which leaves the 7th open for John Mason Neale.

August 27. MONNICA

Her death date is unknown, but was placed by the Order of St. Augustine in the 15th century on May 4, prior to their feast of St. Augustine. The new Roman Calendar has now shifted her day to the eve of the feast of St. Augustine on August 28th. We retain the LFF date.

September 3. GREGORY THE GREAT

His death was on March 12. It is removed here in the new Roman Calendar, to get it out of Lent, and placed on the date of his consecration as pope. We retain the March date in line with other Anglican Calendars—Gregory being especially associated with the conversion of the English.

September 13. JOHN CHRYSOSTOM

This is the date in the Eastern Calendars—the day before his death on the 14th (preempted by the major festival of the Exaltation of the Holy Cross). The new Roman Calendar has adopted this date in preference to its traditional date of January 27, commemorating his translation to Constantinople. This requires the transfer of Cyprian to the 16th. We retain the LFF dates for Chrysostom and Cyprian.

November 17. ELIZABETH OF HUNGARY

The new Roman Calendar shifts to this date, the day of her death. The older date of the 19th was the anniversary of her translation. We retain the 19th rather than displace Hugh (17th) and Hilda (18th).

3. New Entries in the Calendar

January 18. THE CONFESSION OF SAINT PETER

The Calendar proposed now unites the feast of the martyrdom of SS. Peter and Paul on June 29th, in accordance with an ancient tradition in the West. This new feast is designed to give commemoration to an event equal in significance to the Conversion of St. Paul on January 25th. It marks the beginning of the Octave of Prayer for Christian Unity, now observed in all Churches, as the feast of St. Paul's Conversion marks its close. By adding this feast, each of the two chief apostles—the one to the Jews, the other to the Gentiles—will have a distinctive observance. The ancient Gallican service books had a feast of the Chair of St. Peter on January 18th (celebrated at Rome on February 22nd); but our new feast is in no way one of Peter's Chair, but of his bold and representative confession of our Lord's Messiahship.

April 2. JAMES LLOYD BRECK, Priest, 1876.

Born June 27, 1818, near Philadelphia; educated at W. A. Muhlenberg's Flushing Academy, the University of Pennsylvania, and the General Theological Seminary. In 1842 he joined a team to help Bishop Kemper in Wisconsin, where they founded Nashotah House. In 1850 he moved to Minnesota where he founded schools for boys and girls and Seabury Divinity School, and also did mission work among the Chippewa Indians. In 1867 he went to California, where again he founded schools for boys and girls and a seminary at Benicia, where he died April 2, 1876. He is honored as a pioneer missionary and educator.

Charles Breck, *Life and Letters of the Rev. James Lloyd Breck* (New York, 1883), is the primary source. Other biographies by T. I. Holcombe, *An Apostle of the Wilderness* (New York, 1903), and E. J. M. Nutter in *Dictionary of American Biography*, II, 3-4.

June 3. THE MARTYRS OF UGANDA, 1886.

Among the new nations of Africa, Uganda is the most predominantly Christian, a fruit that was seeded in martyrdom. We observe on October 29 the martyr witness of Bishop Hannington, which occurred on his way to Uganda. This date is selected in view of Pope Paul VI's canonization in 1964 of the numerous native converts, mostly youths, put to death by King Mwanga, especially those burned at the stake in Namugongo on June 3,1886. Both Roman Catholic and Anglican men suffered in the persecution—a fact specially mentioned by Pope Paul in his canonization, at which the Anglican Archbishop of Uganda was present as an honored guest.

For the general history, see J. V. Taylor, *The Growth of the Church in Buganda* (SCM Press, 1958). On the martyrs in particular: J. P. Thoonen, *Black Martyrs* (Sheed and Ward, 1941); J. F. Faupel, *African Holocaust, The Story of the Uganda Martyrs* (New York: P. J. Kenedy and Sons, 1962).

June 18. BERNARD MIZEKI, Martyr in Rhodesia, 1896.

Born c. 1861 in Portuguese East Africa. Escaped in early teenage to Capetown, South Africa, where he was converted by Anglican missionaries and baptized, March 9, 1886. In 1891 he volunteered as a catechist for the pioneer mission in Mashonaland, where he was stationed at Nhowe. In June 1896 an uprising of natives against the Europeans and their African friends marked out Bernard especially; and though warned to flee, he refused to leave his converts. In a mysterious way, his stabbed body was never found and the exact site of his burial is unknown. A shrine near his place of martyrdom attracts many pilgrims today. He is listed in the Calendar of the South African Prayer Book, and is commemorated in the Church of the Province of Central Africa as its primary native martyr and witness.

A definitive biography by Jean Farrant, *Mashonaland Martyr, Bernard Mizeki and the Pioneer Church* (Cape Town: Oxford University Press, 1966).

August 7. JOHN MASON NEALE, Priest, 1866.

Born January 24, 1818, in London; educated at Trinity College, Cambridge. One of the founders of the Camden Society (later Ecclesiological Society), 1839. Warden of Sackville College, East Grinsted, 1846 until his death, August 6, 1866. Founder of the sisterhood of St. Margaret. Leader in the Catholic revival of the Church of England; eminent scholar of the history and liturgy of the Church; author and translator of hymns and prayers of the Greek and Latin liturgies; writer of books for children's worship. A modest, patient and devoted priest, Neale is remembered for his single-minded pursuit of all than enriches the spirituality of the Church.

The basic biography is E. A. Towle, *John Mason Neale, D.D., A Memoir* (Longmans, Green and Co., 1906); shorter accounts by J. H. Overton in *Dictionary of National Biography*, XIV, 143-146, and by H. A. L. Rice, *The Bridge Builders* (Darton, Longman, and Todd, 1961), chap. VI. Special studies: A. G. Lough, *The Influence of John Mason Neale* (S.P.C.K., 1962); James F. White, *The Cambridge Movement, The Ecclesiological and the Gothic Revival* (Cambridge University Press, 1962).

August 18. WILLIAM PORCHER DUBOSE, Priest, 1918.

Born April 11, 1836, near Winnsboro, S.C.; educated at the Military College of S.C. (The Citadel), and the University of Virginia. Staff officer and chaplain, the Confederate Army. Ordained priest, 1865, and served parishes in Winnsboro and Abbeville, S.C. Professor at the University of the South, Sewanee, Tenn., 1871, and Dean of its Theological School, 1894 until retirement in 1908. Died at Sewanee, August 18, 1918. The outstanding theologian of the Episcopal Church, and teacher of a generation of its clergy. His many books, based upon a profound knowledge of Greek philosophy, provide a solid theological commentary upon the New Testament and the ancient fathers and ecumenical councils.

In addition to his books, his articles in "The Constructive Quarterly" have been edited by W. Norman Pittenger, *Unity in the Faith* (Seabury Press, 1957). The standard biography is by Theodore DuBose Bratton, *An Apostle of Reality* (Longmans, Green and Co., 1936); and a shorter notice by one of his pupils, G. B. Myers, in *Dictionary of American Biography*, III, 472-73.

September 2. THE MARTYRS OF NEW GUINEA, 1942.

New Guinea is one of the last frontiers of Christian mission, difficult because of the terrain and the primitive character of its native people. The suffering of missionaries and native Christians during World War II was great. This day, observed in the Diocese of New Guinea and other dioceses of the Church of Australia, marks the particular witness of eight missionaries and two Papuan martyrs, but includes all the faith and devotion of Papuan Christians of all Churches who risked their lives to care for the wounded and save the lives of many who otherwise would have perished.

See Peter Robin, "New Guinea Journey," *Anglican World*, Vol. 1, No. 4 (1961), pp. 37-40.

October 9. ROBERT GROSSETESTE, Bishop of Lincoln, 1253.

Born c. 1168 in Suffolk; educated at Oxford and Paris. First Chancellor of Oxford University, 1221. Bishop of Lincoln, 1235-1253. Died October 9, 1253, at Buckden, Huntingdonshire. Several efforts at his canonization did not succeed. One of the model bishops of the Middle Ages, both for his zeal in reform and his diligent pastoral visitations of his large diocese. Grosseteste was also one of the greatest scholars of his time, in philosophy and theology, Biblical exegesis, and science. He knew both Hebrew and Greek, and translated a number of important works of the Greek fathers into Latin.

An older standard biography is G. G. Perry, *Life and Times of Bishop Grosseteste* (S.P.C.K., 1891); recent short accounts by H. R. Luard in *Dictionary of National Biography*, VIII, 718-21, and J. A. Weisheipl in *The New Catholic Encyclopedia*, XII, 530-32. Special studies: S. H. Thomson, *The Writings of Robert Grosseteste* (New York, 1940); A. C. Crombie, *Robert Grosseteste and the Orgins of Experimental Science* (Oxford, 1953) ; D. A. Collins (ed.), *Robert Grosseteste: Scholar and Bishop* (Oxford, 1955). For background, with many references, J. R. H. Moorman, *Church Life in England in the Thirteenth Century* (Cambridge University Press, 1945).

November 2. COMMEMORATION OF ALL FAITHFUL DEPARTED.

Popularly known as "All Souls' Day," its institution goes back to Eastern custom, but it was popularized in the West on this date by the great monastery of Cluny, where it was established in 998 by Abbot Odilo, as an extension of the All Saints' Day observance. It was officially adopted at Rome in the 13th century. The new Roman Calendar accounts it a "Solemnity," but forbids its observance on a Sunday.

For popular custom, see F. X. Weiser, *The Holy Day Book* (Harcourt, Brace and Co., 1956), pp. 123-34.

December 1. NICHOLAS FERRAR, Deacon, 1637.

Born 1592, in London; educated at Clare Hall, Cambridge. Extensive travel on the Continent 1613-18. Member of Parliament, 1624. Retired to Little Gidding, Huntingtonshire, where he was ordained deacon, 1626, by William Laud. With his family and friends, he established a semi-monastic community, which he served as chaplain and spiritual director. A school, dispensary, and infirmary were provided for the surrounding area. Though there was no rule of celibacy, the Puritans contemptuously referred to it as the "protestant nunnery," and broke up the community ten years after Ferrar's death on December 4, 1637. He is commemorated in the Calendar of the South African Prayer Book.

Sources: Nicholas Ferrar, *Two Lives*, edited by J. E. B. Mayor (Cambridge, 1855); and *The Story Books of Little Gidding*, edited by E. C. Sharland (New York: E. P. Dutton and Co., 1899). Among biographies, see: H. P. K. Skipton, *The Life and Times of Nicholas Ferrar* (Mowbray, 1907); A. L. Maycock, *Nicholas Ferrar of Little Gidding* (S.P.C.K., 1938); Mandell Creighton, in *Dictionary of National Biography*, VI, 1241-44.

Appendix II: The Collects

1. Sources of the Collects

Abbreviations:

BCP	*The Book of Common Prayer.* (Date after BCP refers to first edition in which the Collect appeared.)
Bright	William Bright, *Ancient Collects*, 5th ed., Oxford-London: James Parker and Co., 1875.
CECal	*The Calendar and Lessons for the Church's Year.* A Report of the Church of England's Liturgical Commission. London: S.P.C.K., 1969.
Colquhoun	*Parish Prayers.* Compiled and edited by Frank Colquhoun. London: Hodder and Stoughton, 1967.
CSI	The Church of South India, *The Book of Common Worship.* London: Oxford University Press, 1963.
GeSacr	Gelasian Sacramentary: *Liber Sacramentorum Romanae Aeclesiae Ordinis Anni Circuli*, ed. by Leo Cunibert Mohlberg, O.S.B. (Rerum Ecclesiasticarum Documenta, Series Maior, Fontes IV.) Rome: Herder, 1960.

GrSacr	Gregorian Sacramentary: *Das Sacramentarium Gregorianum nach dem Aachener Urexemplar*, ed. by Hans Lietzmann. (Liturgiegeschichtliche Quellen, Heft 3.) Munster in Westf.: Aschendroff, 1921.
LeSacr	Leonine Sacramentary: *Sacramentarium Veronense*, ed. by Leo Cunibert Mohlberg, O.S.B. (Rerum Ecclesiasticarum Documenta, Series Maior, Fontes I.) Rome: Herder, 1956.
LFF	Lesser Feasts and Fasts: *The Calendar and The Collects, Epistles, and Gospels for the Lesser Feasts and Fasts and for Special Occasions.* Prepared by the Standing Liturgical Commission. New York: The Church Pension Fund, 1963.
rev.	revised.
trans.	translation.

Note: The Arabic numerals before a date refer to the Sunday; those after a date refer to the number of the proper for that date; *e.g.*, 1 Christmas = The First Sunday after Christmas; Christmas 1 = the first proper for Christmas Day.

1 Advent. BCP 1549 rev.

2 Advent. New. Cf. CSI for 2 and 3 Advent.

3 Advent. BCP 1549 for 4 Advent rev. Cf. GeSacr No. 1121.

4 Advent. GeSacr No. 1127; trans. by Bright, p. 16, rev.

Christmas Day 1. BCP 1549 rev. GeSacr No. 1156; GrSacr No. 5; cf. trans. A. M. Y. Baylay, *A Century of Collects* (Alcuin Club, 1913), p. 6; and Bright, p. 21.

Christmas Day 2. BCP 1928 American for 2 Christmas rev. GrSacr No. 7; trans. Baylay, op. cit., p. 8, and Bright, p. 25.

Christmas Day 3. BCP 1549 rev.

1 Christmas. LeSacr No. 1248; cf. trans. Bright, p. 22.

Holy Name. *The Cambridge Bede Book*, 1936, rev.

2 Christmas. LeSacr No. 1239. Cf. BCP 1928 English for a Christmas; Offertory prayer in Roman Missal.

Epiphany. BCP 1549 rev. GrSacr No. 17.

Epiphany. New, for Baptism of Christ. Cf. CSI, for 6 Christmas, rev. in CECal for 5 Christmas.

2 Epiphany. New. Cf. CSI for 6 Christmas, rev. in CECa1 for 5 Christmas.

3 Epiphany. New. Cf. Collects for apostles Andrew, James, and Matthew.

4 Epiphany. BCP 1549 for 2 Advent, rev.

5 Epiphany. CSI for 20 Pentecost, rev.

6 Epiphany. BCP 1549 for 1 Trinity, rev. GeSacr No. 566 for 6 after Octave of Easter.

7 Epiphany. BCP 1549 for Quinquagesima, rev.

8 Epiphany. Bright, pp. 234-235, rev. Cf. BCP 1928, p. 596.

Last Epiphany. BCP 1928 English for Transfiguration; also in South African and Indian Prayer Books for the feast.

Ash Wednesday. BCP 1549 rev. (Invitation in Penitential Order from Canadian Prayer Book; litany new; absolution based on BCP forms.)

1 Lent. Bright, pp. 237-238, rev. Cf. CECal for 6 before Easter.

2 Lent. *Common Service Book of the Lutheran Church*, 1917, p. 141. Cf. GeSacr No. 413.

3 Lent. BCP 1549 for 2 Lent, rev. GrSacr No. 45.

4 Lent. F. B. MacNutt, *The Prayer Manual* (Mowbray, 1952).

5 Lent. BCP 1549 for 4 Easter; rev. 1661. GeSacr No. 551 for 4 Easter.

Passion (or Palm) Sunday. a) Blessing of Palms and Procession: 1st Collect, BCP 1928 American for Wednesday in Holy Week; cf. GeSacr No. 74 for Sexagesima; 2nd Collect, *The Kingdom, the Power and the Glory* ("The Grey Book"; Oxford, 1933), pp. 23-24, rev. b) At the Eucharist: BCP 1549 rev. GeSacr No. 329; GrSacr No. 73.

Monday in Holy Week. BCP 1928 American; by the Rev. William Reed Huntington, *Materia Ritualis*, 1882; the preamble from BCP 1549, exhortation in Visitation of the Sick.

Tuesday in Holy Week. BCP 1928 English for Holy Cross Day, rev.; also in Indian Prayer Book and LFF for the feast.

Wednesday in Holy Week. BCP 1928 American for Tuesday in Holy Week; from *The Book Annexed*, 1883, prepared for the BCP 1892.

Maundy Thursday. BCP 1928 American, rev.; certain phrases from the Rev. William Reed Huntington, *Materia Ritualis*, 1882, p. 56.

Good Friday.

- a. Collect, BCP 1549 for Morning Prayer; since BCP 1552, first of three Collects of Liturgy. GrSacr No. 76, "Super populum" for Wednesday in Holy Week.
- b. Intercessions:
    1. BCP 1549 rev. GeSacr No. 405; GrSacr No. 79, 6.
    2. BCP 1928 English, p. 132, "For the Peace of the World," by Bishop Francis Paget of Oxford (d. 1911) ; also in South African, Indian, and Canadian Prayer Books, CECal; and LFF, p. 182.
    3. Eugene Bersier (d. 1889) , rev. Taken from Hugh Martin, *Prayers in Time of War* (SCM Press, 1939), pp. 89—90.
    4. BCP 1549, rev. 1928 American, rev.

5. GeSacr No. 432, second Collect at Easter Vigil, rev. (Bidding from the Taize liturgy.)

c. Final Collect: a medieval devotion in the Office of the Hours, trans. Eric Milner-White, *A Procession of Passion Prayers* (S.P.C.K., 1956), p. xiii.

Holy Saturday. BCP 1661, rev. Cf. BCP 1637 for Scotland.

Easter Eve. BCP 1549 for the procession; restored BCP 1892. GrSacr No. 76, for Wednesday before Easter.

Easter Day. BCP 1549, from GrSacr No. 88; rev. according to GeSacr No. 463.

Monday in Easter Week. BCP 1928 American, for Easter Tuesday. GrSacr No. 94, for Easter Saturday.

Tuesday in Easter Week. Colquhoun, No. 302, rev.

Wednesday in Easter Week. BCP 1928 American, for Easter Monday (cf. 3 Easter), rev.; by the Rev. John W. Suter, Sr. (d. 1942).

Thursday in Easter Week. GrSacr No. 93, for Easter Friday; trans. Bright, pp. 56-57, rev. Cf. 2 Easter.

Friday in Easter Week. BCP 1549 for Easter 2, Easter Tuesday, and 1 Easter, rev.

Saturday in Easter Week. Mozarabic rite; trans. Bright, p. 58, rev.

2 Easter. Same as Thursday in Easter Week.

3 Easter. Same as Wednesday in Easter Week.

4 Easter. New. Cf. *The Kingdom, the Power and the Glory* ("The Grey Book"; Oxford, 1933), p. 71; Colquhoun, No. 324; CECal for 2 Easter.

5 Easter. BCP 1549 for SS. Philip and James, rev.

6 Easter. BCP 1549 for 6 Trinity. GeSacr No. 1178. Ascension Day. BCP 1549 rev. GrSacr No. 108.

7 Easter. Scottish Prayer Book 1912, post-communion for Ascension. LeSacr No. 169.

Pentecost 1. New. Cf. CSI, Collect for Pentecost.

Pentecost 2. BCP 1549 rev. GrSacr No. 112.

Trinity Sunday (1 Pentecost). BCP 1549 rev. From a votive mass of Alcuin, source unknown; but cf. GeSacr No. 680, preface for Octave of Pentecost.

2 Pentecost. BCP 1549 for 14 Trinity, rev. LeSacr No. 598; GeSacr No. 1209.

3 Pentecost. BCP 1549 for 12 Trinity. GeSacr No. 1201.

4 Pentecost. New. Preamble, cf. BCP 1549, 5 Epiphany and 22 Trinity.

5 Pentecost. CSI for 1 Easter, rev.

6 Pentecost. BCP 1549 for 11 Trinity, rev. GeSacr No. 1198.

7 Pentecost. LeSacr No. 971; Bright, p. 77; cf. CECal for 14 Pentecost; Colquhoun No. 1555.

8 Pentecost. BCP 1549 for 17 Trinity. GrSacr No. 204, 24.

9 Pentecost. BCP 1549 for 5 Trinity. LeSacr No. 633.

10 Pentecost. BCP 1549 for 1 Epiphany. GrSacr No. 16, for Sunday after Christmas.

11 Pentecost. BCP 1549, one of Collects after Offertory when there was no Communion; cf. American Prayer Book, pp. 49-50.

12 Pentecost. BCP 1549 for 16 Trinity. GeSacr No. 1218.

13 Pentecost. BCP 1549 for 9 Trinity, rev. LeSacr No. 1015.

14 Pentecost. BCP 1549 for SS. Simon and Jude, rev.

15 Pentecost. BCP 1549 for 2 Easter, rev.

16 Pentecost. BCP 1928 American, for Tuesday in Whitsun Week.

17 Pentecost. LeSacr No. 540; Bright, p. 74.

18 Pentecost. BCP 1549 for 19 Trinity; rev. 1661. GeSacr No. 1230.

19 Pentecost. LeSacr No. 976; trans. Armitage Robinson, taken into BCP 1928 English; cf. CECal for 4 Christmas.

20 Pentecost. BCP 1549 for 4 Trinity, rev. GrSacr (Padua D 47), for 4 Pentecost.

21 Pentecost. LeSacr No. 173; Bright, p. 79.

22 Pentecost. *The Kingdom, the Power and the Glory* ("The Grey Book"; Oxford, 1933), p. 72, rev.

23 Pentecost. BCP 1549 for 7 Trinity, rev. GeSacr No. 1182.

24 Pentecost. BCP 1549 for 5 Easter, rev. GeSacr No. 556.

25 Pentecost. GeSacr No. 401, intercession for Good Friday; trans. Bright, p. 98, rev.

26 Pentecost. Eric Milner-White and G. W. Briggs, *Daily Prayer* (Penguin, 1959), p. 20.

27 Pentecost. BCP 1661, for 6 Epiphany.

Last Pentecost. Roman Missal, Feast of Christ the King; cf. LFF, "For the Reign of Christ," p. 173.

Andrew. BCP 1552, rev.

Thomas. New. Cf. CECal, p. 82.

Stephen. BCP 1549; rev. 1661; rev. GrSacr No. 10

John BCP 1549 rev. Cf. GrSacr No. 11.

Holy Innocents. New.

Confession of St. Peter. New.

Conversion of St. Paul. BCP 1549, rev. Late GrSacr.

Presentation. BCP 1549 rev. GrSacr No. 27.

Matthias. BCP 1549 rev. Cf. CECal.

Joseph. Indian Prayer Book 1960, rev. Cf. LFF.

Annunciation. BCP 1549 rev. GrSacr No. 31, post-communion.

Mark. New. Cf. rev. of BCP Collect in CSI.

Philip and James. South African Prayer Book 1954, Common of a Bishop, rev. (BCP Collect on 5 Easter.)

Visitation. Bright, p. 236, rev. Cf. LFF.

Barnabas. Colquhoun, No. 561, rev.

Nativity of St. John Baptist. BCP 1549 rev. Cf. Colquhoun Nos. 563 and 564.

Peter and Paul. LeSacr No. 280, rev.

Independence Day. BCP 1928 American.

Mary Magdalene. BCP 1928 English, rev. Cf. LFF.

James. BCP 1549 rev.

Transfiguration. BCP 1892 American; by the Rev. William Reed Huntington, rev.

Mary the Virgin. South African Prayer Book 1954. Cf. LFF.

Bartholomew. BCP 1549 rev. From Sarum; but cf. LeSacr No. 1273 for John the Evangelist.

Holy Cross Day. New. Cf. Colquhoun No. 483.

Matthew. New. Cf. Collects for Andrew and James.

Michael and All Angels. BCP 1549 rev. GrSacr No. 169.

Luke. BCP 1928 American, rev.; by the Rev. Charles Morris Addison.

James of Jerusalem. LFF rev.

Simon and Jude. New. Cf. Colquhoun Nos. 585 and 591. (BCP Collect assigned to 14 Pentecost.)

All Saints. BCP 1549 rev.

Thanksgiving Day. New. (Litany, new.)

Martyr. 1) Canadian Prayer Book 1962, rev. 2) BCP 1928 American, rev.; cf. *Missale Gothicum* (ed. Mohlberg, No. 455); Bright, p. 69.

Missionary. BCP 1928 English, and Indian Prayer Book 1960, rev.

Pastor. CSI, "For Pastors," rev.

Theologian or Teacher. New. Cf. Canadian Prayer Book and CSI ("For Doctors").

Monastic. Indian Prayer Book Supplement 1960, rev. ("Of a Religious").

Saint. 1) BCP 1928 American. 2) Bright, p. 236 rev. Cf. LFF.

Commemoration of All Faithful Departed. BCP 1928 American, "At the Burial of the Dead"; by Bishop John Wordsworth of Salisbury (d. 1911).

Holy Trinity. New.

Holy Spirit. BCP 1928 American, for Whitsunday 1. Cf. LFF. Holy Angels. See St. Michael and All Angels. Cf. LFF.

Incarnation. See Christmas Day 2.

Holy Eucharist. St. Thomas Aquinas, for feast of Corpus Christi. Cf. LFF, rev.

Holy Cross. Eric Milner-White and G. W. Briggs, *Daily Prayer* (Penguin Books, 1959), p. 41, rev. Cf. LFF.

All Baptized Christians. New, based on Col. 4:22.

Reign of Christ. See Last Sunday after Pentecost. Cf. LFF.

Church Convention. Composed from phrases in South African, Indian, and Canadian Prayer Books, "For Synods." Cf. LFF. Dedication of a Church. New; suggested by CECal, p. 89. Education. BCP 1928 American, pp. 42-43, rev.; by the Rev. John W. Suter, Jr., *A Book of Collects*, 1919.

Ministry (Ember Days). 1) Ordinal 1550, rev. 2) BCP 1928 American, rev. 3) See Good Friday, intercessions 1. Cf. LFF.

Mission of the Church. 1) BCP 1892 American, rev.; by Bishop George E. L. Cotton of Calcutta (d. 1866). Cf. LFF. 2) Indian Prayer Book Supplement, 1960, rev.

Nation. New. Cf. Colquhoun, No. 1114, by the Rev. Henry Scott Holland.

Peace. See Good Friday intercessions 2. Cf. LFF.

Rogation Days. 1) BCP 1928 American, rev.; by Bishop John Cosin, *Devotions*, 1626. Cf. Colquhoun, No. 348. 2) New; cf. Colquhoun Nos. 346, 354, and 356; CECa1, pp. 88-89. 3) New. Cf. BCP 1928 American, "For Faithfulness in the Use of this World's Goods."

Sick. New. Cf. BCP 1928 American, "For the Recovery of a Sick Person" (from Scottish Prayer Book 1912).

Social Justice. BP 1928 American, rev. Cf. LFF.

Social Service. BCP 1928 American, rev. Cf. LFF.

Unity of the Church. New, based on one of Archbishop William Temple (d. 1944); cf. Colquhoun, No. 494.

Vocation in Daily Work. BCP 1928 American, rev. Cf. LFF.

2. Prayer Book Collects Omitted in Present Proposals or Superseded by New Collects

3 Advent   Cf. new Collect for 2 Advent
Holy Innocents
Circumcision
2 Epiphany
3 Epiphany
4 Epiphany   In revised LFF for Lenten weekdays
5 Epiphany   Cf. 4 Pentecost
Septuagesima
Sexagesima
1 Lent
3 Lent
4 Lent

5 Lent
3 Easter   Cf. new Collect for 2 Easter
Sunday after Ascension Day
Monday in Whitsun Week
2 Trinity
3 Trinity
8 Trinity
10 Trinity
13 Trinity
15 Trinity
18 Trinity   In revised LFF for Lenten weekdays
20 Trinity
21 Trinity   In revised LFF for Lenten weekdays
22 Trinity   Cf. 4 Pentecost
23 Trinity
24 Trinity
Sunday next before Advent
St. Mark
St. Barnabas
St. Peter
St. Matthew
Dedication of a Church
Rogation Days
Thanksgiving Day

Appendix III: Index of Psalms

Psalm	Holy Day	Order
1	23 Pentecost	1
	James of Jerusalem	1
	Common of a Saint	1
	Vocation in Daily Work	1
2:1-8	Easter Eve	1
3	Sick	1
4	24 Pentecost	1
8	Easter Thursday	2
	Holy Name	2
	Vocation in Daily Work	2

Psalm	Holy Day	Order
9:11-14	Holy Innocents	1
16-20	Holy Innocents	2
11:1-6	Matthias	2
13	Sick	2
15	5 Epiphany	2
	2 Pentecost	2
	Matthias	1
	Common of a Saint	2
	Ministry 3	2
16:1-12	6 Pentecost	2
9-12	Easter Monday	2
9-12	All Baptized Christians	2
17:1-7	23 Pentecost	2
18:1-7	Peter and Paul	1
1-7	All Baptized Christians	1
21-29	19 Pentecost	1
19:1-6	Christmas 1	1
1-6	Easter Eve	
1-6	Mark	1
7-14	4 Epiphany	2
7-14	19 Pentecost	2
20	6 Easter	1
21:1-6	Reign of Christ	2
22:1-11	Good Friday	1
23-28	Passion (Palm) Sunday	2
23-28	Social Service	2
23	4 Easter	2
	9 Pentecost	2
	John Apostle and Evengelist	2
	Visitation of B.V.M.	2
	Common of a Pastor	2
24:1-6	Rogation 3	1
1-10	Last Pentecost	1

Psalm	Holy Day	Order
7-10	Ascension Day	2
25:1-4	Philip and James	1
1-6	1 Advent	2
3-9	Education	2
5-10	2 Lent	1
14-21	3 Lent	2
27:1-6	Holy Cross	1
1-7	Last Epiphany	2
1-7	12 Pentecost	2
1-7	Ministry 1	2
4-7	Transfiguration	2
8-16	3 Lent	1
28:1-3,7-10	5 Lent	2
29	1 Epiphany	2
30:1-5	Stephen	1
1-13	Easter Eve	
6-13	3 Pentecost	2
31:1-6	Holy Saturday	1
1-6	Stephen	2
32:1-8	24 Pentecost	2
33:1-6	6 Epiphany	1
1-11	Easter Eve	
12-21	Easter Eve	
12-14, 17-21	Pentecost 2	2
13-18	James the Apostle	2
17-21	Easter Tuesday	2
34:1-4	Blessed Virgin Mary	1
1-8	12 Pentecost	1
1-10	4 Lent	1
3-10	Common of a Saint	2
4-9	All Saints	2
11-19	8 Epiphany	1
36:5-10	2 Epiphany	2

Psalm	Holy Day	Order
5-10	Commemoration of Departed	1
5-12	11 Pentecost	2
37:4-9	7 Epiphany	2
23-28	8 Epiphany	2
23-28	Barnabas	2
38-41	Luke	2
40:1-7	26 Pentecost	2
5-10	Holy Cross (Votive)	2
42:1-7	2 Lent	2
1-7	Easter Eve	
43	Maundy Thursday	1
46	Last Pentecost	2
47	7 Easter	2
	Nation	2
48:1-7	Thomas	1
8-13	7 Easter	1
8-13	Presentation	2
50:1-6	1 Advent	1
7-15	3 Pentecost	1
51:1-18	Ash Wednesday	
10-13	Holy Spirit	2
54	18 Pentecost	2
55:1-8	Monday in Holy Week	1
56:1-4	Holy Cross (Votive)	1
1-11	Monday in Holy Week	2
57:8-12	26 Pentecost	1
59:1-4, 8-9	Tuesday in Holy Week	1
60:1-5	Tuesday in Holy Week	2
61:1-8	Ministry 2	1
1-5,8	Wednesday in Holy Week	1
62:1-8	Wednesday in Holy Week	2
1-8	13 Pentecost	2
7-12	Simon and Jude	1

Psalm	Holy Day	Order
63:1-8	2 Epiphany	1
1-8	Common of a Saint	1
1-9	Ministry 2	2
65:1-5	Matthew	1
4-8	3 Epiphany	2
9-14	8 Pentecost	1
9-14	Thanksgiving Day	2
66:1-7	Mission	2
1-8	Conversion of St. Paul	1
1-11	Easter Day	2
14-18	Blessed Virgin Mary	2
67	5 Epiphany	1
	5 Easter	2
	Conversion of St. Paul	2
	Nation	1
68:1-4, 18-20	Pentecost 1	1
4-6	Luke	1
32-35	Pentecost 1	2
69:1-9, 13-22	Good Friday	2
30-37	5 Pentecost	1
71:1-7	14 Pentecost	1
18-23	3 Easter	1
72:1-4, 12-14	Social Justice	1
1-8	Epiphany	1
10-17	Epiphany	2
75:1-8	James the Apostle	1
1-12	Social Justice	2
78:1-8	Education	1
14-21, 24-26	Maundy Thursday	2
80:1-7	2 Advent	1
7-14	18 Pentecost	1
14-19	20 Pentecost	1

Psalm	Holy Day	Order
81:1-10	2 Pentecost	1
9-15	Nativity John Baptist	2
82	3 Advent	1
	16 Pentecost	2
84:1-5	Presentation	1
1-7	2 Christmas	1
1-7	21 Pentecost	2
1-7	Dedication of a Church	2
8-13	3 Epiphany	1
85:1-3, 10-13	Holy Name	1
4-9	2 Advent	2
7-13	Nativity John Baptist	1
7-13	Peace	1
8-13	8 Pentecost	2
86:1-7	Ash Wednesday	1
11-17	9 Pentecost	1
87	Peter and Paul	2
	Unity	2
89:1-2, 16-19	6 Pentecost	1
1-4, 27-30	Christmas 1	2
9-18	Confession of St Peter	1
90:1-8, 12	27 Pentecost	1
13-17	27 Pentecost	2
91:1-4	Bartholomew	1
1-8	1 Lent	1
9-16	1 Lent	2
92:1-5, 11-14	21 Pentecost	1
11-14	John Apostle and Evangelist	1
93	1 Epiphany	1
94:8-15	4 Pentecost	1
16-22	4 Pentecost	2
95:1-7	11 Pentecost	1
96:1-7	Common of a Missionary	1

Psalm	Holy Day	Order
1-8	22 Pentecost	1
1-13	Christmas 2	1
1-13	Mission	1
8-13	Common of a Missionary	2
97:1-6	1 Christmas	1
8-12	1 Christmas	2
98:1-4	Holy Cross	2
1-10	Christmas 3	1
1-10	Easter Eve	
99:1-5	Reign of Christ	1
1-9	Last Epiphany	1
5-9	Transfiguration	1
102:15-22	6 Epiphany	2
15-22	Andrew	2
103:1-6	7 Epiphany	1
1-12	17 Pentecost	1
8-14	Ash Wednesday	2
13-22	17 Pentecost	2
15-22	Commemoration of Departed	2
19-22	Michael and All Angels	2
19-22	Holy Angels	1
104:1, 13-15, 23-31	Rogation 3	2
1-4	Holy Angels	2
105:1-8	Easter Wednesday	2
1-8	25 Pentecost	1
107:1-9	Rogation 2	1
21-32	Rogation 2	2
23-32	5 Pentecost	2
108:1-6	5 Easter	1
110:1-4	Ascension Day	1
111:1-4, 8-9	Incarnation	2
1-10	25 Pentecost	2
112:1-6	Barnabas	1

Psalm	Holy Day	Order
1-7	4 Epiphany	1
1-9	Common of a Pastor	1
1-9	Ministry 3	2
1-10	15 Pentecost	1
113	Christmas 2	2
	Easter Eve	
	15 Pentecost	2
	Annunciation	1
	Incarnation	1
114	Easter Eve	2
	Easter Thursday	2
116:1-9	Easter Friday	2
1-9	4 Easter	1
5-9	Mary Magdalene	2
11-16	3 Easter	2
11-16	Holy Eucharist	2
117	Andrew	1
118:1-6, 14-18	Easter Day	1
14-18	Easter Saturday	2
19-24	Easter Week	1
19-29	Passion (Palm) Sunday	1
119:9-16	Mark	2
33-40	Matthew	2
33-40	Theologian or Teacher	1
41-48	Philip and James	2
57-64	Joseph	2
97-104	Theologian or Teacher	2
129-136	10 Pentecost	2
137-144	Simon and Jude	2
145-152	James of Jerusalem	2
161-168	Bartholomew	2
161-168	Peace	2
121	22 Pentecost	2

Psalm	Holy Day	Order
	Visitation B.V.M.	1
	Common of a Martyr	2
122	Pentecost	1
	Dedication of a Church	1
	Unity	1
123	7 Pentecost	2
124	2 Easter	1
125	14 Pentecost	2
	Church Convention	2
126	3 Advent	2
	2 Easter	2
	Thomas	2
	Common of a Martyr	1
127:1-4	Joseph	1
128	2 Christmas	2
	20 Pentecost	2
130	Holy Saturday	2
131	Annunciation	2
132:8-15	4 Advent	1
8-18	Ministry 1	1
133	Confession of St. Peter	2
134	Common of a Monastic	1
138:1-5	Mary Magdalene	1
1-8	7 Pentecost	1
139:6-11	Holy Spirit	1
13-18	Common of a Monastic	2
142	5 Lent	1
144:9-15	6 Easter	2
9-15	Rogation 1	2
145:1-9	Christmas 3	2
1-9	Independence Day	1
14-18	Holy Eucharist	1
14-21	10 Pentecost	1

Psalm	Holy Day	Order
14-21	Independence Day	2
15-21	4 Lent	2
146:1-10	16 Pentecost	1
1-10	Church Convention	1
1-10	Social Service	1
4-10	4 Advent	2
147:1-7	13 Pentecost	1
5-11	Rogation 1	1
7-11	Thanksgiving Day	1
148:1-5	Michael and All Angels	1
1-6	Holy Trinity	1
1-13	Trinity Sunday	1
7-13	Holy Trinity	2
149	All Saints	1
150	Trinity Sunday	2

Appendix IV: Index of Scripture Lessons*

Lesson	Holy Day	New Roman Lectionary
Genesis		
1:1-2:2	Easter Eve (Vigil)	Same
2:7-9, 15-17, 3:1-7a	1 Lent A	Gen. 2:7-9; 3:1-7
2:18-24	20 Pentecost B	Same (27)
3:9-15	3 Pentecost B	Same (10)
12:1-8	2 Lent A	Gen. 12:1-4a
15:1-6	12 Pentecost C	Wisd. 18:6-9 (19)
18:1-10a	9 Pentecost C	Same (16)
18:20-32	10 Pentecost C	Same (17)

---

* Editor's Note: The lectionary presented here is not the lectionary currently in use in the Episcopal Church. This was a lectionary adapted from the Common Lectionary, but retaining the option for an Old Testament reading with a typological connection to the appointed Gospel. In 2006, the Episcopal Church adopted the Revised Common Lectionary with use of the prayer book lectionary only on the permission of the bishop.

The Church Year The Calendar and the Proper of the Sundays 99

Lesson	Holy Day	New Roman Lectionary
22:1-14	1 Lent B	Gen. 9:8-15, (Gen. 22 on 2 Lent B)
22:1-18	Easter Eve (Vigil)	Same
28:10-17	Michaelmas	Dan. 7:9-10, 13-14
28:11-17	2 Lent B	Gen. 22:1-2, 9a, 10-13, 15-18
45:1-7	7 Epiphany C	1 Sam. 26:2, 7-9, 12-13, 22-23 (7)
Exodus		
3:1-8b, 10-15	3 Lent B	Ex. 20:1-17 (Ex. 3 on 3 Lent C)
3:1-6	Trinity Sunday B	Deut. 4:32-34, 39-40
3:11-15	Holy Trinity (Votive)	
12:1-14a	Maundy Thursday	Ex. 12:1-8, 11-14
14:15-15:1	Easter Eve (Vigil)	Same
16:2-4, 12-15	11 Pentecost B	Same (18)
16:2-8, 13-15	4 Lent B	2 Chron. 36:14-16, 19-23
17:8-12	22 Pentecost C	Ex. 17:8-13 (29)
19:2-6a	4 Pentecost A	Same (11)
19:3-8	Ministry 3 (Votive)	
22:21-27	23 Pentecost A	Same (30)
24:12, 15-18	Last Epiphany A	Same (3 Lent A)
32:7-11, 13-14	17 Pentecost C	Same (24)
34:29-35	Transfiguration	Dan. 7:9-10, 13-14
Leviticus		
19:1-2, 15-18	7 Epiphany A	Lev. 19:1-2, 17-18 (7)
Numbers		
6:22-27	Trinity Sunday C	Prov. 8:22-31
11:16-17, 24-29	Ministry 1 (Votive)	
11:25-29	19 Pentecost B	Same (26)
Deuteronomy		
4:1-2, 6b-8	15 Pentecost B	Same (22)
5:1, 6-21	3 Lent A	Ex. 17:3-7
5:6-21 (or, vss. 12-15)	2 Pentecost B	Same (9)

Lesson	Holy Day	New Roman Lectionary
6:1-6	24 Pentecost B	Deut. 6:2-6 (31)
6:4-9, 20-25	Education (Votive)	
8:1-3, 5-6	Last Epiphany C	
8:2-3	Holy Eucharist (Votive)	Same
8:6-11	Thanksgiving Day	
8:7-18	4 Lent A	1 Sam. 16:1b, 6-7, 10-13
11:18-21, 26-28	2 Pentecost A	Deut. 11:18, 26-28 (9)
18:15-18	Bartholomew	
18:15-20	4 Epiphany B	Same (4)
26:5-10	1 Lent C	Deut. 26:4-10
30:10-14	8 Pentecost C	Same (15)
30:11-14	Andrew	
32:1-4	Simon and Jude	
Joshua		
24:1-2a, 14-18	14 Pentecost B	Josh. 24:1-2a, 15-17, 18b (21)
Ruth		
1:8-19a	21 Pentecost C	2 Kings 5:14-17 (28)
1 Samuel		
3:1-10	2 Epiphany B	1 Sam. 3:3b-10, 19 (2)
3:1-10	Ministry 2 (Votive)	Same
16:1-13	3 Lent C	Ex. 3:1-8a, 13-15
2 Samuel		
7:1-5, 8b-11, 16	4 Advent B	Same
12:7-10, 13	4 Pentecost C	Same (11)
1 Kings		
3:5-12	10 Pentecost A	1 Kings 3:5, 7-12 (17)
8:22-30	Dedication of Church	
8:41-43	2 Pentecost C	Same (9)
17:10-16	25 Pentecost B	Same (32)
17:17-24	3 Pentecost C	Same (10)
19:4-8	12 Pentecost B	Same (19)
19:4-12	Last Epiphany B	

Lesson	Holy Day	New Roman Lectionary
19:9-12	12 Pentecost A	1 Kings 19:9a, 11-13a (19)
19:15-16, 19-21	6 Pentecost C	1 Kings 19:16b, 19-21 (13)
2 Kings		
4:42-44	10 Pentecost B	Same (17)
5:1-14	6 Epiphany B	Lev. 13:1-2, 44-46 (6)
20:1-5	Sick (Votive)	2 Kings 20:1-6
2 Chronicles		
24:17-22	Stephen	
Job		
14:1-14	Holy Saturday	
19:23-29	25 Pentecost C	2 Macc. 7:1-2, 9-14
29:11-16	Barnabas	
38:1-11, 16-18	5 Pentecost B	Job 38:1, 8-11 (12)
38:1-18	Rogation 3	
Proverbs		
3:1-6	Matthew	
8:22-30	John	
9:1-6	13 Pentecost B	Same (20)
31:10-13, 19-20, 30-31	27 Pentecost A	Same (33)
Ecclesiastes		
1:2; 2:18-23	11 Pentecost C	Eccles. 1:2; 2:21-23 (18)
3:1, 9-13	Vocation in Daily Work (Votive)	
Song of Songs		
8:6-7	Monastic (Votive)	Same
Isaiah		
2:1-5	1 Advent A	Same
2:2-4	Mission (Votive)	
2:10-17	6 Pentecost A	2 Kings 4:8-11, 14-16a (13)
4:2-6	Easter Eve (Vigil)	
5:1-7	20 Pentecost A	Same (27)
6:1-8	5 Epiphany C	Isa. 6:1-2a, 3-8 (5)
6:1-8	Trinity Sunday A	Ex. 34:4b-6, 8-9

Lesson	Holy Day	New Roman Lectionary
7:10-14	4 Advent A	Same
7:10-14; 8:10c	Annunciation	Isa. 7:10-14
9:1-4	3 Epiphany A	Same (3)
9:2-4, 6-7	Christmas Day	Same
9:2-4, 6-7	Holy Name	
11:1-10	2 Advent A	Same
11:1-10	Incarnation (Votive)	
12	4 Lent C	Josh. 5:9a, 10-12
22:15-16, 19-23	14 Pentecost A	Isa. 22:19-23 (21)
25:6-9	Easter Day	
25:6-9	Commemoration of Faithful Departed	Same
25:6-10a	21 Pentecost A	Same (28)
26:1-8	Nation (Votive)	
30:18-21	Philip and James	
35:1-10	3 Advent A	35:1, 6a, 10
35:1-10	Unity	
35:4-7a	16 Pentecost B	Same (23)
40:1-5, 9-11	2 Advent B	Same
40:1-11	Nativity John Baptist	Jer. 1:4-10
42:1-7	1 Epiphany	Isa. 42:1-4, 6-7
42:1-7	Monday Holy Week	Same
42:1-8	Social Justice	
43:16-21	5 Lent C	Same
43:18-19, 22, 24b-25	7 Epiphany B	Isa. 43:18-19, 21-22, 24b-25 (7)
45:1, 4-6	22 Pentecost A	Same (29)
45:21-25	Holy Cross	Num. 21:4-9
49:1-7	2 Epiphany A	Isa. 49:3, 5-6 (2)
49:1-9a	Tuesday Holy Week	Isa. 49:1-6
49:5-13	Mission	
49:13-15	8 Epiphany A	Isa. 49:14-15 (8)
50:4-9a	Wednesday Holy Week	Same

Lesson	Holy Day	New Roman Lectionary
Isaiah		
50:5-9a	17 Pentecost B	Same (24)
52:7-10	Christmas 3	Same
52:7-10	Missionary	Same (Pastors)
52:12-15; 53:10-12	Holy Cross (Votive)	Same
52:13-53:12	Good Friday	Same
53:10-11	22 Pentecost B	Same (30)
55:1-3	11 Pentecost A	Same (18)
55:1-11	Easter Eve (Vigil)	Same
55:1-13	Church Convention	
55:6-9	18 Pentecost A	Same (25)
55:10-11	8 Pentecost A	Same (15)
55:10-13	8 Epiphany C	Ecclus. 27:5-8
56:1, 6-7	13 Pentecost A	Same (20)
58:8-12	5 Epiphany A	Isa. 58:7-10 (5)
60:1-6	Epiphany	Same
60:13-21	1 Christmas	Ecclus. 3:3-7, 14-17a
61:1-3, 10-11	3 Advent B	Isa. 61:1-2a, 10-11
61:1-3	Holy Spirit	
61:1-6	3 Epiphany C	Neh. 8:1-4a, 5-6, 8-10
61:7-11	Blessed Virgin Mary	1 Chron. 15:3-4, 15-16; 16:1-2
61:10-62:3	2 Christmas	Ecclus. 24:1-2, 8-12, but Isa. 62:1-4 (Christmas Eve)
62:2-5	2 Epiphany C	Isa. 62:1-5
62:6-8, 10-12	Mark	
62:10-12	Christmas 2	Isa. 62:10-12
63:7-9, 16	Joseph	2 Sam. 7:4-5a, 12-14a, 16
63:16b-64:8	1 Advent B	Isa. 63:16b-17; 64:1, 3b-8
66:10-14	7 Pentecost C	Same (14)
66:18b-23	14 Pentecost C	Isa. 66:18-21 (21)
Jeremiah		
1:4-10	4 Epiphany C	Jer. 4:4-5, 17-19 (4)

Lesson	Holy Day	New Roman Lectionary
17:5-8	6 Epiphany C	Same (6)
17:7-8	All Baptized Christians	
20:7-9	15 Pentecost A	Same (22)
20:7-13	5 Pentecost A	Jer. 20:10-13 (12)
23:1-6	9 Pentecost B	Same (16)
23:2-6	Last Pentecost C	2 Sam. 5:1-3
23:23-29	13 Pentecost C	Jer. 38:4-6, 8-10 (20)
Jeremiah		
26:1-9	25 Pentecost A	
31:7-9	23 Pentecost B	Same (30)
31:15-20	Holy Innocents	
31:31-34	5 Lent B	Same
33:14-16	1 Advent C	Same
45:1-5	James the Apostle	
Ezekiel		
2:2-5	7 Pentecost B	Same (14)
3:4-11	Confession St. Peter	
17:22-24	4 Pentecost B	Same (11)
18:25-28	19 Pentecost A	Same (26)
33:7-9	16 Pentecost A	Same (23)
34:11-16	Peter and Paul	
34:11-16	Pastor	
34:11-17	Last Pentecost A	
34:25-31	Rogation 1	
36:22-28	2 Lent C	Gen. 15:5-12, 17-18
36:24-28	Easter Eve (Vigil)	Ezek. 36:16-28
37:1-3, 11-14	5 Lent A	Ezek. 37:12-14
Daniel		
7:9-10a	Holy Angels (Votive)	Same (Michaelmas)
7:9-12	26 Pentecost B	
7:13-14	Last Pentecost B	
7:13-14	Reign of Christ	
12:1-3	27 Pentecost B	Same (33)

Lesson	Holy Day	New Roman Lectionary
Hosea		
2:14-23	8 Epiphany B	Hos. 2:14b-15b, 19-20
6:3-6	3 Pentecost A	Same (10)
Joel		
2:12-19	Ash Wednesday	Joel 2:12-18
2:28-32	Pentecost 1	Same (Vigil)
Amos		
6:1, 3-7	19 Pentecost C	Amos 6:1a, 4-7 (26)
7:10-15	8 Pentecost B	Amos 7:12-15 (15)
8:4-7	18 Pentecost C	Same (25)
Jonah		
3:1-5, 10	3 Epiphany B	Same (3)
Micah		
4:1-5	Independence Day	
4:1-5	Peace	(Same; Time of War)
5:2-5a	4 Advent C	Same
6:6-8	Saint	Same
Habakkuk		
1:2-3; 2:2-4	20 Pentecost C	Same (27)
2:1-4	Thomas	
Zephaniah		
3:9-13	4 Epiphany A	Zeph. 2:3; 3:12-13
3:14-17	Visitation B.V.M.	Zeph. 3:14-18a
3:14-18a	3 Advent C	Same
3:14-20	5 Epiphany B	Job 7:1-4, 6-7
3:14-17, 19-20	Easter Eve (Vigil)	
Zechariah		
8:3-12, 16-17	Social Service	
9:9-10	7 Pentecost A	Same (14)
9:9-12	Palm Sunday	Isa. 50:4-7
12:9-11	5 Pentecost C	Zech. 12:10-11
Malachi		
1:14b-2:2b, 8-10	24 Pentecost A	Same (31)

Lesson	Holy Day	New Roman Lectionary
3:1-4	Presentation	Same
3:1-5; 4:5-6	27 Pentecost C	
4:1-2a	26 Pentecost C	Same (33)
2 Esdras 2:42-48	Martyr	
Wisdom		
1:13-15; 2:23-24	6 Pentecost B	Same (13)
2:1, 12-20	18 Pentecost B	Wisd. 2:17-29 (25)
3:1-9	Saint; Comm. Departed	
6:12-16	26 Pentecost A	Same (32)
7:7-11	21 Pentecost B	Same (28)
7:7-14	Theologian or Teacher	Wisd. 7:7-10, 15-16
9:13-18	16 Pentecost C	Same (23)
11:23-12:2	24 Pentecost A	Same (31)
12:13, 16-19	9 Pentecost A	Same (16)
Ecclesiasticus		
2:7-11	Common of a Saint	
3:17-18, 20, 28-29	15 Pentecost C	Same (22)
15:14-20	6 Epiphany A	Ecclus. 15:16-21 (6)
27:29-28:7	17 Pentecost A	Same (24)
35:12-14, 16-19	23 Pentecost C	Ecclus. 35:12-14, 16-18
38:1-4, 6-10, 12-14	Luke	
44:1-10, 13-14	All Saints	
51:1-12	Martyr	Same
Baruch		
5:1-9	2 Advent C	Same
Matthew		
1:18-25	4 Advent A	Same
2:1-12	Epiphany	Same
2:13-15, 19-23	2 Christmas	Same on 1 Christmas
2:13-18	Holy Innocents	Same
3:1-12	2 Advent A	Same
3:13-17	1 Epiphany A	Same
4:1-11	1 Lent A	Same

Lesson	Holy Day	New Roman Lectionary
Matthew		
4:12-23	3 Epiphany A	Same (3)
4:18-22	Andrew	Same
5:1-12	All Saints	Same
5:1-12a	4 Epiphany A	Same (4)
5:13-24	5 Epiphany A	Matt. 5:13-16 (5)
5:27-37	6 Epiphany A	Matt. 5:17-37 (6)
5:38-48	7 Epiphany A	Same (7)
5:43-48	Independence Day	
6:1-6, 16-21	Ash Wednesday	Matt. 6:1-6, 16-18
6:19-24	Rogation 2	
6:19-24	Vocation Daily Work	Matt. 6:31-34
6:24-34	8 Epiphany A	Same (8)
6:25-33	Thanksgiving Day	
7:21-27	2 Pentecost A	Same (9)
9:9-13	3 Pentecost A	Same (10)
9:9-13	Matthew	Same
9:35-38	Ministry 2	Same
9:36-10:8	4 Pentecost A	Same (11)
10:16-22	Martyr	Matt. 10:17-22
10:26-33	5 Pentecost A	Same (12)
10:32-42	Social Justice	
10:34-42	6 Pentecost A	Same (13)
11:2-11	3 Advent A	Same
11:25-30	7 Pentecost A	Same (14)
11:25-30	Education	
13:1-9, 18-23	8 Pentecost A	Same (15)
13:24-34	9 Pentecost A	Same (16)
13:44-49a	10 Pentecost A	Matt. 13:44-52 or 44-46
13:54-58	James of Jerusalem	
14:13-21	11 Pentecost A	Same (18)
14:22-33	12 Pentecost A	Same (19)
15:21-28	13 Pentecost A	Same (20)

Lesson	Holy Day	New Roman Lectionary
Matthew		
16:13-19	Confession St. Peter	Same (Feb. 22 feast)
16:13-20	14 Pentecost A	Same (21)
16:21-26	15 Pentecost A	Matt. 16:21-27 (22)
16:24-27	Ministry 3	
17:1-9	Last Epiphany A	Same on 2 Lent A
18:15-20	16 Pentecost A	Same (23)
18:21-35	17 Pentecost A	Same (24)
20:1-16	18 Pentecost A	Same (25)
20:20-28	James the Apostle	Same
21:1-11	Blessing of Palms A	Same
21:12-16	Dedication Church	
21:28-32	19 Pentecost A	Same (26)
21:33-43	20 Pentecost A	Same (27)
22:1-14	21 Pentecost A	Matt. 22:1-10 (28)
22:15-21	22 Pentecost A	Same (29)
22:34-40	23 Pentecost A	Same (30)
23:1-12	24 Pentecost A	Same (31)
23:34-39	Stephen	Matt. 10:17-22
24:4-14	25 Pentecost A	
24:37-44	1 Advent A	Same
25:1-13	26 Pentecost A	Same (32)
25:1-13	Common of a Saint	
25:14-15, 19-30	27 Pentecost A	Same (33)
25:31-40	Saint	
25:31-46	Last Pentecost A	Same (34)
26:1-5, 14-25	Wednesday Holy Week	Matt. 26:14-25
26:36-27:54	Palm Sunday A	Matt. 26:14-27:66
27:57-66	Holy Saturday	
28:1-10	Easter Eve	Same (A)
28:1-10	Easter Day A (alt)	
28:9-15	Easter Monday	Matt. 28:8-15
28:16-20	Trinity Sunday A	Same in year B

Lesson	Holy Day	New Roman Lectionary
28:16-20	Mission	Matt. 28:19-20
28:18-20	Holy Trinity (Votive)	
Mark		
1:1-8	2 Advent B	Same
1:7-11	1 Epiphany B	Mark 1:6b-11
1:9-13	1 Lent B	Same
1:14-20	3 Epiphany B	Same (3)
1:21-28	4 Epiphany B	Same (4)
1:29-39	5 Epiphany B	Same (5)
1:40-45	6 Epiphany B	Same (6)
2:1-12	7 Epiphany B	Same (7)
2:1-12	Sick (Votive)	
2:18-22	8 Epiphany B	Same (8)
2:23-28	2 Pentecost B	Same (9)
3:20-35	3 Pentecost B	Same (10)
3:31-35	James of Jerusalem	
4:26-34	4 Pentecost B	Same (11)
4:35-41	5 Pentecost B	Mark 4:35-41 (12)
5:21-24, 35b-43	6 Pentecost B	Same (13)
6:1-6	7 Pentecost B	Same (14)
6:7-13	8 Pentecost B	Same (15)
6:30-34	9 Pentecost B	Same (16)
6:35-44	to Pentecost B	John 6:1-15 (17)
7:1-8, 14-15, 21-23	15 Pentecost B	Same (22)
7:31-37	16 Pentecost B	Same (23)
8:12-21	4 Lent B	John 3:14-21
8:27-38	17 Pentecost B	Mark 8:27-35 (24)
9:2-9	Last Epiphany B	Same on 2 Lent B
9:30-37	18 Pentecost B	Same (25)
9:38-43, 45, 47-48	19 Pentecost B	Same (26)
10:2-9	20 Pentecost B	Mark 10:2-16 (27)
10:17-27	21 Pentecost B	Same (28)
10:23-31	Barnabas	Matt. 10:7-13

Lesson	Holy Day	New Roman Lectionary
Mark		
10:32-45	2 Lent C	Luke 9:28b-36
10:35-45	22 Pentecost B	Same (29)
10:35-45	All Baptized Christians	
10:42-52	Social Service	
10:46-52	23 Pentecost B	Same (30)
11:1-11a	Blessing of Palms B	Mark 11:1-10
12:1-11	5 Lent C	John 8:1-11
12:13-17	Nation	
12:28b-34	24 Pentecost B	Same (31)
12:38-44	25 Pentecost B	Same (32)
13:1-10	Mark	Mark 16:15-20
13:14-23	26 Pentecost B	
13:24-32	27 Pentecost B	Same (33)
13:33-37	1 Advent B	Same
14:3-9	Monday Holy Week	
14:32-15:39	Palm Sunday B	Mark 14:1-15:47
16:1-8	Easter Day B	Mark 16:1-8 (Vigil)
16:9-15, 20	Easter Saturday	Mark 16:9-15
Luke		
1:26-38	4 Advent B	Same
1:26-38	Annunciation	Same
1:26-38	Incarnation (Votive)	
1:39-49	4 Advent C	Luke 1:39-47
1:39-49	Visitation	Luke 1:39-56
1:46-55	Blessed Virgin Mary	Luke 11:27-28
1:57-80	Nativity John Baptist	Luke 1:5-17
2:1-14	Christmas 1	Same
2:15-21	Holy Name	Same
2:15b-20	Christmas 2	Same
2:22-40	Presentation	Same
2:41-51a	Joseph	Matt. 1:16, 18-21, 24a
2:41-52	2 Christmas	Same for 1 Christmas

Lesson	Holy Day	New Roman Lectionary
Luke		
3:1-6	2 Advent C	Same
3:7-18	3 Advent C	Luke 3:10-18
3:15-16, 21-22	1 Epiphany C	Same
4:1-13	I Lent C	Same
4:14-21	3 Epiphany C	Luke 1:1-4; 4:14-2
4:14-21	Luke	Luke 10:1-9
4:21-30	4 Epiphany C	Same (4)
5:1-11	5 Epiphany C	Same (5)
6:17-23	Saint	
6:20-26	6 Epiphany C	Luke 6:7, 20-26 (6)
6:27-38	7 Epiphany C	Same (7)
6:39-45	8 Epiphany C	Same (8)
7:1-10	2 Pentecost C	Same (9)
7:11-17	3 Pentecost C	Same (10)
7:36-50	4 Pentecost C	Same (11)
9:18-24	5 Pentecost C	Same (12)
9:28-36	Last Epiphany C	Same for 2 Lent C
9:28-36	Transfiguration	Same
9:51-62	6 Pentecost C	Same (13)
10:1-9	Missionary	
10:1-9	Mission	
10:1-9, 16-20	7 Pentecost C	Luke 10:1-12, 17-20 (14)
10:25-37	8 Pentecost C	Same (15)
10:38-42	9 Pentecost C	Same (16)
11:1-13	to Pentecost C	Same (17)
11:5-13	Rogation 1	
11:9-13	Pentecost 1	John 7:37-39
11:9-13	Holy Spirit (Votive)	
12:2-12	Martyr	
12:13-21	11 Pentecost C	Same (18)
12:16-31	Rogation 3	
12:32-40	12 Pentecost C	Same (19)

Lesson	Holy Day	New Roman Lectionary
Luke		
12:33-37	Monastic	
12:49-56	13 Pentecost C	Luke 12:49-53 (20)
13:1-9	3 Lent C	Same
13:22-30	14 Pentecost C	Same (21)
14:1, 7-14	15 Pentecost C	Same (22)
14:25-33	16 Pentecost C	Same (23)
15:1-10	17 Pentecost C	Luke 15:1-32 (24)
15:11-32	4 Lent C	Luke 15:1-3, 11-32
16:10-13	18 Pentecost C	Luke 16:1-13 (25)
16:19-31	19 Pentecost C	Same (26)
17:5-10	20 Pentecost C	Same (27)
17:11-19	21 Pentecost C	Same (28)
18:1-8a	22 Pentecost C	Same (29)
18:9-14	23 Pentecost C	Same (30)
19:29-10	24 Pentecost C	Same (31)
19:28-40	Blessing of Palms	Same
20:27, 34-38	25 Pentecost C	Same (32)
21:5-19	26 Pentecost C	Same (33)
21:10-19	Conversion St. Paul	Matt. 16:15-18
21:25-31	1 Advent C	Luke 21:25-31, 34-36
21:32-36	27 Pentecost C	
22:14-30	Maundy Thursday (alt)	
22:24-30	Bartholomew	John 1:45-51
22:39-23:49	Palm Sunday C	Luke 22:14-23:56
23:35-43	Last Pentecost C	Same
24:1-10	Easter Day C	Same for Easter Vigil C
24:13-35	3 Easter A	Same
24:13-35	Easter Wednesday	Same
24:35-48	3 Easter B	Same
24:36b-48	Easter Thursday	Luke 24:35-48
24:49-53	Ascension Day	Luke 24:36, 46-53 (C)

Lesson	Holy Day	New Roman Lectionary
John		
1:1-14	Christmas 3	John 1:1-18
1:1-18	1 Christmas	
1:6-8, 19-28	3 Advent B	Same
1:29-41	2 Epiphany A	John 1:29-34 (2)
1:43-51	2 Epiphany B	John 1:35-42
1:47-51	Michaelmas	Same
1:47-51	Holy Angels (Votive)	
2:1-12	2 Epiphany C	Same
2:13-22	2 Lent B	Mark 9:1-9 (3 Lent B, John 2:13-25)
3:1-16	Trinity Sunday B	John 3:16-18, Trinity A (3:1-16, 4 Lent B)
3:14-21	3 Lent B	
4:5-26	2 Lent A	Matt. 17:1-9 (John 4:5-42, 3 Lent A)
4:31-38	Ministry 1	
6:4-15	4 Lent A	John 9:1-41
6:24-35	11 Pentecost B	Same (18)
6:41-51	12 Pentecost B	Same (19)
6:47-59	Holy Eucharist (Votive)	John 6:51-59
6:53-58	13 Pentecost B	John 6:51-58 (20)
6:60-69	14 Pentecost B	Same (21)
9:1-13, 24-28	3 Lent A	John 9:1-41, on 4 Lent A
10:1-10	4 Easter A	Same
10:11-16	4 Easter B	John 10:11-18
10:22-30	4 Easter C	John 10:27-30
11:21-27	Commemoration Departed	John 11:17-27
11:18-44	5 Lent A	John 11:1-45
12:1-11	Monday Holy Week	Same
12:20-33	5 Lent B	Same
12:23-33	Holy Cross (Votive)	John 12:31-36a
12:31-36	Holy Cross Day	John 3:13-17

Lesson	Holy Day	New Roman Lectionary
John		
12:37-38, 42-50	Tuesday Holy Week	
13:1-15	Maundy Thursday	Same
13:21-35	Wednesday Holy Week	
13:31-35	5 Easter C	John 13:31-33a, 34-35
14:1-12	5 Easter A	Same
14:6-13a	Philip and James	John 14:6-14
14:8-17	Trinity Sunday C	John 16:12-15
14:15-21	6 Easter A	Same
14:21-27	Simon and Jude	Luke 6:12-16
14:23-29	6 Easter C	Same
15:1, 6-16	Matthias	John 15:9-17
15:1-11	5 Easter B	John 15:1-8
15:1-8	Church Convention	
15:9-17	6 Easter B	Same
16:23-33	Peace (Votive)	
17:1-11a	7 Easter A	Same
17:11b-19	7 Easter B	Same
17:15-23	Unity (Votive)	John 17:11b-19, or 20-26
17:18-23	Theologian or Teacher	
17:20-26	7 Easter C	Same
18:1-19:37	Good Friday	John 18:1-19:42
18:33-37	Last Pentecost	Same
18:33-37	Reign of Christ (Votive)	
19:38-42	Holy Saturday (alt)	
20:1-9	Easter Day A	Same
20:11-18	Easter Tuesday	Same
20:11-18	Mary Magdalene	John 20:1-2, 11-18
20:19-23	Pentecost 2	Same
20:19-31	2 Easter A B C	Same
20:24-29	Thomas	Same
21:1-14	Easter Friday	Same
21:1-14	3 Easter C	John 21:1-19

Lesson	Holy Day	New Roman Lectionary
21:15-17	Pastor	Same
21:15-19	Peter and Paul	Same
21:19-24	John the Apostle	John 20:2-8
Acts		
1:1-9	Missionary	
1:1-11	Ascension Day	Same
1:8-14	7 Easter A	Acts 1:12-14
1:15-26	7 Easter B	Acts 1:15-17, 20-26
1:15-26	Matthias	Acts 1:15-17, 20-26
2:1-11	Pentecost 2	Same
2:14, 22-32	Easter Monday	Same
2:14a, 36-41	4 Easter A	Same
2:22-32	3 Easter A	Acts 2:14, 22-28
2:32-39	Trinity Sunday B	Romans 8:14-17
2:36-41	Easter Tuesday	Same
2:42-47	2 Easter A	Same
3:1-10	Easter Wednesday	Same
3:11-26	Easter Thursday	Same
3:13-15, 17-21	3 Easter B	Acts 3:13-15, 17
4:1-12	Easter Friday	Same
4:5, 7-12	4 Easter B	Acts 4:8-21
4:8-13	Confession St. Peter	
4:13-21	Easter Saturday	Same
4:32-35	2 Easter B	Same
5:12-16	2 Easter C	Same
5:27-35	3 Easter C	Acts 5:27b-32
6:1-7a	5 Easter A	Same
7:55-60	7 Easter C	Same
7:55-60	Stephen	Acts 6:8-10; 7:54-59
8:5-8, 4-17	6 Easter A	Same
9:26-31	5 Easter B	Same
10:34-38	1 Epiphany	Same
10:34-43	Easter Day (alt)	

Lesson	Holy Day	New Roman Lectionary
11:5a, 11-18	6 Easter B	Acts 10:25-26, 34-35, 44-48
11:22-30	Barnabas	Acts 11:21b-26; 13:1-3
11:27-12:2	James the Apostle	2 Cor. 4:7-15
13:14b-26	Nativity John Baptist	1 Peter 1:8-12
13:16, 26-33	4 Easter C	Acts 13:14, 43-52
13:27-31	Mary Magdalene	Song of Songs 3:1-4a
13:44-52	5 Easter C	Acts 14:20b-26
15:1-6, 22-29	6 Easter C	Acts 15:1-2, 22-29
15:12-22	James of Jerusalem	
20:32-35	Rogation 2	
26:9-20	Conversion St. Paul	Acts 22:3-16
Romans		
1:1-7	Holy Name	Same for 4 Advent A
3:21-25a, 28	2 Pentecost A	Same (9)
4:2-3, 20-25	1 Lent B	1 Pet. 3:18-22
4:18-25	3 Pentecost A	Same (10)
5:1-10	2 Lent A	Rom. 5:1-5 (3 Lent A)
5:6-11	4 Pentecost A	Same (11)
5:12-15	5 Pentecost A	Same (12)
5:12-19	1 Lent A	Same
6:3-11	Easter Eve	Same
6:3-11	All Baptized Christians	
6:3-11	6 Pentecost A	Rom. 6:3-4, 8-11 (13)
8:1-10	3 Lent B	Rom. 5:1-2, 5-8
8:9-17	9 Pentecost A	Rom. 8:9, 11-13 (14)
8:11-19	4 Lent A	Eph. 5:8-14
8:12-17	Trinity Sunday C	Rom. 5:1-5
8:18-23	8 Pentecost A	Same (15)
8:14-17, 22-27	Pentecost 1	Rom. 8:22-27 (Vigil)
8:26-27	9 Pentecost A	Same (16)
8:28-30	10 Pentecost A	Same (17)
8:31b-39	5 Lent A	Rom. 8:31b-34 (2 Lent B)

Lesson	Holy Day	New Roman Lectionary
8:35-39	11 Pentecost A	Rom. 8:35, 37-39 (18)
9:1-5	12 Pentecost A	Same (19)
9:1-5	4 Advent A	Rom. 1:1-7
10:8-13	2 Lent B	Same, 1 Lent C
10:8-18	Andrew	
11:13-15, 29-32	13 Pentecost A	Same (20)
11:33-36	14 Pentecost A	Same (21)
11:33-36	Holy Trinity (Votive)	
12:1-2	15 Pentecost A	Same (22)
12:9-18	Rogation 2	
13:1-10	Nation (Votive)	
13:8-10	16 Pentecost A	Same (23)
13:8-14	1 Advent A	Rom. 13:11-14
14:7-9	17 Pentecost A	Same (24)
15:4-13	2 Advent A	Rom. 15:4-9
16:25-27	4 Advent B	Same
1 Corinthians		
1:3-9	1 Advent B	Same
1:10-13, 17	3 Epiphany A	Same (3)
1:18-24	Holy Cross (Votive)	1 Cor. 1:18-25
1:18-31	Tuesday Holy Week	
1:26-31	4 Epiphany A	Same (4)
1:26-31	Common of a Saint	
2:1-5	5 Epiphany A	Same (5)
2:6-10	6 Epiphany A	Same (6)
2:6-10, 13-16	Theologian or Teacher	1 Cor. 2:1-10a, or 10b-16
3:5-11	Ministry 1	
3:6-9	Rogation 1	
3:16-23	7 Epiphany A	Same (7)
4:1-5	8 Epiphany A	Same (8)
4:9-15	Bartholomew	Rev. 21:9b-14
4:9-16	2 Epiphany A	1 Cor. 1:1-3
6:13b-20	2 Epiphany B	1 Cor. 6:13c-15a, 17-20

Lesson	Holy Day	New Roman Lectionary
7:17-23	3 Epiphany B	1 Cor. 7:29-31
8:1b-13	4 Epiphany B	1 Cor. 7:32-35
9:16-23	5 Epiphany B	
10:1-13	2 Lent C	Same on 3 Lent C
11:23-26	Maundy Thursday	Same
12:4-13	Pentecost 2	1 Cor. 12:3b-7, 12-13
12:4-11	2 Epiphany C	Same (2)
12:4-14	Holy Spirit (Votive)	
12:12-27	3 Epiphany C	1 Cor. 12:12-30 (3)
12:31-13:13	Last Epiphany A	Same on 4 Epiphany C
14:12b-17, 33, 40	4 Epiphany C	1 Cor. 12:31-13:13
15:1-11	5 Epiphany C	Same (5)
15:1-11	James of Jerusalem	
15:12, 16-20	6 Epiphany C	Same (6)
15:20-26, 28	Last Pentecost A	Same
15:44b-49	7 Epiphany C	1 Cor. 15:45-49
15:50-58	Commemoration Departed	1 Cor. 15:51-57
15:54-58	8 Epiphany C	Same (8)
2 Corinthians		
1:18-22	7 Epiphany B	Same (7)
3:17-4:2	8 Epiphany B	2 Cor. 3:1b-6
4:1-6	Philip and James	1 Cor. 15:1-8
4:1-10	Church Convention	
4:3-6	Last Epiphany B	
4:7-11	2 Pentecost B	2 Cor. 4:6-11 (9)
4:13-5:1	3 Pentecost B	Same (10)
4:16b-18	6 Epiphany B	1 Cor. 10:31-11:1
5:6-10	4 Pentecost B	Same (11)
5:14-17	5 Pentecost B	Same (12)
5:14-18	Mary Magdalene	
5:17-21	3 Lent C	Same on 4 Lent C
5:20b-6:10	Ash Wednesday	2 Cor. 5:20-6:2

Lesson	Holy Day	New Roman Lectionary
8:1-9, 13-15	6 Pentecost B	2 Cor. 8:7, 9, 13-15 (13)
12:7-10	7 Pentecost B	Same (14)
Galatians		
1:1-10	2 Pentecost C	Gal. 1:1-2, 6-10 (9)
1:11-19	3 Pentecost C	Same (10)
1:11-24	Conversion St. Paul	
2:11-21	4 Pentecost C	Gal. 2:16, 19-21 (11)
3:23-29	5 Pentecost C	Gal. 2:26-28 (12)
4:4-7	1 Christmas	Same on Octave
4:4-7	Blessed Virgin Mary	1 Cor. 15:54-57
4:26-5:1	4 Lent B	Eph. 2:4-10
4:31-5:1, 13-18	6 Pentecost C	Same (13)
6:14-18	7 Pentecost C	Same (14)
Ephesians		
1:3-14	8 Pentecost B	Same (15)
1:3-6, 15-18	2 Christmas	Same
1:16-23	Ascension Day	Eph. 1:17-23
2:4-10	4 Lent C	Same in year B
2:11-18	9 Pentecost B	Eph. 2:13-18 (16)
2:13-22	Simon and Jude	Eph. 2:19-22
2:13-18	Peace	
2:13-22	Mission	
3:1-12	Mission	Eph. 3:2-12
3:1-12	Epiphany	Eph. 3:2-3a, 5-6
4:1-6	10 Pentecost B	Same (17)
4:1-6	Unity	Same
4:7-8, 11-16	Mark	1 Peter 5:5b-14
4:11-16	Ministry 2	
4:17-24	11 Pentecost B	Eph. 4:17, 20-24 (18)
4:30-5:2	12 Pentecost B	Same (19)
5:8-14	3 Lent B	Same on 4 Lent A
5:15-20	13 Pentecost B	Same (20)
5:18b-20	Visitation	
5:21-32	14 Pentecost B	Same (21)

Lesson	Holy Day	New Roman Lectionary
Philippians		
1:3-11	2 Advent C	Phil. 1:4-6, 8-11
1:20c-24, 27a	18 Pentecost A	Same (25)
2:1-11	19 Pentecost A	Same (26)
2:5-11	Palm Sunday	Phil. 2:6-11
2:5-11	Holy Cross	Phil. 2:6-11
2:12-15	5 Lent C	Phil. 3:8-14
3:7-15	Monastic (Votive)	
3:7-15	Last Epiphany C	Same on 5 Lent C
3:13-21	Matthias	
4:4-7	3 Advent C	Same
4:4-9	Saint	Same
4:4-8	20 Pentecost A	Phil. 4:6-9 (27)
4:5-8, 9b	Joseph	Rom. 4:13, 16-18, 22
4:10-13	21 Pentecost A	Phil. 4:12-14, 19-20 (28)
Colossians		
1:1-12	8 Pentecost C	Col. 1:15-20 (15)
1:12-20	Last Pentecost C	Same
1:12-20	Reign of Christ	
1:21-28	9 Pentecost C	Col. 1:24-28 (16)
2:6-15	10 Pentecost C	Col. 2:12-14 (17)
3:1-5, 9-11	11 Pentecost C	Same (18)
3:1-4	Easter Day	Same
1 Thessalonians		
1:1-5b	22 Pentecost A	Same (29)
1:5c-10	23 Pentecost A	Same (30)
2:7-13	24 Pentecost A	1 Thess. 2:7b-9,13 (31)
3:7-13	25 Pentecost A	
3:9-13	1 Advent C	Same
4:12-17	26 Pentecost A	Same (32)
5:1-10	27 Pentecost A	1 Thess. 5:1-6 (33)
5:16-24	3 Advent B	Same
2 Thessalonians		
1:1-5, 11-12	24 Pentecost C	2 Thess. 1:11-2:2 (31)

The Church Year The Calendar and the Proper of the Sundays   121

Lesson	Holy Day	New Roman Lectionary
2:15-3:5	25 Pentecost C	Same (32)
3:7-12	26 Pentecost C	Same (33)
1 Timothy		
1:12-17	17 Pentecost C	Same (24)
2:1-8	18 Pentecost C	Same (25)
6:7-10, 17-19	Rogation 3	
6:11-16	19 Pentecost C	Same (26)
2 Timothy		
1:6-14	20 Pentecost C	2 Tim. 1:6-8, 13-14 (27)
2:8-13	21 Pentecost C	Same (28)
3:14-17	Matthew	Eph. 4:1-7, 11-13
3:14-4:2	22 Pentecost C	Same (29)
3:14-4:5	Education (Votive)	
4:1-8	Peter and Paul	Gal. 1:11-20
4:5-13	Luke	2 Tim. 4:9-17a
4:6-8, 16-18	23 Pentecost C	Same (30)
Titus		
2:11-14	Christmas 1	Same
3:4-7	Christmas 2	Same
Philemon		
1:7-17	16 Pentecost C	Philem. 1:9b-10, 12-17 (23)
Hebrews		
1:1-6	Christmas 3	Same
2:9-18	20 Pentecost B	Heb. 2:9-11 (27)
3:1-6	21 Pentecost B	Heb. 4:12-13 (28)
4:12-16	22 Pentecost B	Heb. 4:14-16 (29)
5:1-9	23 Pentecost B	Heb. 5:1-6 (30)
5:5-9	5 Lent B	Heb. 5:7-10
7:23-28	24 Pentecost B	Same (31)
9:11-15, 24-28	Wednesday Holy Week	
9:24-28	25 Pentecost B	Same (32)
10:1-25	Good Friday	
10:4-10	Annunciation	Same

Lesson	Holy Day	New Roman Lectionary
10:5-10	4 Advent C	Same
10:11-14, 18	26 Pentecost B	Same (33)
10:31-33, 35-39	27 Pentecost B	
10:35-11:1	Thomas	Eph. 2:19-22
11:1-2, 8-16	12 Pentecost C	Heb. 11:1-2, 8-19 (19)
11:8-16	Independence Day	
11:39-12:3	Monday Holy Week	
12:1-2	Saint	
12:1-4	13 Pentecost C	Same (20)
12:5-7, 11-13	14 Pentecost C	Same (21)
12:18-19, 22-24	15 Pentecost C	Same (22)
James		
1:12-18	1 Lent C	Rom. 10:8-13
1:16-21	Thanksgiving Day	
1:17-18, 21b-22, 27	15 Pentecost B	Same (22)
2:1-5	i6 Pentecost B	Same (23)
2:5-9, 12-17	Social Justice	
2:14-18	17 Pentecost B	Same (24)
3:16-4:3	18 Pentecost B	Same (25)
5:1-6	19 Pentecost B	Same (26)
5:7-10	3 Advent A	Same
5:13-16	Sick (Votive)	Same
1 Peter		
1:3-9	2 Easter A	Same
1:17-23	3 Easter A	1 Peter 1:17-21
2:1-9	Dedication Church	
2:1-10	5 Easter A	1 Peter 2:4-9
2:11-17	Vocation Daily Work	
2:19-25	4 Easter A	1 Peter 2:20b-25
3:12-18	Martyr	1 Peter 3:14-17
3:15-18	6 Easter A	Same
4:1-8	Holy Saturday	
4:7-11	Ministry 3	

Lesson	Holy Day	New Roman Lectionary
4:7-11	Social Service	
4:12-19	7 Easter A	1 Peter 4:13-16
4:17-19	27 Pentecost C	
5:1-4	Pastor	Same
2 Peter		
1:13-21	Transfiguration	2 Peter 1:16-19
3:8-14	2 Advent B	Same
1 John		
1:1-5	John the Apostle	1 John 1:1-4.
1:3-2:5a	3 Easter B	1 John 2:1-5a
3:1-8	4 Easter B	1 John 3:1-2
3:1-8	Presentation	Heb. 2:14-18
3:18-24	5 Easter B	Same
4:1-11	Incarnation (Votive)	
4:7-21	6 Easter B	1 John 4:7-10
5:1-6	2 Easter B	Same
5:9-15	7 Easter B	1 John 4:11-16
Revelation		
1:4b-8	Last Pentecost B	Rev. 1:5-8
1:4-10a, 12-18	2 Easter C	Rev. 1:9-11a, 12-13, 17-19
4:1-11	Trinity Sunday A	2 Cor. 13:11-13
5:6-14	3 Easter C	Rev. 5:11-14
5:11-14	Holy Angels (Votive)	
7:9-17	4 Easter C	Rev. 7:9, 14b-17
7:9-17	All Saints	Rom. 7:2-4, 9-14
7:13-17	Martyr	Rev. 7:9-17
12:7-11	Michaelmas	Rev. 12:7-12a
19:1, 4-9	5 Easter C	Rev. 21:1-5a
19:1-2a, 4-9	Holy Eucharist (Votive)	
21:3-5	Holy Innocents	1 John 1:5-2:2
21:2-4, 14, 22-24	6 Easter C	Rev. 21:10-14, 22-23
22:12-14, 16-17, 20	7 Easter C	Same

Appendix V: Bibliography

Episcopal Church

The Book of Common Prayer, in its several editions since the first Book of 1549.

Reports of the Joint Commission on the Book of Common Prayer appointed by The General Convention of 1913. Five reports were issued for the Conventions of 1916, 1919, 1922, 1925, and 1928. The first four contain materials on the revision of the Calendar and the proper of the Eucharist.

Prayer Book Studies. The Standing Liturgical Commission. New York: The Church Pension Fund. See especially:
II. *The Liturgical Lectionary*, 1950.
IX. *The Calendar*, 1957.
XII. *The Propers for the Minor Holy Days*, 1958.
XII Supplement. *The Collects, Epistles, and Gospels for the Lesser Feasts and Fasts*, 1960.
XVI. *The Calendar and the Collects, Epistles and Gospels for the Lesser Feasts and Fasts*. A Supplementary Revision of Prayer Book Studies IX and XII, 1963.

The Book of Offices, Services for Certain Occasions not provided in the Book of Common Prayer. Third Edition. New York: The Church Pension Fund, 1960.

Holy Week Offices. Edited by Massey H. Shepherd, Jr., for the Associated Parishes, Incorporated. Published under the auspices of the Adult Division of the Department of Christian Education. Protestant Episcopal Church. Greenwich: The Seabury Press, 1958.

A Suggested Lectionary 1966, With Lessons, Introductions and 1967 Supplement; The Suggested Lectionary and the Holy Communion, With an appraisal of the Sunday Collects, Epistles and Gospels. (Prepared under the auspices of the Department of Christian Education, Diocese of Central New York.)

Other Anglican Churches

The Calendar and Lessons for the Church's Year. A Report submitted by the Church of England Liturgical Commission to the Archbishops of Canterbury and York, November 1968. London: S.P.C.K., 1969.

Lectionary Committee, General Synod of The Church of Ireland.
Report to the General Synod 1968.
Report to the General Synod 1969.
Dublin University Press, Ltd., Trinity College.

The Church in Wales. *The Calendar, Tables and Rules, 1963. Additional Collects, Epistles and Gospels for Use with the Revised Calendar, 1965.* Penarth: Church in Wales Publications.

The Canadian Book of Occasional Offices. Services for Certain Occasions not provided in The Book of Common Prayer. Published at the request of the House of Bishops of the Anglican Church of Canada. Compiled by the Most Reverend Harold E. Sexton, Archbishop of British Columbia. 1964.

The Supplement to the Book of Common Prayer. Madras-Delhi-Lahore: I.S.P.C.K., 1960.

Prayer Book Revision in Australia. Report of a Commission of the General Synod appointed to explore the possibilities of revision of, and addition to, the Book of Common

Prayer for the Church of England in Australia, 1966. Sydney: The Standing Committee of the General Synod, 1966.

The Liturgy or Eucharist of the Church of the Province of New Zealand. An alternative Order approved for experimental use upon certain conditions by the General Synod, 1966. Published by the Association of Anglican Bookrooms in New Zealand.

Roman Catholic Church

Calendarium Romanum. Ex decreto Sacrosancti Oecumenici Concilii Vaticani II instauratum auctoritate Pauli PP. VI promulgatum. Typis Polyglottis Vaticanis, 1969.

Ordo Lectionum Missae. Missale Romanum, ex decreto Sacrosancti Oecumenici Concilii Vaticani II instauratum auctoritate Pauli PP. VI promulgatum. Typis Polyglottis Vaticanis, 1969.

Priere du temps present. Le nouvel Office Divin, Texte liturgique approuve. Desclee de Brouwer, 1969.

Lectionary. Order of Readings for Use at Mass According to the Cycle of Readings Promulgated by His Holiness Pope Paul VI, Using the Jerusalem Bible Version of Scripture. Approved for Use in the Churches of England, Wales, Scotland and Ireland. London: Geoffrey Chapman, 1969.

Other Churches and Groups

The Calendar and Lectionary, A Reconsideration. By the Joint Liturgical Group. Edited by Ronald C. D. Jasper. London: Oxford University Press, 1967.

The Daily Office. By the Joint Liturgical Group. Edited by Ronald C. D. Jasper. London: S.P.C.K. and The Epworth Press, 1968. ("The Collects," pp. 78-88.)

The Church of South India. *The Book of Common Worship.* As Authorized by the Synod 1962. London: Oxford University Press, 1963.

Common Service Book of the Lutheran Church. Authorized by The United Lutheran Church in America. Philadelphia: The Board of Publication, The United Lutheran Church in America, 1917.

Service Book and Hymnal of the Lutheran Church in America. Authorized by the Churches cooperating in The Commission on the Liturgy and The Commission on the Hymnal. 1958.

The Book of Common Order of the Church of Scotland. By Authority of the General Assembly. Edinburgh: Oxford University Press, 1940. 2nd ed. With New Lectionary, 1952.

The Book of Common Worship. Approved by the General Assembly of the Presbyterian Church in the United States of America. Philadelphia: The Publication Division of the Board of Christian Education, 1946.

The Book of Worship for Church and Home. Nashville: The Methodist Publishing House, 1964.

L'Office Divin de Chaque Jour, (Eglise et Liturgie). 3rd edition Neuchatel: Editions Delachaux et Niestle, 1961.

Liturgikon. "Messbuch" der byzantinischen Kirche. Edited by Neophytos Edelby. Recklinghausen: Aurel Bongers, 1967.

Service Book of the Holy Orthodox-Catholic Apostolic Church. Compiled, Translated, etc. by Isabel Florence Hapgood. Boston: Houghton, Mifflin and Co, 1906.

A Manual of Eastern Orthodox Prayers. New York: Macmillan, 1945. (The Calendar, pp. 82-113.)

Anthologies of Prayers

Baylay, Atwell M. Y., *A Century of Collects*, Selected and Translated. (Alcuin Club Prayer Book Revision Pamphlets III.) London: A. R. Mowbray and Co. Ltd., 1913.
Bright, William, *Ancient Collects and Other Prayers*, Selected for Devotional Use from Various Rituals; With an Appendix, on the Collects in the Prayer-Book. Fifth Edition. Oxford-London: James Parker and Co., 1875.
Colquhoun, Frank, *Parish Prayers*. Compiled and Edited. With a Foreword by the Archbishop of York. London: Hodder and Stoughton, 1967.
The Kingdom, the Power and the Glory. Services of Praise and Prayer for Occasional Use in Churches. An American Edition of The Grey Book. New York: Oxford University Press, 1933.
MacNutt, Frederick Brodie, *The Prayer Manual*, for private devotions or for public use on divers occasions. Compiled from all sources, ancient, medieval, and modern, with a Foreword by the Archbishop of Canterbury. London: A. R. Mowbray and Co. Ltd., 1951. 2nd edition, 1952.
Martin, Hugh, *Prayers in Time of War*, for Private and Corporate Use. Edited. London: Student Christian Movement Press, 1939.
Milner-White, Eric, *After the Third Collect*. Prayers and Thanksgivings for use in Public Worship, previously published as 'Memorials upon Several Occasions.' Edited. Fourth edition revised. London: A. R. Mowbray and Co. Ltd., 1952.
Milner-White, Eric, *A Procession of Passion Prayers*. London: S.P.C.K., 1962.
Milner-White, Eric, and Briggs, G. W., *Daily Prayer*. Compiled. (Pelican Books.) Penguin Books, 1959. (First published in 1941 by Oxford University Press.)
Morning Prayers. For Use at the Daily Services in The Memorial Church of Harvard University. Privately Printed for The Memorial Church.
Suter, John Wallace, Jr., *The Book of English Collects*. From the Prayer Books of the Anglican Communion, etc., With Notes, and an Essay on the Collect Form. New York-London: Harper and Brothers, 1940.
Williams, Rowland, *Psalms and Litanies, Counsels and Collects, for Devout Persons*. Edited by his Widow. Popular Edition. London: Henry S. King and Co., 1876.

Selected Modern Works

(See Bibliographies in *Prayer Book Studies IX* and *XVI*.)

Boeckh, Jurgen, "Die Entwicklung der altkirchlichen Pentekoste," *Jahrbuch für Liturgik und Hymnologie*, V (1960), 1-45.
Botte, Bernard, *Les origines de la Noël et de l'Épiphanie*. Étude historique. (Textes et Études liturgiques, I.) Louvain: Abbaye du Mont Cesar, 1932.
Brook, Stella, *The Language of the Book of Common Prayer*. New York: Oxford University Press, 1965.
Cabie, Robert, *La Pentecôte*. L'évolution de la Cinquantaine pascale au cours des cinq premiers siecles. (Bibliothèque de Liturgie.) Tournai: Desclée et Cie., 1965.

Callewaert, Camillus, *Sacris Erudiri*. Fragmenta liturgica collects a monachis Sancti Petri de Aldenburgo in Steenbrugge ne pereant. Steenbrugge: Abbatia S. Petri de Aldenburgo, 1950. (A collection of his articles.)
Casel, Odo, "Art und Sinn der altesten christlichen Osterfeier," *Jahrbuch für Liturgiewissenschaft*, XIV (1938), 1-78.
The Commemoration of Saints and Heroes of the Faith in the Anglican Communion. The Report of a Commission Appointed by the Archbishop of Canterbury. London: S.P.C.K., 1957.
Colson, F. H., *The Week*. Cambridge University Press, 1926.
Cowley, Patrick, *Advent, Its Liturgical Significance*. London: The Faith Press Ltd., 1960.
Croce, Walter, "Die Adventliturgie im Licht ihrer geschichtlichen Entwicklung," *Zeitschrift für katholische Theologie*, LXXVI (1954), 258-296.
Denis-Boulet, Noele M., *The Christian Calendar*. Translated from the French by P. Hepburne-Scott. (Twentieth Century Encyclopedia of Catholicism, Vol. 113.) New York: Hawthorn Books, 1960.
Devereux, James A., "Reformed Doctrine in the Collects of the First Book of Common Prayer," *The Harvard Theological Review*, LVIII (1965), 49-68.
Dublanchy, E., "Dimanche," *Dictionnaire de Théologie catholique*, IV, 1308-1348.
Duchesne, Louis, *Christian Worship, Its Origin and Evolution*. A Study of the Latin Liturgy up to the Time of Charlemagne. Translated by M. L. McLure. 5th edition, London: S.P.C.K., 1919, pp. 228-291.
Fendt, Leonhard, "Der heutige Stand der Forschung fiber das Geburtsfest Jesu am 25. XII und über Epiphanias," Theologische Literaturzeitung, LXXVIII (1953), 1-10.
Goulburn, Edward Meyrick, *The Collects of the Day*, An Exposition Critical and Devotional of the Collects Appointed at the Communion. 2 vols. New York: Pott, Young, and Co., 1880.
Holl, Karl, "Der Ursprung des Epiphanienfestes," Gesammelte Aufsätze zur Kirchengeschichte, II (Tübingen: J. C. B. Mohr, 1928), 123-154.
James, E. O., *Seasonal Feasts and Festivals*. London: Thames and Hudson, 1961.
Jones, C. P. M., (ed.), *A Manual for Holy Week*. (Alcuin Club Edition.) London: S.P.C.K. 1967.
Jungmann, Josef Andreas, "Advent und Voradvent. Überreste des gallischen Advents in der römischen Liturgie," *Gewordene Liturgie*, Studien und Durchblicke. Innsbruck: Felizian Rauch, 1941, pp. 232-94.
Jungmann, Josef Andreas, "Die Nachfeier vom Epiphanie im Missale Romanum," *Zeitschrift für katholischer Theologie*, LXVI (1942), 39-46.
Jungmann, Josef A., *Public Worship, A Survey*. Translated by Clifford Howell. Collegeville, Minn.: The Liturgical Press, 1957, pp. 178-238.
Lemarié, Joseph, *La manifestation du Seigneur*, La Liturgie de Noël et de l'Épiphanie. (Lex Orandi 23.) Paris: Les éditions du Cerf, 1957.
La Maison-Dieu. Revue de Pastorale liturgique. No. 52 (1957), on the Sanctorale; No. 59 (1959), on Advent and Christmas.
McArthur, A. Allan, *The Evolution of the Christian Year*. Greenwich: The Seabury Press, 1953.
McArthur, A. Allan, *The Christian Year and Lectionary Reform*. London: SCM Press Ltd., 1958.
Miller, John H., *Fundamentals of the Liturgy*. Notre Dame: Fides Publishers Association, 1959, pp. 345-424.

Mohrmann, Christine, "Epiphania," *Études sur le latin des chrétiens*, Tome I. 2nd edition. Rome: Edizioni di storia e letteratura, 1961, pp. 245-275.
Nikolasch, Franz, "Zum Ursprung des Epiphaniefestes," *Ephemerides liturgicae*, LXXXII (1968). 393-429.
Noël-Épiphanie, Retour du Christ. By Various Authors. (Lex Orandi 40.) Paris: Les éditions du Cerf, 1967.
Porter, H. B., *The Day of Light: The Biblical and Liturgical Meaning of Sunday*. Greenwich: The Seabury Press, 1960.
Rahner, Hugo, *Greek Myths and Christian Mystery*. With a Foreword by E. O. James. London: Burns and Oates, 1963.
Rordorf, Willy, *Sunday. The History of the Day of Rest and Worship in the Earliest Centuries of the Christian Church*. Translated by A. A. K. Graham. Philadelphia: The Westminster Press, 1968.
Seidenspinner, Clarence, *Great Protestant Festivals*. New York: Henry Schuman, 1952.
Shepherd, Massey H., Jr., *The Paschal Liturgy and the Apocalypse*. (Ecumenical Studies in Worship. No. 6.) Richmond: John Knox Press, 1960.
Thurston, H., *Lent and Holy Week*. London: Longmans, Green and Co., 1904.
Tyrer, J. W., *Historical Survey of Holy Week. Its Services and Ceremonial*. (Alcuin Club Collections, No. XXIX.) London: Oxford University Press, 1932.
Weiser, Francis X., *Handbook of Christian Feasts and Customs*. The Year of the Lord in Liturgy and Folklore. New Yorker: Harcourt, Brace and Co., 1958.
Willis, G. G., *Essays in Early Roman Liturgy*. (Alcuin Club Collections, No. XLVI.) London: S.P.C.K., 1964.
Willis, G. G, *Further Essays in Early Roman Liturgy*. (Alcuin Club Collections, No. 50.) London: S.P.C.K., 1968.

PART II
THE CALENDAR
OF THE CHURCH YEAR

Observed in This Church

THE CHURCH YEAR consists of two cycles of feasts and holy days: the one is dependent upon the movable date of the Sunday of the Resurrection or Easter Day; the other, upon the fixed date of December 25, the feast of our Lord's Nativity or Christmas Day.

Easter Day is always the first Sunday after the full moon that falls on or after March 21. It cannot occur before March 22 or after April 25.

The sequence of all Sundays of the Church Year depends upon the date of Easter Day. But the Sundays in Advent are always the four Sundays prior to Christmas Day, whether it occurs on a Sunday or a weekday. The date of Easter also determines the beginning of Lent on Ash Wednesday, and the feast of the Ascension on a Thursday forty days after Easter.

1. Sundays

All Sundays of the year are feasts of our Lord Jesus Christ. Only the following feasts of our Lord Jesus Christ, appointed on fixed days, take precedence of a Sunday:

Christmas Day	The Presentation
The Holy Name	The Transfiguration
The Epiphany	All Saints' Day

All Saints' Day may always be observed on the Sunday following November 1, in addition to its observance on the fixed date. All other feasts appointed on fixed days in the Calendar, which may occur on a Sunday, are observed on the nearest open day following. But the patronal or dedication feasts of a church may be observed on a Sunday, except those in the seasons of Advent, Lent, and Easter. With the express permission of the Ordinary, and for urgent and sufficient reason, some other special occasion may be observed on a Sunday.

2. Holy Days

The following Holy Days are regularly observed throughout the year. Unless otherwise ordered in the preceding rules concerning Sundays, they have precedence over all other days of commemoration or of special observance:

Feasts of our Lord

Christmas Day	The Visitation
The Holy Name	The Nativity of Saint John
The Epiphany	the Baptist
The Presentation	The Transfiguration
The Annunciation	Holy Cross Day
Ascension Day	All Saints' Day

Other Major Feasts

All feasts of Apostles	Saint Mary the Virgin
All feasts of Evangelists	Saint Michael and All Angels
Saint Stephen	Saint James, the Brother
The Holy Innocents	of our Lord
Saint Joseph	Independence Day
Saint Mary Magdalene	Thanksgiving Day

Fasts

Ash Wednesday	Good Friday

Feasts appointed on fixed days in the Calendar are not observed on the days of Holy Week or of Easter Week. Major feasts falling in these weeks are transferred to the first open day following the Second Sunday of Easter.

Feasts appointed on fixed days in the Calendar do not take precedence of Ash Wednesday or of Ascension Day.

Feasts of our Lord and other major feasts appointed on fixed days, which may fall upon or be transferred to a weekday, may be observed on any open day within the week in which they occur, except Christmas Day, the Epiphany, and All Saints' Day.

3. Days of Special Devotion

The following days are observed by special acts of discipline and self-denial:

> Ash Wednesday and the other weekdays of Lent and of Holy Week, except the feast of the Annunciation and other major feasts.
>
> Good Friday and all other Fridays of the year, in commemoration of the Lord's crucifixion, except on Fridays in the Christmas and Easter seasons, and on any major feasts which may occur on a Friday.

4. Days of Optional Observance

Subject to the rules of precedence governing Sundays and holy days listed above, the following days may be observed, with the proper prayers and lessons duly authorized by this Church:

> Other commemorations listed in the Calendar
>
> The Common of Saints
>
> Special Occasions

Provided, that there is no celebration of the Eucharist for any special occasion on Ash Wednesday, Maundy Thursday, Good Friday, and Holy Saturday; and *provided further*, that no proper appointed for a special occasion is used as a substitute for, or as an addition to the proper appointed on Christmas Day, Easter Day, Ascension Day, and the Day of Pentecost.

The proper appointed for the Sunday serves for celebrations of the Eucharist on the weekdays following, unless otherwise ordered for holy days and special occasions.

The Collect appointed for any Sunday or other feast may be used at the evening service of the day before.

JANUARY

1	A	THE HOLY NAME OF OUR LORD JESUS CHRIST
2	b	
3	c	
4	d	
5	e	
6	f	THE EPIPHANY OF OUR LORD JESUS CHRIST
7	g	
8	A	
9	b	
10	c	William Laud, Archbishop of Canterbury, 1645
11	d	
12	e	
13	f	Hilary, Bishop of Poitiers, 367
14	g	
15	A	
16	b	
17	c	Antony, Abbot in Egypt, 356
18	d	THE CONFESSION OF SAINT PETER THE APOSTLE
19	e	Wulstan, Bishop of Worcester, 1095
20	f	Fabian, Bishop of Rome, and Martyr, 250
21	g	Agnes, Martyr at Rome, 304
22	A	Vincent, Deacon of Saragossa, and Martyr, 304
23	b	Phillips Brooks, Bishop of Massachusetts, 1893
24	c	
25	d	THE CONVERSION OF SAINT PAUL THE APOSTLE
26	e	Timothy and Titus, Companions of Saint Paul
27	f	John Chrysostom, Bishop of Constantinople, 407
28	g	Thomas Aquinas, Friar, 1274
29	A	
30	b	
31	c	

FEBRUARY

1	d	
2	e	THE PRESENTATION OF OUR LORD JESUS CHRIST IN THE TEMPLE
3	f	Anskar, Archbishop of Hamburg, Missionary to Denmark and Sweden, 865
4	g	Cornelius the Centurion
5	A	The Martyrs of Japan, 1597
6	b	
7	c	
8	d	
9	e	
10	f	
11	g	
12	A	
13	b	
14	c	Cyril, Monk, and Methodius, Bishop, Missionaries to the Slavs, 869, 885
15	d	Thomas Bray, Priest and Missionary, 1730
16	e	
17	f	
18	g	
19	A	
20	b	
21	c	
22	d	
23	e	Polycarp, Bishop and Martyr of Smyrna, 156
24	f	SAINT MATTHIAS THE APOSTLE
25	g	
26	A	
27	b	George Herbert, Priest, 1633
28	c	
29		

MARCH

	1	d	David, Bishop of Menevia, Wales, c. 544
	2	e	Chad, Bishop of Lichfield, 672
	3	f	John and Charles Wesley, Priests, 1791, 1788
	4	g	
	5	A	
	6	b	
	7	c	Perpetua and her Companions, Martyrs of Carthage,
	8	d	
	9	e	Gregory, Bishop of Nyssa, c. 394
	10	f	
	11	g	
	12	A	Gregory the Great, Bishop of Rome, 604
	13	b	
	14	c	
	15	d	
	16	e	
	17	f	Patrick, Bishop and Missionary of Ireland, 461
	18	g	Cyril, Bishop of Jerusalem, 386
	19	A	SAINT JOSEPH
	20	b	Cuthbert, Bishop of Lindisfarne, 687
	21	c	Thomas Ken, Bishop of Bath and Wells, 1711
14	22	d	James De Koven, Priest, 1879
3	23	e	Gregory the Illuminator, Bishop and Missionary of Armenia, c. 332
	24	f	
11	25	g	THE ANNUNCIATION OF THE BLESSED VIRGIN MARY
	26	A	
19	27	b	
8	28	c	
	29	d	John Keble, Priest, 1866
16	30	e	
5	31	f	John Donne, Priest, 1631

APRIL

	1	g	Frederick Denison Maurice, Priest, 1872
13	2	A	James Lloyd Breck, Priest, 1876
2	3	b	Richard, Bishop of Chichester, 1253
	4	c	
10	5	d	
	6	e	
18	7	f	
7	8	g	William Augustus Muhlenberg, Priest, 1877
	9	A	William Law, Priest, 1761
15	10	b	
4	11	c	
	12	d	George Augustus Selwyn, First Missionary Bishop of New Zealand, 1878
12	13	e	
1	14	f	
	15	g	
9	16	A	
17	17	b	
6	18	c	
	19	d	Alphege, Archbishop of Canterbury, and Martyr, 1012
	20	e	
	21	f	Anselm, Archbishop of Canterbury, 1109
	22	g	
	23	A	
	24	b	
	25	c	SAINT MARK THE EVANGELIST
	26	d	
	27	e	
	28	f	
	29	g	Catherine of Siena, 1380
	30	A	

MAY

1	b	SAINT PHILIP AND SAINT JAMES, APOSTLES
2	c	Athanasius, Bishop of Alexandria, 373
3	d	
4	e	Monnica, Mother of Augustine of Hippo, 387
5	f	
6	g	
7	A	
8	b	
9	c	Gregory of Nazianzus, Bishop of Constantinople, 389
10	d	
11	e	
12	f	
13	g	
14	A	
15	b	
16	c	
17	d	
18	e	
19	f	Dunstan, Archbishop of Canterbury, 988
20	g	Alcuin, Deacon, and Abbot of Tours, 804
21	A	
22	b	
23	c	
24	d	Jackson Kemper, First Missionary Bishop in the United States, 1870
25	e	Bede, The Venerable, Priest, and Monk of Jarrow, 735
26	f	Augustine, First Archbishop of Canterbury, 605
27	g	
28	A	
29	b	
30	c	
31	d	THE VISITATION OF THE BLESSED VIRGIN MARY

JUNE

1	e	Justin, Martyr at Rome, c. 167
2	f	The Martyrs of Lyons, 177
3	g	The Martyrs of Uganda, 1886
4	A	
5	b	Boniface, Archbishop of Mainz, Missionary to Germany, Martyr, 754
6	c	
7	d	
8	e	
9	f	Columba, Abbot of Iona, 597
10	g	Ephrem of Edessa, Syria, Deacon, 373
11	A	SAINT BARNABAS THE APOSTLE
12	b	
13	c	
14	d	Basil the Great, Bishop of Caesarea, 379
15	e	
16	f	Joseph Butler, Bishop of Durham, 1752
17	g	
18	A	Bernard Mizeki, Martyr in Rhodesia, 1896
19	b	
20	c	
21	d	
22	e	Alban, First Martyr of Britain, c. 304
23	f	
24	g	THE NATIVITY OF SAINT JOHN BAPTIST
25	A	
26	b	
27	c	
28	d	Irenaeus, Bishop of Lyons, c. 202
29	e	SAINT PETER AND SAINT PAUL, APOSTLES
30	f	

JULY

1	g	
2	A	
3	b	
4	c	INDEPENDENCE DAY
5	d	
6	e	
7	f	
8	g	
9	A	
10	b	
11	c	Benedict of Nursia, Abbot of Monte Cassino, c. 540
12	d	
13	e	
14	f	
15	g	
16	A	
17	b	William White, Bishop of Pennsylvania, 1836
18	c	
19	d	
20	e	
21	f	
22	g	SAINT MARY MAGDALENE
23	A	
24	b	Thomas a Kempis, Priest, 1471
25	c	SAINT JAMES THE APOSTLE
26	d	The Parents of the Blessed Virgin Mary
27	e	William Reed Huntington, Priest, 1909
28	f	
29	g	Mary and Martha of Bethany
30	A	William Wilberforce, 1833
31	b	Joseph of Arimathaea

AUGUST

1	c	
2	d	
3	e	
4	f	Dominic, Friar, 1221
5	g	
6	A	THE TRANSFIGURATION OF OUR LORD JESUS CHRIST
7	b	John Mason Neale, Priest, 1866
8	c	
9	d	
10	e	Laurence, Deacon, and Martyr at Rome, 258
11	f	Clare of Assisi, 1253
12	g	
13	A	Hippolytus, Bishop and Martyr, c. 235
14	b	Jeremy Taylor, Bishop of Down, Connor, and Dromore, 1667
15	c	SAINT MARY THE VIRGIN, MOTHER OF OUR LORD JESUS CHRIST
16	d	
17	e	
18	f	William Porcher DuBose, Priest, 1918
19	g	
20	A	Bernard, Abbot of Clairvaux, 1153
21	b	
22	c	
23	d	
24	e	SAINT BARTHOLOMEW THE APOSTLE
25	f	Louis, King of France, 1270
26	g	
27	A	
28	b	Augustine, Bishop of Hippo, 430
29	c	
30	d	
31	e	Aidan, Bishop of Lindisfarne, 651

SEPTEMBER

1	f	
2	g	The Martyrs of New Guinea, 1942
3	A	
4	b	
5	c	
6	d	
7	e	
8	f	
9	g	
10	A	
11	b	
12	c	John Henry Hobart, Bishop of New York, 1830
13	d	Cyprian, Bishop of Carthage, and Martyr, 258
14	e	HOLY CROSS DAY
15	f	
16	g	Ninian, Bishop in Galloway, c. 430
17	A	
18	b	
19	c	Theodore of Tarsus, Archbishop of Canterbury, 690
20	d	John Coleridge Patteson, Bishop of Melanesia, and his Companions, Martyrs, 1871
21	e	SAINT MATTHEW, APOSTLE AND EVANGELIST
22	f	
23	g	
24	A	
25	b	Sergius, Abbot of Holy Trinity, Moscow, 1392
26	c	Lancelot Andrewes, Bishop of Winchester, 1626
27	d	
28	e	
29	f	SAINT MICHAEL AND ALL ANGELS
30	g	Jerome, Priest, and Monk of Bethlehem, 420

OCTOBER

1	A	Remigius, Bishop of Rheims, c. 530
2	b	
3	c	
4	d	Francis of Assisi, Friar, 1226
5	e	
6	f	William Tyndale, Priest, and Martyr, 1536
7	g	
8	A	
9	b	Robert Grossteste, Bishop of Lincoln, 1253
10	c	
11	d	
12	e	
13	f	
14	g	
15	A	Samuel Isaac Joseph Schereschewsky, Bishop of Shanghai, 1906
16	b	Hugh Latimer and Nicholas Ridley, Bishops, 1555
17	c	Ignatius, Bishop of Antioch, and Martyr, c. 115
18	d	SAINT LUKE THE EVANGELIST
19	e	Henry Martyn, Priest, and Missionary to India and Persia, 1812
20	f	
21	g	
22	A	
23	b	SAINT JAMES OF JERUSALEM, BROTHER OF OUR LORD JESUS CHRIST, AND MARTYR, C. 62
24	c	
25	d	
26	e	Alfred the Great, King of England, 899
27	f	
28	g	SAINT SIMON AND SAINT JUDE, APOSTLES
29	A	James Hannington, Bishop of Eastern Equatorial Africa, and Martyr, 1885
30	b	
31	c	

NOVEMBER

1	d	ALL SAINTS
2	e	Commemoration of All Faithful Departed
3	f	Richard Hooker, Priest, 1600
4	g	
5	A	
6	b	
7	c	Willibrord, Archbishop of Utrecht, Missionary to Frisia, 738
8	d	
9	e	
10	f	Leo the Great, Bishop of Rome, 461
11	g	Martin, Bishop of Tours, 397
12	A	Charles Simeon, Priest, 1836
13	b	
14	c	Consecration of Samuel Seabury, First American Bishop, 1784
15	d	
16	e	Margaret, Queen of Scotland, 1093
17	f	Hugh, Bishop of Lincoln, 1200
18	g	Hilda, Abbess of Whitby, 680
19	A	Elizabeth, Princess of Hungary, 1231
20	b	
21	c	
22	d	
23	e	Clement, Bishop of Rome, c. 100
24	f	
25	g	
26	A	
27	b	
28	c	
29	d	
30	e	SAINT ANDREW THE APOSTLE

DECEMBER

1	f	Nicholas Ferrar, Deacon, 1637
2	g	Channing Moore Williams, Missionary Bishop in China and Japan, 1910
3	A	
4	b	John of Damascus, Priest, c. 760
5	c	Clement of Alexandria, Priest, c. 210
6	d	Nicholas, Bishop of Myra, c. 342
7	e	Ambrose, Bishop of Milan, 397
8	f	
9	g	
10	A	
11	b	
12	c	
13	d	
14	e	
15	f	
16	g	
17	A	
18	b	
19	c	
20	d	
21	e	Saint Thomas the Apostle
22	f	
23	g	
24	A	
25	b	The Nativity of Our Lord Jesus Christ
26	c	Saint Stephen, Deacon and Martyr
27	d	Saint John, Apostle and Evangelist
28	e	The Holy Innocents
29	f	
30	g	
31	A	

THE TITLES OF THE SEASONS SUNDAYS AND MAJOR HOLY DAYS

Observed in this Church Throughout the Year

ADVENT SEASON
    The First Sunday in Advent
    The Second Sunday in Advent
    The Third Sunday in Advent
    The Fourth Sunday in Advent

CHRISTMAS SEASON
    The Nativity of Our Lord Jesus Christ, or Christmas Day
        December 25
    The First Sunday after Christmas Day
    The Holy Name of Our Lord Jesus Christ
        January 1
    The Second Sunday after Christmas Day

EPIPHANY SEASON
    The Epiphany, or The Manifestation of Christ to the Gentiles
        January 6
    The First Sunday after The Epiphany, The Baptism of Our Lord Jesus Christ
    The Second Sunday after The Epiphany
    The Third Sunday after The Epiphany
    The Fourth Sunday after The Epiphany
    The Fifth Sunday after The Epiphany
    The Sixth Sunday after The Epiphany
    The Seventh Sunday after The Epiphany
    The Eighth Sunday after The Epiphany
    The Last Sunday after The Epiphany

LENTEN SEASON
    The First Day of Lent, or Ash Wednesday
    The First Sunday in Lent
    The Second Sunday in Lent
    The Third Sunday in Lent

The Fourth Sunday in Lent
The Fifth Sunday in Lent

HOLY WEEK

The Sunday of the Passion, or Palm Sunday
Monday in Holy Week
Tuesday in Holy Week
Wednesday in Holy Week
Maundy Thursday
Good Friday
Holy Saturday

EASTER SEASON

Easter Eve
The Sunday of the Resurrection, or Easter Day
Monday in Easter Week
Tuesday in Easter Week
Wednesday in Easter Week
Thursday in Easter Week
Friday in Easter Week
Saturday in Easter Week
The Second Sunday of Easter
The Third Sunday of Easter
The Fourth Sunday of Easter
The Fifth Sunday of Easter
The Sixth Sunday of Easter
Ascension Day
The Seventh Sunday of Easter
The Day of Pentecost, or Whitsunday

THE SEASON AFTER PENTECOST

The First Sunday after Pentecost, or Trinity Sunday
The Second Sunday after Pentecost
The Third Sunday after Pentecost
The Fourth Sunday after Pentecost
The Fifth Sunday after Pentecost
The Sixth Sunday after Pentecost
The Seventh Sunday after Pentecost

The Eighth Sunday after Pentecost
The Ninth Sunday after Pentecost
The Tenth Sunday after Pentecost
The Eleventh Sunday after Pentecost
The Twelfth Sunday after Pentecost
The Thirteenth Sunday after Pentecost
The Fourteenth Sunday after Pentecost
The Fifteenth Sunday after Pentecost
The Sixteenth Sunday after Pentecost
The Seventeenth Sunday after Pentecost
The Eighteenth Sunday after Pentecost
The Nineteenth Sunday after Pentecost
The Twentieth Sunday after Pentecost
The Twenty-First Sunday after Pentecost
The Twenty-Second Sunday after Pentecost
The Twenty-Third Sunday after Pentecost
The Twenty-Fourth Sunday after Pentecost
The Twenty-Fifth Sunday after Pentecost
The Twenty-Sixth Sunday after Pentecost
The Twenty-Seventh Sunday after Pentecost
The Last Sunday after Pentecost, or The Sunday before Advent

HOLY DAYS

Saint Andrew the Apostle
   November 30
Saint Thomas the Apostle
   December 21
Saint Stephen, Deacon and Martyr
   December 26
Saint John, Apostle and Evangelist
   December 27
The Holy Innocents
   December 28
The Confession of Saint Peter the Apostle
   January 18
The Conversion of Saint Paul the Apostle
   January 25

The Presentation of Our Lord Jesus Christ in the Temple, also called the Purification of Saint Mary the Virgin
February 2

Saint Matthias the Apostle
February 24

Saint Joseph
March 19

The Annunciation of Our Lord Jesus Christ to the Blessed Virgin Mary
March 25

Saint Mark the Evangelist
April 25

Saint Philip and Saint James, Apostles
May 1

The Visitation of the Blessed Virgin Mary
May 31

Saint Barnabas the Apostle
June 11

The Nativity of Saint John the Baptist
June 24

Saint Peter and Saint Paul, Apostles
June 29

Independence Day
July 4

Saint Mary Magdalene
July 22

Saint James the Apostle
July 25

The Transfiguration of Our Lord Jesus Christ
August 6

Saint Mary the Virgin
August 15

Saint Bartholomew the Apostle
August 24

Holy Cross Day
September 14

Saint Matthew, Apostle and Evangelist
   September 21
Saint Michael and All Angels
   September 29
Saint Luke the Evangelist
   October 18
Saint James of Jerusalem, Brother of Our Lord Jesus Christ, and Martyr
   October 23
Saint Simon and Saint Jude, Apostles
   October 28
All Saints' Day
   November 1
Thanksgiving Day

PART III
THE PROPER

General Directions

The Psalms or selections from Psalms appointed in the proper are for optional use at any place in the Liturgy where the rubrics allow the use of a Psalm, Hymn, or Anthem. They may be lengthened or shortened, at the discretion of the Minister, and may be used with or without the Gloria Patri.

The first Psalm listed in the proper has been chosen as especially suitable for use at the Entrance of the Ministers; the second one, as especially suitable for use between the Lessons.

Three Lessons have been provided in each set of proper. According to the rubrics of the Liturgy, the Minister may use all three Lessons, or he may omit either the first or the second Lesson. The Lesson from the Gospels is always read.

Year C of the three-year cycle of Lessons begins on the First Sunday in Advent, 1970.

The Proper Preface appointed with each set of proper is to be used according to the rubrics of the Liturgy. But the Priest may, at his discretion, omit the Proper Preface indicated in "The Common of Saints" and "Special Occasions," or use the Proper Preface of the Season.

In each proper, two forms of the Collect are given: The first is always in contemporary language, the second is in traditional wording.

The First Sunday in Advent

The Collect

ALMIGHTY GOD, give us grace to cast away the works of darkness, and put on the armor of light, now in the time of this mortal life, in which your Son Jesus Christ came to visit us in great humility; that in the last day, when he shall come again in his glorious majesty to judge the living and the dead, we may rise to the life immortal, through him who lives and reigns with you and the Holy Spirit, one God, now and ever. *Amen.*

ALMIGHTY GOD, give us grace to cast away the works of darkness, and put on us the armor of light, now in the time .of this mortal life, in which thy Son Jesus Christ came to visit us in great humility; that in the last day, when he shall come again in his glorious majesty to judge both the living and the dead, we may rise to the life immortal, through him who liveth and reigneth with thee and the Holy Spirit, one God, now and ever. *Amen.*

The Psalms

[Entrance Psalm]	50:1-6
[Between Readings]	25:1-6

The Lessons

	Isaiah 2:1-5		Isaiah 63:16b-64:8		Jeremiah 33:14-16
A	Romans 13:11-14	B	1 Corinthians 1:3-9	C	Thessalonians 3:9-13
	Matthew 24:37-44		Mark 13:33-37		Luke 21:25-31

PROPER PREFACE OF ADVENT

The Second Sunday in Advent

The Collect

MERCIFUL GOD, who sent your messengers the prophets, to preach repentance and prepare the way for our salvation: Give us grace to heed their warning and forsake our sins, that we may greet with joy the coming of our Redeemer, Jesus Christ our Lord, who lives and reigns with you and the Holy Spirit, one God, now and for ever. *Amen.*

MERCIFUL GOD, who hast sent thy messengers the prophets, to preach repentance and prepare the way for our salvation: Give us grace to heed their warning and forsake our sins, that we may greet with joy the coming of our Redeemer, Jesus Christ our Lord, who liveth and reigneth with thee and the Holy Spirit, one God, now and for ever. *Amen.*

The Psalms

| [Entrance Psalm] | 80:1-7 |
| [Between Readings] | 85:4-9 |

The Lessons

	Isaiah 11:1-10		Isaiah 40:1-5,9-11		Baruch 5:1-9
A	Romans 15:4-13	B	2 Peter 3:8-14	C	Philippians 1:3-11
	Matthew 3:1-12		Mark 1:1-8		Luke 3:1-6

PROPER PREFACE OF ADVENT

The Third Sunday in Advent

The Collect

RAISE UP your mighty power, O LORD, and come; and, because we are hindered and bound by our sins, let your plentiful grace and mercy speedily help and deliver us; through Jesus Christ our Lord, to whom with you and the Holy Spirit be honor and glory, one God, now and for ever. *Amen.*

RAISE UP thy mighty power, O LORD, and come; and, because we are hindered and bound by our sins, let thy plentiful grace and mercy speedily help and deliver us; through Jesus Christ our Lord, to whom with thee and the Holy Spirit be honor and glory, one God, now and for ever. *Amen.*

The Psalms

| [Entrance Psalm] | 82 |
| [Between Readings] | 126 |

The Lessons

	A		B		C
	Isaiah 35		Isaiah 61:1-3,10-1		Zephaniah 3:14-18a
	James 5:7-10		1 Thessalonians 5:16-24		Philippians 4:4-7
	Matthew 11:2-11		John 1:6-8, 19-28		Luke 3:7-18

PROPER PREFACE OF ADVENT

The Fourth Sunday in Advent

The Collect

MIGHTY LORD, cleanse our consciences, we pray, and bring light to the darkness of our hearts by the visitation of our Savior Jesus Christ; that when he comes, he may find in us a mansion prepared for himself, who now lives and reigns with you in the unity of the Holy Spirit, one God, for ever and ever. *Amen.*

MIGHTY LORD, we beseech thee to cleanse our consciences, and bring light to the darkness of our hearts by the visitation of our Savior Jesus Christ; that when he comes, he may find in us a mansion prepared for himself, who now liveth and reigneth with thee in the unity of the Holy Spirit, one God, for ever and ever. *Amen.*

The Psalms

| [Entrance Psalm] | 132:8-15 |
| [Between Readings] | 146:4-10 |

The Lessons

	A		B		C
	Isaiah 7:10-14		2 Samuel 7:1-5, 8b-11, 16		Micah 5:2-5a
	Romans 9:1-5		Romans 16:25-27		Hebrews 10:5-10
	Matthew 1:18-25		Luke 1:26-38		Luke 1:39-49

PROPER PREFACE OF ADVENT

The Nativity of our Lord Jesus Christ or Christmas Day

DECEMBER 25

When there is more than one celebration of the Liturgy on this day, any of the collects and lessons appointed may be used, at the discretion of the Priest; but the Gospel lesson from John 1:1-14 shall be read at one of them at least.

The Collect

O GOD, in our joyful remembrance of the birth of your only Son Jesus Christ, grant us to receive him so faithfully as our Redeemer, that we may with sure confidence behold him when he shall come to be our Judge, who lives and reigns with you and the Holy Spirit, one God, now and for ever. *Amen.*

O GOD, who makest us glad with the yearly remembrance of the birth of thine only Son Jesus Christ: Grant that as we joyfully receive him for our Redeemer, so we may with sure confidence behold him when he shall come to be our Judge, who liveth and reigneth with thee and the Holy Spirit, one God, now and for ever. *Amen.*

The Psalms

[Entrance Psalm]	19:1-6
[Between Readings]	89:1-4, 27-30

The Lessons

Isaiah 9:2-4, 6-7
Titus 2:11-14
Luke 2:1-14

PROPER PREFACE OF CHRISTMAS

A Second Proper for Christmas Day

The Collect

ALMIGHTY FATHER, by whom the world has been filled with the new light of your beloved Son, the incarnate Word: Grant, we pray, that as he kindles the flame of faith and love in our hearts, so his light may shine forth in our lives, who now lives and reigns with you in the unity of the Holy Spirit, one God, now and for ever. *Amen.*

ALMIGHTY FATHER, who hast filled the world with the new light of thy beloved Son, the incarnate Word: Grant, we beseech thee, that as he enkindles the flame of faith and love in our hearts, so his light may shine forth in our lives, the same thy Son, Jesus Christ our Lord, who liveth and reigneth with thee in the unity of the Holy Spirit, one God, now and for ever. *Amen.*

The Psalms

| [Entrance Psalm] | 96 |
| [Between Readings] | 113 |

The Lessons

| Isaiah 62:10-12 |
| Titus 3:4-7 |
| Luke 2:15b-20 |

PROPER PREFACE OF CHRISTMAS

A Third Proper for Christmas Day

The Collect

ALMIGHTY GOD, who gave us your only-begotten Son to take our nature upon him, and to be born of a pure virgin: Grant that we, who have been born again in him, and made your children by adoption and grace, may daily be renewed by your Holy Spirit; through our Lord Jesus Christ, to whom with you and the Spirit be all honor and glory, one God, now and for ever. *Amen.*

ALMIGHTY GOD, who hast given us thine only-begotten Son to take our nature upon him, and to be born of a pure virgin: Grant that we, being born again in him and made thy children by adoption and grace, may daily be renewed by thy Holy Spirit; through the same our Lord Jesus Christ, who liveth and reigneth with thee and the same Spirit, one God, now and for ever. *Amen.*

The Psalms

[Entrance Psalm]	98
[Between Readings]	145:1-9

The Lessons

Isaiah 52:7-10
Hebrews 1:1-6
John 1:1-14

PROPER PREFACE OF CHRISTMAS

The First Sunday after Christmas Day

The Collect

ALMIGHTY GOD, who revealed in the incarnation of your eternal Word, our Savior Jesus Christ, the source and perfection of all true religion: Grant that we may entrust our lives to him, on whom is built the whole salvation of mankind, and who now lives and reigns with you and the Holy Spirit, one God, in glory evermore. *Amen.*

ALMIGHTY GOD, who hast revealed in the incarnation of thine eternal Word, our Savior Jesus Christ, the source and perfection of all true religion: Grant that we may entrust our lives to him, on whom is built the whole salvation of mankind, the same Jesus Christ our Lord, who now liveth and reigneth with thee and the Holy Spirit, one God, in glory evermore. *Amen.*

The Psalms

[Entrance Psalm]	97:1-6
[Between Readings]	97:8-12

The Lessons

Isaiah 60:13-21
Galatians 4:4-7
John 1:1-18

PROPER PREFACE OF CHRISTMAS

The Holy Name of our Lord Jesus Christ

JANUARY 1

The Collect

ETERNAL FATHER, who gave to your incarnate Son the name of Jesus, to be the sign of our salvation: Plant in every heart, we pray, the love of him who is the Savior of the world, and who now lives and reigns with you and the Holy Spirit, one God, in glory everlasting. *Amen.*

ETERNAL FATHER, who didst give to thine incarnate Son the name of Jesus, to be the sign of our salvation: Plant in every heart, we beseech thee, the love of him who is the Savior of the world, even our Lord Jesus Christ, who now liveth and reigneth with thee and the Holy Spirit, one God, in glory everlasting. *Amen.*

The Psalms

| [Entrance Psalm] | 85:1-3, 10-13 |
| [Between Readings] | 8 |

The Lessons

| Isaiah 9:2-4, 6-7 |
| Romans 1:1-7 |
| Luke 2:15-21 |

PROPER PREFACE OF CHRISTMAS

The Second Sunday after Christmas Day

The Collect

O GOD, who wonderfully created us in the dignity of your own image, and yet more wonderfully restored us after the likeness of your Son Jesus Christ: Make us worthy, we pray, to partake of his divine life, who for our sake came to share our human nature, and who now lives and reigns with you in the unity of the Holy Spirit, one God, for ever and ever. *Amen.*

O GOD, who hast wonderfully created us in the dignity of thine own image, and hast yet more wonderfully restored us after the likeness of thy Son Jesus

Christ: Make us worthy, we beseech thee, to partake of his divine life, who for our sake came to share our human nature, the same Jesus Christ our Lord, who now liveth and reigneth with thee in the unity of the Holy Spirit, one God, for ever and ever. *Amen.*

The Psalms

| [Entrance Psalm] | 84:1-7 |
| [Between Readings] | 128 |

The Lessons

| Isaiah 61:10-62:3 |
| Ephesians 1:3-6, 15-18 |
| Matthew 2:13-15, 19-23 or Luke 2:41-52 |

PROPER PREFACE OF CHRISTMAS

The Epiphany, or the Manifestation of Christ to the Gentiles

JANUARY 6

The Collect

O GOD, who guided by a star the wise men of the Gentiles to the worship of your only Son: Lead all peoples of the earth to know him now by faith, and in the world to come to see him in the splendor of his glory, where he lives and reigns with you and the Holy Spirit, one God, now and ever. *Amen.*

    O GOD, who by a star didst guide the wise men of the Gentiles to the worship of thine only Son: Lead all the peoples of the earth to know him now by faith, and in the world to come to see him in the splendor of his glory, where he liveth and reigneth with thee and the Holy Spirit, one God, now and ever. *Amen.*

The Psalms

| [Entrance Psalm] | 72:1-8 |
| [Between Readings] | 72:10-17 |

The Lessons

| Isaiah 60:1-6 |
| Ephesians 3:1-12 |
| Matthew 2:1-12 |

PROPER PREFACE OF EPIPHANY

The First Sunday after the Epiphany, the Baptism of our Lord Jesus Christ

The Collect

FATHER IN HEAVEN, who at the baptism of our Savior Jesus Christ declared him to be your beloved Son, and endowed him with the mighty power of the Holy Spirit: Grant that all who are baptized into his Name may be found worthy of their calling to be your adopted sons, and heirs with him of everlasting life, who lives and reigns with you and the Holy Spirit, one God, now and ever. *Amen.*

FATHER IN HEAVEN, who at the baptism of our Savior Jesus Christ didst declare him to be thy beloved Son, and didst endow him with the mighty power of the Holy Spirit: Grant, we beseech thee, that all who are baptized into his Name may be found worthy of their calling to be thine adopted sons, and heirs with him of everlasting life, the same thy Son Jesus Christ our Lord, who liveth and reigneth with thee and the Holy Spirit, one God, now and ever. *Amen.*

The Psalms

| [Entrance Psalm] | 93 |
| [Between Readings] | 29 |

The Lessons

Isaiah 42:1-7	A Matthew 3:13-17
Acts 10:34-38	B Mark 1:7-11
	C Luke 3:15-16, 21-22

PROPER PREFACE OF EPIPHANY

The Second Sunday after the Epiphany

The Collect

God, the giver of all grace: Set us free from the bondage of our sins; and give us, we pray, that abundant life and liberty of sonship which you have made known in your Son our Savior Jesus Christ, who lives and reigns with you in the unity of the Holy Spirit, one God, now and for ever. *Amen.*

God, the giver of all grace: Set us free from the bondage of our sins; and give us, we pray, that abundant life and liberty of sonship which thou hast manifested to us in thy Son our Savior Jesus Christ, who liveth and reigneth with thee in the unity of the Holy Spirit, now and for ever. *Amen.*

The Psalms

[Entrance Psalm]	63:1-8
[Between Readings]	36:5-10

The Lessons

A	Isaiah 49:1-7	B	1 Samuel 3:1-10	C	Isaiah 62:2-5
	1 Corinthians 4:9-16		1 Corinthians 6:13b-20		1 Corinthians 12:4-11
	John 1:29-41		John 1:43-51		John 2:1-12

PROPER PREFACE OF EPIPHANY

The Third Sunday after the Epiphany

The Collect

Give us grace, heavenly Father, to answer readily the call of our Savior Jesus Christ to follow him in his service, that, in proclaiming to all men the good news of his salvation, we may perceive the glory of his marvelous works; through Jesus Christ our Lord, who lives and reigns with you and the Holy Spirit, one God, for ever and ever. *Amen.*

Give us grace, heavenly Father, to answer readily the call of our Savior Jesus Christ to follow him in his service, that, in proclaiming to all men the good news of his salvation, we may perceive the glory of his marvelous works; through the same Jesus Christ our Lord, who liveth and reigneth with thee and the Holy Spirit, one God, for ever and ever. *Amen.*

The Psalms

[Entrance Psalm]	84:8-13
[Between Readings]	65:4-8

The Lessons

A	Isaiah 9:1-4	B	Jonah 3:1-5, 10	C	Isaiah 61:1-6
	1 Corinthians 1:10-13, 17		1 Corinthians 7:17-23		1 Corinthians 12:12-27
	Matthew 4:12-23		Mark 1:14-20		Luke 4:14-21

PROPER PREFACE OF EPIPHANY

The Fourth Sunday after the Epiphany

BLESSED LORD, who caused all holy Scriptures to be written for our learning: Grant us so to hear them, read, mark, learn, and inwardly digest them, that we may embrace and ever hold fast the hope of everlasting life, which you have given us in our Savior Jesus Christ, who lives and reigns with you and the Holy Spirit, one God, now and ever. *Amen.*

BLESSED LORD, who hast caused all holy Scriptures to be written for our learning: Grant that we may in such wise hear them, read, mark, learn, and inwardly digest them, that by patience and comfort of thy holy Word, we may embrace, and ever hold fast, the blessed hope of everlasting life, which thou hast given us in our Savior Jesus Christ, who liveth and reigneth with thee and the Holy Spirit, one God, now and ever. *Amen.*

The Psalms

[Entrance Psalm]	112:1-7
[Between Readings]	19:7-14

The Lessons

A	Zephaniah 3:9-13	B	Deuteronomy 18:15-20	C	Jeremiah 1:4-10
	1 Corinthians 1:26-31		1 Corinthians 8:1b-13		1 Corinthians 14:12b-17, 33, 40
	Matthew 5:1-12a		Mark 1:21-28		Luke 4:21-30

PROPER PREFACE OF EPIPHANY

The Fifth Sunday after the Epiphany

The Collect

ALMIGHTY GOD, who gave your Son our Savior Jesus Christ to be the light of the world: Nourish us, your people, by your Word and Sacraments, that we may be strengthened to serve all men with the immeasurable riches of Christ, so that he may be known, worshiped, and obeyed to the ends of the earth; through Jesus Christ our Lord, who lives and reigns with you and the Holy Spirit, one God, now and for ever. *Amen.*

ALMIGHTY GOD, who didst give thy Son our Savior Jesus Christ to be the light of the world: Nourish thy people, we beseech thee, by thy Word and Sacraments, that we may be strengthened to serve all men with the immeasurable riches of Christ, so that he may be known, worshiped, and obeyed to the ends of the earth; through the same Jesus Christ our Lord, who liveth and reigneth with thee and the Holy Spirit, one God, now and for ever. *Amen.*

The Psalms

| [Entrance Psalm] | 67 |
| [Between Readings] | 15 |

The Lessons

	Isaiah 58:8-12		Zephaniah 3:14-20		Isaiah 6:1-8
A	1 Corinthians 2:1-5	B	1 Corinthians 9:16-23	C	1 Corinthians 15:1—11
	Matthew 5:13-24		Mark 1:29-39		Luke 5:1-11

PROPER PREFACE OF EPIPHANY

The Sixth Sunday after the Epiphany

The Collect

GOD, the strength of all who put their trust in you: Mercifully accept our prayers; and because, through the weakness of our nature, we can do nothing that is good without you, grant us the help of your grace, that in keeping your commandments we may please you both in will and deed; through Jesus Christ our Lord, who lives and reigns with you and the Holy Spirit, one God, now and for ever. *Amen.*

O GOD, the strength of all those who put their trust in thee: Mercifully accept our prayers; and because, through the weakness of our mortal nature, we can do no good thing without thee, grant us the help of thy grace, that in keeping thy commandments we may please thee both in will and deed; through Jesus Christ our Lord, who liveth and reigneth with thee and the Holy Spirit, one God, now and for ever. *Amen.*

The Psalms

| [Entrance Psalm] | 33:1-6 |
| [Between Readings] | 102:15-22 |

The Lessons

	Ecclesiasticus 15:14-20		2 Kings 5:1-14		Jeremiah 17:5-10
A	1 Corinthians 2:6-10	B	2 Corinthians 4:16b-18	C	1 Corinthians 15:12, 16-20
	Matthew 5:27-37		Mark 1:40-45		Luke 6:20-26

PROPER PREFACE OF EPIPHANY

The Seventh Sunday after the Epiphany

The Collect

O LORD, who taught us in your holy Word that anything we do without love is worth nothing: Pour into our hearts that most excellent gift of love, the true bond of peace and all virtues, without which whoever lives is counted dead before you. Grant this for the sake of your only Son Jesus Christ, who lives and reigns with you and the Holy Spirit, one God, now and ever. *Amen.*

O LORD, who hast taught us in thy holy Word that all our doings without charity are nothing worth: Send thy Holy Spirit, and pour into our hearts that most excellent gift of charity, the very bond of peace and of all virtues, without which whosoever liveth is counted dead before thee. Grant this for thine only Son Jesus Christ's sake, who liveth and reigneth with thee and the same Spirit, one God, now and ever. *Amen.*

The Psalms

| [Entrance Psalm] | 103:1-6 |
| [Between Readings] | 37:4-9 |

The Lessons

	A		B		C	
A	Leviticus 19:1-2, 15-18	B	Isaiah 43:18-19, 22, 24b-25	C	Genesis 45:1-7	
	1 Corinthians 3:16-23		2 Corinthians 1:18-22		1 Corinthians 15:44b-49	
	Matthew 5:38-48		Mark 2:1-12		Luke 6:27-38	

PROPER PREFACE OF EPIPHANY

The Eighth Sunday after the Epiphany

The Collect

MOST LOVING FATHER, whose will it is for us to cast all our care on you, who care for us: Preserve us from faithless fears and worldly anxieties, that no clouds of this mortal life may hide from us the light of that love which you have made known to us in your Son, Jesus Christ our Lord, who lives and reigns with you in the unity of the Holy Spirit, one God, now and ever. *Amen.*

MOST LOVING FATHER, who willest us to cast all our care on thee, who carest for us: Preserve us from faithless fears and worldly anxieties, and grant that no clouds of this mortal life may hide from us the light of that love which thou hast manifested unto us in thy Son, Jesus Christ our Lord, who liveth and reigneth with thee in the unity of the Holy Spirit, one God, now and ever. *Amen.*

The Psalms

[Entrance Psalm]	34:11-19
[Between Readings]	37:23-28

The Lessons

	A		B		C	
	Isaiah 49:13-15		Hosea 2:14-23		Isaiah 55:10-13	
A	1 Corinthians 4:1-5	B	2 Corinthians 3:17-4:2	C	1 Corinthians 15:54-58	
	Matthew 6:24-34		Mark 2:18-22		Luke 6:39-45	

PROPER PREFACE OF EPIPHANY

The Last Sunday after the Epiphany

The proper for this Sunday is always to be used on the Sunday before the beginning of Lent on Ash Wednesday, whether the Sundays after the Epiphany be four or more in number.

The Collect

O GOD, who before the passion of your only-begotten Son revealed his glory upon the holy mountain: Grant to us your servants that, in faith beholding the light of his countenance, we may be strengthened to bear the cross, and be changed into his likeness from glory to glory; through Jesus Christ your Son our Lord, who lives and reigns with you and the Holy Spirit, one God, for ever and ever. *Amen.*

O GOD, who before the passion of thine only-begotten Son didst reveal his glory upon the holy mount: Grant unto us thy servants that, in faith beholding the light of his countenance, we may be strengthened to bear the cross, and be changed into his likeness from glory to glory; through the same thy Son Jesus Christ our Lord, who liveth and reigneth with thee and the Holy Spirit, one God, for ever and ever. *Amen.*

The Psalms

[Entrance Psalm]	99
[Between Readings]	27:1-7

The Lessons

A	Exodus 24:12, 15-18	B	1 Kings 19:4-12	C	Deuteronomy 8:1-3, 5-6
	1 Corinthians 12:31-13:13		2 Corinthians 4:3-6		Philippians 3:7-15
	Matthew 17:1-9		Mark 9:2-9		Luke 9:28-36

PROPER PREFACE OF EPIPHANY

Lenten Season

The First Day of Lent, or Ash Wednesday

On this day, the Liturgy begins with the Collect of the Day, the Minister first saying

	The Lord be with you.
Answer	And also with you.
Minister	Let us pray.

The Collect

ALMIGHTY AND EVERLASTING GOD, who hate nothing that you have made, and forgive the sins of all who are penitent, create and make in us new and contrite hearts, that we, worthily lamenting our sins and acknowledging our wretchedness, may obtain of you, God of all mercy, perfect forgiveness and peace; through Jesus Christ our Lord. *Amen.*

ALMIGHTY AND EVERLASTING GOD, who hatest nothing that thou hast made, and dost forgive the sins of all those who are penitent: Create and make in us new and contrite hearts, that we, worthily lamenting our sins, and acknowledging our wretchedness, may obtain of thee, the God of all mercy, perfect forgiveness and peace; through Jesus Christ our Lord. *Amen.*

The Psalms

[Entrance Psalm]	86:1-7
[Between Readings]	103:8-14

The Lessons

Joel 2:12-19
2 Corinthians 5:20b-6:10
Matthew 6:1-6,16-21

After the Sermon, all stand, and the Priest or Minister appointed invites the People to the observance of a Holy Lent, saying

DEAR PEOPLE OF GOD: The first Christians observed with great devotion the days of our Lord's Passion and Resurrection; and it became the custom of the Church to prepare for them by a season of penitence and fasting. This season of Lent provided a time in which converts to the faith were prepared for holy Baptism. It was also a time when those who, because of notorious sins, had been separated from the body of the faithful were reconciled by penitence and forgiveness, and restored to the fellowship of the Church. Thereby the whole congregation was put in mind of the message of pardon and absolution set forth in the gospel of our Savior, and of the need which all Christians continually have to renew their repentance and faith.

I invite you, therefore, in the name of the Church, to the observance of a holy Lent, by self-examination and repentance; by prayer, fasting, and self-denial; and by reading and meditating on God's holy Word. And, to make a right beginning of repentance and as a mark of our mortal nature, let us now kneel before the Lord, our Maker and Redeemer.

Silence is then kept for a time, all kneeling, after which the Minister may say

> Remember, O man, that dust you are,
> and to dust shall you return.

The following Psalm is then sung or said [PSALM 51:1-18]:

Have mercy on me, O GOD,
according to your loving-kindness;
   in your great compassion blot out my offences.

Wash me through and through from my wickedness,
   and cleanse me from my sin.
For I know my transgressions only too well,
   and my sin is ever before me.
Against you only have I sinned,
   and done what is evil in your sight.
And so you are justified when you speak,
   and upright in your judgment.
Indeed, I have been wicked from my birth,
   a sinner from my mother's womb.
For behold, you look for truth in the inward parts,
   and shall make me understand wisdom secretly.
Take away my sin, and I shall be pure;
   wash me, and I shall be cleaner than snow.
Make me hear of joy and gladness,
   that the body you have broken may rejoice.
Hide your face from my sins,
   and blot out all my iniquities.
Create in me a clean heart, O GOD,
   and renew a right spirit within me.
Cast me not away from your presence,
   and take not your holy Spirit from me.
Give me the joy of your saving help again,
   and sustain me with your bountiful spirit.
I shall teach your ways to the wicked,
   and sinners shall return unto you.

Deliver me from death, O God,
    and my tongue shall sing of your righteousness,
    O God of my salvation.
Open my lips, O Lord,
    and my mouth shall show forth your praise.
Had you desired it, I would have offered sacrifice;
    but you take no delight in burnt-offerings.
The sacrifice of God is a troubled spirit;
    a broken and contrite heart, O God, you will not despise.

The Minister then leads the People, all kneeling, in the following

Litany of Penitence

All say together

Most holy and merciful Father:

We confess to you and to one another,
    and to the whole communion of saints
    in heaven and earth,
    that we have sinned in thought, word, and deed,
    by what we have done, and by what we have left undone.

Minister

We have not loved you with our whole heart and mind and strength;
    We have not loved our neighbors as ourselves;
    We have not forgiven others, as we have been forgiven.
    Have mercy on us, Lord.

We have been deaf to your call to serve, as Christ served us;
    We have not had in us the mind of Christ;
    We have grieved your Holy Spirit.
    Have mercy on us, Lord.

We confess to you, Lord, all our past unfaithfulness:
    The pride, hypocrisy, and impatience of our lives,
    We confess to you, Lord.

    Our negligence in prayer and worship, and our failure to commend the faith that is in us,
    We confess to you, Lord.

Our dishonesty in daily life and work, and our intemperate love of worldly goods and comforts,
We confess to you, Lord.

Accept our repentance, Lord, for the wrongs we have done to our fellow men:
For our blindness to human need and suffering, and our indifference to injustice and cruelty,
Accept our repentance, Lord.

For all false judgments, and uncharitable thoughts toward our neighbors, and for our prejudice and contempt toward those who differ from us,
Accept our repentance, Lord.

For our waste and pollution of your creation, and our lack of concern for those who come after us,
Accept our repentance, Lord.

Restore us, good Lord, and let your anger depart from us.
Favorably hear us, for your mercy is great.
Accomplish in us the work of your salvation,
That we may show forth your glory in the world.
By the cross and passion of your Son our Lord,
Bring us and all men to the joy of his resurrection.

The Minister then says

MAY THE ALMIGHTY and merciful God, the Father of our Lord Jesus Christ, who desires not the death of sinners, but rather that we turn from our wickedness and live, accept our repentance, forgive us our sins, and restore us by his Holy Spirit to newness of life. *Amen.*

The Ministers and People then exchange the Peace.

In the absence of a Priest or Deacon, all that precedes may be led by a Lay Reader.

When Communion follows, the service continues with the Offertory.

PROPER PREFACE OF LENT

Note: The Litany of Penitence may be used at other times and may be preceded by an appropriate invitation and a penitential Psalm.

The First Sunday in Lent

The Collect

ALMIGHTY GOD, whose blessed Son our Savior was in every way tempted as we are, yet did not sin: Strengthen us, we pray, to withstand the assaults of our many temptations; and as you know our weaknesses, so may we find you mighty to save; through Jesus Christ your Son our Lord, who lives and reigns with you and the Holy Spirit, one God, now and for ever. *Amen.*

ALMIGHTY GOD, whose blessed Son our Savior was in every way tempted as we are, yet did not sin: Strengthen us, we pray, to withstand the assaults of our manifold temptations; and, as thou knowest our weaknesses, so may we find thee mighty to save; through the same Jesus Christ thy Son our Lord, who liveth and reigneth with thee and the Holy Spirit, one God, now and for ever. *Amen.*

The Psalms

| [Entrance Psalm] | 91:1-8 |
| [Between Readings] | 91:9-16 |

The Lessons

A	Genesis 2:7-9, 15-17; 3:1-7a	B	Genesis 22:1-14	C	Deuteronomy 26:5-10
	Romans 5:12-19		Romans 4:2-3, 20-25		James 1:12-18
	Matthew 4:1-11		Mark 1:9-13		Luke 4:1-13

PROPER PREFACE OF LENT

The Second Sunday in Lent

The Collect

HEAVENLY FATHER, whose glory it is always to have mercy: Be gracious, we pray, to all who have erred and gone astray from your holy Word, and bring them again in steadfast faith, to receive and hold fast your unchangeable truth; through Jesus Christ our Lord, who lives and reigns with you and the Holy Spirit, one God, now and for ever. *Amen.*

HEAVENLY FATHER, whose glory it is always to have mercy: Be gracious, we beseech thee, to all who have erred and gone astray from thy holy Word, and bring them again in steadfast faith, to receive and hold fast thine unchangeable truth; through Jesus Christ our Lord, who liveth and reigneth with thee and the Holy Spirit, one God, now and for ever. *Amen.*

The Psalms

| [Entrance Psalm] | 25:5-10 |
| [Between Readings] | 42:1-7 |

The Lessons

A	Genesis 12:1-8	B	Genesis 28:11-17	C	Ezekiel 36:22-28
	Romans 5:1-10		Romans 10:8-13		1 Corinthians 10:1-13
	John 4:5-26		John 2:13-22		Mark 10:32-45

PROPER PREFACE OF LENT

The Third Sunday in Lent

The Collect

ALMIGHTY GOD, since we have no power of ourselves to help ourselves, keep us, we pray, both outwardly in our bodies and inwardly in our souls, that we may be defended from all adversities which may happen to the body, and from all evil thoughts which may assault and hurt the soul; through Jesus Christ our Lord, who lives and reigns with you in the unity of the Holy Spirit, one God, for ever and ever. *Amen.*

ALMIGHTY GOD, who seest that we have no power of ourselves to help ourselves: Keep us both outwardly in our bodies, and inwardly in our souls; that we may be defended from all adversities which may happen to the body, and from all evil thoughts which may assault and hurt the soul; through Jesus Christ our Lord, who liveth and reigneth with thee in the unity of the Holy Spirit, one God, for ever and ever. *Amen.*

The Psalms

| [Entrance Psalm] | 27:8-16 |
| [Between Readings] | 25:14-21 |

The Lessons

A	Deuteronomy 5:1,6-21	B	Exodus 3:1-8b, 10-15	C	1 Samuel 16:1-13
	Romans 8:1-10		Ephesians 5:8-14		2 Corinthians 5:17-21
	John 9:1-13, 24-28		John 3:14-21		Luke 13:1-9

PROPER PREFACE OF LENT

The Fourth Sunday in Lent

The Collect

GRACIOUS FATHER, whose blessed Son came down from heaven to be the true bread of life for the world: Feed us continually, we pray, with this bread, that he may evermore live in us, and we in him, our Savior Jesus Christ, who lives and reigns with you and the Holy Spirit, one God, now and for ever. *Amen.*

GRACIOUS FATHER, whose blessed Son came down from heaven to be the true bread of life for the world: Feed us continually, we beseech thee, with this bread; that he may evermore live in us, and we in him, even our Savior Jesus Christ, who liveth and reigneth with thee and the Holy Spirit, one God, now and for ever. *Amen.*

The Psalms

[Entrance Psalm]	34:1-10
[Between Readings]	145:15-21

The Lessons

A	Deuteronomy 8:7-18	B	Exodus 16:2-8, 13-15	C	Isaiah 12
	Romans 8:11-19		Galatians 4:26-5:1		Ephesians 2:4-10
	John 6:4-15		Mark 8:12-21		Luke 15:11-32

PROPER PREFACE OF LENT

The Fifth Sunday in Lent

The Collect

ALMIGHTY GOD, who alone can order the unruly wills and affections of sinful men: Grant your people grace to love what you command and desire what you promise; that among the swift and varied changes of the world, our hearts may surely there be fixed, where true joys are to be found; through Jesus Christ our Lord, who lives and reigns with you and the Holy Spirit, one God, now and for ever. *Amen.*

ALMIGHTY GOD, who alone canst order the unruly wills and affections of sinful men: Grant unto thy people, that they may love the thing which thou commandest, and desire that which thou dost promise; that so, among the sundry and manifold changes of the world, our hearts may surely there be fixed, where true joys are to be found; through Jesus Christ our Lord, who liveth and reigneth with thee and the Holy Spirit, one God, now and for ever. *Amen.*

The Psalms

| [Entrance Psalm] | 142 |
| [Between Readings] | 28:1-3, 7-10 |

The Lessons

	Ezekiel 37:1-3, 11-14		Jeremiah 31:31-34		Isaiah 43:16-21
A	Romans 8:31b-39	B	Hebrews 5:5-9	C	Philippians 2:12-15
	John 11:18-44		John 12:20-33		Mark 12:1-11

PROPER PREFACE OF LENT

Holy Week
The Sunday of the Passion or Palm Sunday

AT THE BLESSING OF PALMS AND PROCESSION

The branches of palm or of other trees to be carried in the Procession may be distributed to the People immediately after the Prayer of Blessing, or before the Service.

The following Anthem is sung or said, the People standing:

Blessed is the King who comes in the name of the Lord.
Peace in heaven and glory in the highest.

The Collect

Minister Let us pray.

Assist us mercifully with your help, O Lord God of our salvation, that we may enter with joy upon the meditation of those mighty acts, whereby you have given us eternal life; through Jesus Christ our Lord. *Amen.*

Here may be read one of the following lessons:

> Matthew 21:1-11
> Mark 11:1-11a
> Luke 19:29-40

When it is desired to ask God's blessing on the branches to be carried in the Procession, the following form may be used:

Minister Let us give thanks to the Lord our God.
Answer It is right to give him thanks and praise.

Minister

We praise *you*, Almighty and Everlasting God, whose Son our Savior Jesus Christ before his passion entered the holy city of Jerusalem, and was triumphantly acclaimed as King by those who spread their garments and branches of palm along his way. Bless, we pray, these branches, and those who bear them in his Name, and grant that we may ever hail him as our King, and follow him in the way that leads to eternal life, who *lives* and *reigns* in glory with *you* and the Holy Spirit, one God, now and for ever. *Amen.*

The following anthem may be sung or said at the distribution of the branches.

> Blessed is he who comes in the name of the Lord:
> *Hosanna in the highest.*

The Procession

Minister Let us go forth in peace.
People In the name of Christ. *Amen.*

During the Procession, appropriate Hymns, Psalms, or Anthems are sung, such as the Hymn "All glory, laud, and honor" and Psalm 118:19-29.

The following Collect may be said, either in the course of the Procession, or at its conclusion.

ALMIGHTY GOD, who showed us in your Son the true way of blessedness: Give us grace to take up our cross and follow him, in the strength of patience and in constancy of faith; and grant us such fellowship with him in his suffering, that we may know the secret of his strength and peace; who now lives and reigns with you in the unity of the Holy Spirit, one God, for ever and ever. *Amen.*

In the absence of a Priest or Deacon, the preceding Service may be led by a Lay Reader.

AT THE EUCHARIST

When the Blessing of Palms and Procession immediately precede the celebration of the Holy Eucharist, the Liturgy begins at once with the Salutation and Collect of the Day.

The Collect

ALMIGHTY AND EVERLIVING GOD, who of your tender love towards mankind sent your Son, our Savior Jesus Christ, to take upon him our nature, and to suffer death upon the cross, that all should follow the example of his great humility: Mercifully grant that we may follow the example of his patience, and become partakers of his resurrection; through Jesus Christ our Lord, who lives and reigns with you and the Holy Spirit, one God, for ever and ever. *Amen.*

ALMIGHTY AND EVERLIVING GOD, who, of thy tender love towards mankind, hast sent thy Son our Savior Jesus Christ, to take upon him our flesh, and to suffer death upon the cross, that all mankind should follow the example of his great humility: Mercifully grant, that we may both follow the example of his patience, and also may be made partakers of his resurrection; through the same Jesus Christ our Lord, who liveth and reigneth with thee and the Holy Spirit, one God, for ever and ever. *Amen.*

The Psalms

| [Entrance Psalm] | 118:19-29 |
| [Between Readings] | 22:23-28 |

The Lessons

| Zechariah 9:9-12 |
| Philippians 2:5-11 |

For the Gospel, the Minister or Ministers appointed read

The passion of our Lord Jesus Christ according to _____.

A	Matthew 26:36-27:54
B	Mark 14:32-15:39
C	Luke 22:39-23:49

When desired, the Passion Gospel may be read or chanted by lay persons.

PROPER PREFACE OF HOLY WEEK

Monday in Holy Week

The Collect

ALMIGHTY GOD, whose most dear Son went not up to joy but first he suffered pain, and entered not into glory before he was crucified: Mercifully grant that we, walking in the way of the cross, may find it none other than the way of life and peace; through Jesus Christ your. Son our Lord. *Amen.*

ALMIGHTY GOD, whose most dear Son went not up to joy but first he suffered pain, and entered not into glory before he was crucified: Mercifully grant that we, walking in the way of the cross, may find it none other than the way of life and peace; through Jesus Christ thy Son our Lord. *Amen.*

The Psalms

[Entrance Psalm]	55:1-8
[Between Readings]	56:1-11

The Lessons

Isaiah 42:1-7
Hebrews 11:39-12:3
John 12:1–11, *or* Mark 14:3-9

PROPER PREFACE OF HOLY WEEK

Tuesday in Holy Week

The Collect

O GOD, who in the passion of your blessed Son made an instrument of shameful death to be to us the sign of life: Grant us so to glory in the cross of Christ that we may gladly suffer shame and loss for the sake of his Name, your Son our Savior Jesus Christ. *Amen.*

O GOD, who in the passion of thy blessed Son didst make an instrument of shameful death to be unto us the sign of life: Grant us so to glory in the cross of Christ, that we may gladly suffer shame and loss for the sake of his Name, even thy Son our Savior Jesus Christ. *Amen.*

The Psalms

| [Entrance Psalm] | 59:1-4, 8-9 |
| [Between Readings] | 60:1-5 |

The Lessons

| Isaiah 49:1-9a |
| 1 Corinthians 1:18-31 |
| John 12:37-38, 42-50 |

PROPER PREFACE OF HOLY WEEK

Wednesday in Holy Week

The Collect

LORD GOD, whose blessed Son our Savior gave his back to the smiters and hid not his face from shame: Give us grace to take joyfully the sufferings of the present time, in full assurance of the glory that shall be revealed; through Jesus Christ your Son our Lord. *Amen.*

LORD GOD, whose blessed Son our Savior gave his back to the smiters and hid not his face from shame: Give us grace to take joyfully the sufferings of the present time, in full assurance of the glory that shall be revealed; through Jesus Christ thy Son our Lord. *Amen.*

The Psalms

| [Entrance Psalm] | 61:1-5, 8 |
| [Between Readings] | 62:1-8 |

The Lessons

| Isaiah 50:4-9a |
| Hebrews 9:11-15, 24-28 |
| John 13:21-35, or Matthew 26:1-5, 14-25 |

PROPER PREFACE OF HOLY WEEK

Maundy Thursday

The Collect

ALMIGHTY FATHER, whose dear Son, on the night before he suffered, instituted the Sacrament of his Body and Blood: Mercifully grant that we may thankfully receive it in remembrance of him, who in these holy mysteries gives us a pledge of life eternal, even Jesus Christ your Son our Lord, who lives and reigns with you and the Holy Spirit, one God, now and for ever. *Amen.*

ALMIGHTY FATHER, whose dear Son, on the night before he suffered, didst institute the Sacrament of his Body and Blood: Mercifully grant that we may thankfully receive the same in remembrance of him, who in these holy mysteries giveth us a pledge of life eternal; the same thy Son Jesus Christ our Lord, who liveth and reigneth with thee and the Holy Spirit, one God, now and for ever. *Amen.*

The Psalms

| [Entrance Psalm] | 43 |
| [Between Readings] | 78:14-21, 24-26 |

The Lessons

| Exodus 12:1-14a |
| 1 Corinthians 11:23-26 |
| John 13:1-15, or Luke 22:14-30 |

PROPER PREFACE OF HOLY WEEK

Good Friday

On this day, the Liturgy begins with the Collect of the Day, the Minister first saying

	The Lord be with you.
Answer	And also with you.
Minister	Let us pray.

The Collect

ALMIGHTY GOD, we pray you graciously to behold this your family, for whom our Lord Jesus Christ was content to be betrayed, and given up into the hands of sinful men, and to suffer death upon the Cross; who now lives and reigns with you and the Holy Spirit, one God, for ever and ever. *Amen.*

ALMIGHTY GOD, we beseech thee graciously to behold this thy family, for which our Lord Jesus Christ was contented to be betrayed, and given up into the hands of wicked men, and to suffer death upon the Cross; who now liveth and reigneth with thee and the Holy Spirit, one God, for ever and ever. *Amen.*

The Psalms

[Entrance Psalm]	22:1-11, or 1-19
[Between Readings]	69:1-9,13-22

The Lessons

Isaiah 52:13-53:12
Hebrews 10:1-25

For the Gospel, the Minister or Ministers appointed read

The Passion of our Lord Jesus Christ according to John.

John 18:1-19:37, or 19:1-37

When desired, the Passion Gospel may be read or chanted by lay persons.

After the Sermon, the Nicene Creed may be said.

Then, all standing, the Priest or Minister appointed says to the People

DEAR PEOPLE OF GOD: Our heavenly Father sent his Son into the world, not to condemn the world, but that the world through him might be saved; that all who believe in him might be delivered from the power of sin and death, and become heirs with him of everlasting life.

We pray, therefore, for all men according to their needs, and for the people of God in every place.

In the biddings which follow, the indented petitions may be adapted by addition or omission, as appropriate, at the discretion of the Minister. The People stand or kneel.

LET US PRAY for the holy Catholic Church of Christ throughout the world; especially,

> For its unity in witness and service
> For all Bishops and other Ministers
>   and the people whom they serve
> For N., our Bishop, and all the people of this Diocese
> For all Christians in this community
> For those preparing to be baptized (particularly, ...)

that God will confirm his Church in faith, increase it in love, and preserve it in peace.

Silence

> ALMIGHTY AND EVERLASTING GOD, by whose Spirit the whole company of your faithful people is governed and sanctified: Receive our prayers which we now offer before you for all members of your holy Church, that in their vocation and ministry they may truly and devoutly serve you, to the glory of your Name; through our Lord and Savior Jesus Christ. *Amen.*

Collect in Traditional Language

> ALMIGHTY AND EVERLASTING GOD, by whose Spirit the whole body of the Church is governed and sanctified: Receive our supplications and prayers, which we offer before thee for all members of thy holy Church, that every member of the same, in his vocation and ministry, may truly and godly serve thee; through our Lord and Savior Jesus Christ. *Amen.*

LET US PRAY for all nations and peoples of the earth, and for those in authority among them; especially,

> For N., the President of the United States
> For the Congress and the Supreme Court

> For the Members and representatives of the United Nations
> For all who serve the common good of men

that by God's help they may seek justice and truth, and live in peace and concord.

Silence

> ALMIGHTY GOD, from whom all thoughts of truth and peace proceed: We pray you to kindle in the hearts of all men the true love of peace; and guide with your pure and peaceable wisdom those who take counsel for the nations of the earth, that in tranquillity your kingdom may go forward, until the earth is filled with the knowledge of your love; through Jesus Christ our Lord. *Amen.*

> ALMIGHTY GOD, from whom all thoughts of truth and peace proceed: Kindle, we pray thee, in the hearts of all men the true love of peace; and guide with thy pure and peaceable wisdom those who take counsel for the nations of the earth; that in tranquillity thy kingdom may go forward, till the earth is filled with the knowledge of thy love; through Jesus Christ our Lord. *Amen.*

LET US PRAY for all who suffer, and are afflicted in body or in mind; especially,

> For the hungry and the homeless, the destitute and the oppressed
> For the sick, the wounded, and the crippled
> For those in loneliness, fear, and anguish
> For those who face temptation, doubt, and despair
> For prisoners and captives, and those in mortal danger
> For the sorrowful and bereaved

that God in his mercy will comfort and relieve them, and grant them the knowledge of his love, and stir up in us the will and patience to minister to their needs.

Silence

> Gracious God, you see all the suffering, injustice, and misery which abound in this world. We implore you to look mercifully upon the poor, the oppressed, and all who are burdened with pain and sorrow. Fill our hearts with your compassion, and give us strength to serve them in their need, for the sake of him who suffered for us, our Savior Jesus Christ. *Amen.*

> Gracious God, who seest all the suffering, injustice, and misery which abound in this world: We beseech thee to look mercifully upon the poor, the oppressed, and all who are burdened with pain and sorrow. Fill our hearts with thy compassion, and give us strength to serve them in their need, for the sake of him who suffered for us, our Savior Jesus Christ. *Amen.*

LET US PRAY for all who, whether in ignorance or in disbelief, have not received the gospel of Christ; especially,

> For those who have never heard the word of Christ
> For those who have lost their faith
> For those hardened by sin or indifference
> For the contemptuous and the scornful
> For those who are enemies of the Cross of Christ, and persecutors of his disciples

that God will open their hearts to the truth, and lead them to faith and obedience.

Silence

> Merciful God, who made all men and hate nothing that you have made; nor do you desire the death of a sinner, but rather that he should be converted and live: Have mercy upon all who know you not as you are revealed in the Gospel of your Son. Take from them all ignorance, hardness of heart, and contempt of your Word. Bring all men home, good Lord, to your fold, so that they may be one flock under the one shepherd, your Son Jesus Christ our Lord. *Amen.*

> Merciful God, who hast made all men, and hatest nothing that thou hast made, nor desirest the death of a sinner, but rather that he should be converted and live: Have mercy upon all who know thee not as thou art revealed in the Gospel of thy Son. Take from them all ignorance, hardness of heart, and contempt of thy Word; and so bring them home, blessed Lord, to thy fold, that they may be made one flock under one shepherd, Jesus Christ our Lord. *Amen.*

LET US COMMIT ourselves to our God, and pray for the grace of a holy life, that, with all who have departed this world and have died in the faith, we may be accounted worthy to enter into the fullness of the joy of our Lord, and receive the crown of life in the day of resurrection.

Silence

> O God of unchangeable power and eternal light: Look favorably on your whole Church, that wonderful and sacred mystery. By the tranquil operation of your providence, carry out the work of man's salvation. Let the whole world see and know that things which were cast down are being raised up, and things which had grown old are being made new, and that all things are being renewed to the perfection of him through whom all things were made, your Son our Lord Jesus Christ, who lives and reigns with you, in the unity of the Holy Spirit, one God, for ever and ever. *Amen.*

O God of unchangeable power and eternal light: Look favorably upon thy whole Church, that wonderful and sacred mystery; and by the tranquil operation of thy providence, carry out the work of man's salvation. Let the whole world see and know that things which were cast down are being raised up, and things which had grown old are being made new, and that all things are being renewed unto the perfection of him through whom all things were made, thy Son our Lord Jesus Christ, who liveth and reigneth with thee in the unity of the Holy Spirit, one God, for ever and ever. *Amen.*

Here, at his discretion, the Minister may add other appropriate devotions set forth by authority.

One or both of the following Anthems may be sung or said:

O Savior of the world, who by your Cross and precious blood have redeemed us:
Save us, and help us, we humbly beseech you, O Lord.

We adore you, O Christ, and we bless you,
Because by your holy Cross you have redeemed the world.

The Minister may conclude the Service with the following Prayer:

Lord Jesus Christ, Son of the living God, set, we pray, your passion, cross, and death between your judgment and our souls, now and in the hour of death. Give mercy and grace to the living, and pardon and rest to the dead. Grant peace and concord to your holy Church, and to us sinners everlasting life and glory; who with the Father and the Holy Spirit live and reign, one God, now and for ever. *Amen.*

The Service ends with an Anthem, or with a Dismissal.

In the absence of a Priest or Deacon, all that precedes may be led by a Lay Reader.

In places where Holy Communion is to be administered from the Reserved Sacrament, the following order is observed before the dismissal of the People:

THE LORD'S PRAYER
A CONFESSION OF SIN
THE COMMUNION
A PRAYER AFTER COMMUNION

Concluding Anthems and Prayers in Traditional Language

O Savior of the world, who by thy Cross and precious blood hast redeemed us:
Save us, and help us, we humbly beseech thee, O Lord.

We adore thee, O Christ and we bless thee:
Because by thy holy Cross thou hast redeemed the world.

LORD JESUS CHRIST, Son of the living God, we beseech thee to set thy passion, cross, and death between thy judgment and our souls, now and in the hour of death. Give mercy and grace to the living, and pardon and rest to the dead. Grant peace and concord to thy holy Church, and to us sinners everlasting life and glory; who with the Father and the Holy Spirit livest and reignest, one God, now and for ever. *Amen.*

Holy Saturday

There is no celebration of the Eucharist on this day, until after the Vigil of Easter Eve.

When there is a Ministry of the Word, the following proper is used:

The Collect

MOST GRACIOUS GOD, as we have been baptized into the death of your Son our Savior Jesus Christ, so in your mercy may we be dead to sin and buried with him; that from the grave and gate of death, we may be raised up with him to newness of life; through Jesus Christ our Lord. *Amen.*

MOST GRACIOUS GOD, who hast baptized us into the death of thy Son our Savior Jesus Christ: Grant in thy mercy that we, being dead to sin, may be buried with him; that through the grave and gate of death, we may be raised up with him unto newness of life; through the same Jesus Christ our Lord. *Amen.*

The Psalms

[Entrance Psalm]	31:1-6
[Between Readings]	130

The Lessons

Job 14:1-14
1 Peter 4:1-8
Matthew 27:57-66, *or* John 19:38-42

Easter Season

EASTER EVE

At the Lighting of the Paschal Candle

The lighting of the Paschal Candle may take place at the beginning of the Vigil, or at some other convenient time before the Liturgy of Easter Day, all standing.

The Deacon or other Minister appointed, standing near the Paschal Candle, sings or says the Exultet, as follows. (The Music of the Exultet will be found in the Altar Book edition.)

When a shorter form is desired, any of the bracketed sections may be omitted.

REJOICE NOW, heavenly hosts and choirs of angels,
    and let your trumpets shout Salvation
    for the victory of our mighty King.
Rejoice and sing now, all the round earth,
    bright with a glorious splendor,
    for darkness has been vanquished by our eternal King.
Rejoice and be glad now, Mother Church,
    and let your holy courts in radiant light
    resound with the praises of your people.

[All you who stand near this marvelous holy flame,
    pray with me to God the Almighty
    for the grace to sing the worthy praise of this great light;
    through Jesus Christ his Son our Lord,
    who lives and reigns with him,
    in the unity of the Holy Spirit,
    one God, for ever and ever. *Amen.*]

	The Lord be with you.
Answer	And also with you.
Minister	Let us give thanks to the Lord our God.
Answer	It is right to give him thanks and praise.

Minister

It is truly right and good, always and everywhere, with our whole heart and mind and voice, to praise you, the invisible, almighty, and eternal God, and your only-begotten Son, our Lord Jesus Christ: For he is the true Paschal Lamb, who at the Feast of the Passover paid for us the debt of Adam's sin, and delivered by his blood your faithful people.

This is the night, when you brought our fathers,
> the children of Israel, out of bondage in Egypt,
> and led them through the Red Sea on dry land.

This is the night, when all who believe in Christ
> are delivered from the shade of sin,
> and are restored to grace and holiness of life.

This is the night, when Christ broke the bonds of death and hell,
> and rose victorious from the grave.

[How wonderful and beyond our knowing, O God,
> is your mercy and loving-kindness to us,
> that to redeem a slave, you gave a Son.

How holy is this night, when wickedness is put to flight,
> and sin is washed away. It restores innocence to the fallen,
> and joy to those who mourn. It casts out pride and hatred,
> and brings peace and concord.

How blessed is this night,
> when earth and heaven are joined,
> and man is reconciled to God.]

If the Paschal Candle was not lit earlier, the Deacon or Minister now lights it; and from its flame other candles and lamps in the church may be lighted; after which he continues

Holy Father, accept our evening sacrifice, the offering of this Candle in your honor.

[May it shine continually to drive away all darkness.
May Christ, the Morning Star who knows no setting,
> find it ever burning—he who gives his light to all creation.]

We pray you, Lord, to direct, sanctify, and govern us your
> servants, and all your faithful family, with your continual
> grace; that we may pass our time in peace and gladness,
> in the festival of our redemption;

Through Jesus Christ your Son our Lord, who lives and
> reigns with you in the unity of the Holy Spirit, one God,
> for ever and ever. *Amen.*

Note: It is customary that the Paschal Candle be burning at all services during the Easter Season.

At the Vigil

At least two of the following Lessons are read, one of which is always the lesson from the Book of Exodus. After each Lesson, an appropriate Psalm, Canticle, or Hymn may be sung; a period of silence may be kept, and an appropriate Collect may be said.

Genesis 1:1-2:2
Genesis 22:1-18
Exodus 14:15-15:1
Isaiah 4:2-6
Isaiah 55:1-11
Ezekiel 36:24-28
Zephaniah 3:14-17, 19-20

Suggested Psalms and Canticles

Psalms 19:1-6; 30:1-13; 33:1-11 *or* 12-21; 42:1-7; 98; 113.

The Song of Moses, Exodus 15:1b-2, 11-13, [17-18]
The First Song of Isaiah, Isaiah 12:2-6

The Litany may then be sung or said.

Holy Baptism [and the Laying on of Hands] may be administered either before or after the Litany; or after the Gospel (and Sermon) in the Eucharist.

In the absence of a Priest or Deacon, all that precedes (except for the ministration of Baptism) may be led by a Lay Reader. He may conclude the Service in the manner described in the following rubric.
    If the Eucharist is not immediately to follow, the Minister may conclude the service with what follows through the Collect of the Day.

At the Eucharist

When the celebration of the Eucharist immediately follows the Vigil, the Liturgy begins with one of the Canticles listed below. Immediately before the Canticle, the Minister may say to the People

              Alleluia! Christ is risen.
Answer   The Lord is risen indeed, Alleluia!

The Canticles

Gloria in excelsis
Te Deum laudamus
Christ our Passover

The Minister then says

              The Lord be with you.
Answer   And also with you.
Minister   Let us pray.

The Collect

ALMIGHTY GOD, who for our redemption gave your only-begotten Son to the death of the Cross, and by his glorious Resurrection delivered us from the power of our enemy: Grant us so to die daily to sin, that we may evermore live with him in the joy of his resurrection; through Jesus Christ your Son our Lord, who lives and reigns with you and the Holy Spirit, one God, now and ever. *Amen.*

ALMIGHTY GOD, who for our redemption didst give thine only-begotten Son to the death of the Cross, and by his glorious Resurrection hast delivered us from the power of our enemy: Grant us so to die daily from sin, that we may evermore live with him in the joy of his resurrection; through the same thy Son Jesus Christ our Lord, who liveth and reigneth with thee and the Holy Spirit, one God, now and ever. *Amen.*

The Psalms

[Entrance Psalm]	2:1-8
[Between Readings]	114

The Lessons

Romans 6:3-11
Matthew 28:1-10

PROPER PREFACE OF EASTER

The Sunday of the Resurrection, or Easter Day

The Collect

ALMIGHTY GOD, who through your only-begotten Son Jesus Christ overcame death, and opened to us the gate of everlasting life: Grant that we, who celebrate with joy the solemnity of the Lord's resurrection, may arise from the death of sin through the renewal of your Holy Spirit; through Jesus Christ our Lord, who now lives and reigns with you and the Holy Spirit, one God, for ever and ever. *Amen.*

ALMIGHTY GOD, who through thine only-begotten Son Jesus Christ hast overcome death, and opened to us the gate of everlasting life: Grant that we, who celebrate with joy the solemnity of the Lord's resurrection, may arise from the death of sin through the renewal of thy Holy Spirit; through Jesus Christ our Lord, who liveth and reigneth with thee and the same Spirit, one God, now and for ever. *Amen.*

The Psalms

[Entrance Psalm]	118:1-6, 14-18
[Between Readings]	66:1-11

The Lessons

Isaiah 25:6-9,	A	John 20:1-9, *or* Matthew 28:1-10
or Acts 10:34-43	B	Mark 16:1-8
Colossians 3:1-4	C	Luke 24:1-10

PROPER PREFACE OF EASTER

Monday in Easter Week

The Collect

GRANT, we pray, ALMIGHTY GOD, that we, who celebrate with reverence the Paschal feast, may be found worthy to attain to everlasting joys; through Jesus Christ our Lord, who lives and reigns with you and the Holy Spirit, one God, now and ever. *Amen.*

GRANT, we beseech thee, ALMIGHTY GOD, that we, who celebrate with reverence the Paschal feast, may be found worthy to attain to everlasting joys; through Jesus Christ our Lord, who liveth and reigneth with thee and the Holy Spirit, one God, now and ever. *Amen.*

The Psalms

[Entrance Psalm]	118:10-24
[Between Readings]	16:9-12

The Lessons

Acts 2:14, 22-32
Matthew 28:9-15

PROPER PREFACE OF EASTER

Tuesday in Easter Week

The Collect

O GOD, who by the glorious resurrection of your Son Jesus Christ destroyed death, and brought life and immortality to light: Grant that we, being raised together with him, may know the strength of his presence, and rejoice in the hope of his eternal glory; through Jesus Christ our Lord, to whom with you and the Holy Spirit, be dominion and praise for ever and ever. *Amen.*

O GOD, who by the glorious resurrection of thy Son Jesus Christ hast destroyed death, and brought life and immortality to light: Grant that we, being raised together with him, may know the strength of his presence, and rejoice in the hope of his eternal glory; through the same Jesus Christ our Lord, to whom with thee and the Holy Spirit, be dominion and praise for ever and ever. *Amen.*

The Psalms

[Entrance Psalm]	118:19-24
[Between Readings]	33:17-21

The Lessons

Acts 2:36-41
John 20:11-18

PROPER PREFACE OF EASTER

Wednesday in Easter Week

The Collect

O GOD, whose blessed Son made himself known to his disciples in the breaking of bread: Open the eyes of our faith, that we may behold him in all his redeeming work; through Jesus Christ your Son our Lord, who lives and reigns with you in the unity of the Holy Spirit, one God, now and ever. *Amen.*

O GOD, whose blessed Son did manifest himself to his disciples in the breaking of bread: Open, we pray thee, the eyes of our faith, that we may behold him in all his redeeming work; through the same thy Son Jesus Christ our Lord, who liveth and reigneth with thee in the unity of the Holy Spirit, one God, now and ever. *Amen.*

The Psalms

| [Entrance Psalm] | 118: 19-24 |
| [Between Readings] | 105:1-8 |

The Lessons

| Acts 3:1-10 |
| Luke 24:13-35 |

PROPER PREFACE OF EASTER

Thursday in Easter Week

The Collect

ALMIGHTY AND EVERLASTING GOD, who established the new covenant of reconciliation in the Paschal mystery of Christ: Grant that all who have been reborn into the fellowship of his Body, may show forth in their lives what they profess by their faith; through Jesus Christ our Lord, who lives and reigns in eternal glory with you and the Holy Spirit, one God, for ever and ever. *Amen.*

ALMIGHTY AND EVERLASTING GOD, who hast established the new covenant of reconciliation in the Paschal mystery of Christ: Grant that all who have been reborn into the fellowship of his Body, may show forth in their lives what they profess by their faith; through Jesus Christ our Lord, who liveth and reigneth in eternal glory with thee and the Holy Spirit, one God, for ever and ever. *Amen.*

The Psalms

[Entrance Psalm]	118:19-24
[Between Readings]	8, or 114

The Lessons

Acts 3: 11-26
Luke 24:36b-48

PROPER PREFACE OF EASTER

Friday in Easter Week

The Collect

ALMIGHTY FATHER, who gave your only Son to die for our sins and to rise for our justification: Give us grace so to put away the leaven of malice and wickedness, that we may always serve you in pureness of living and truth; through Jesus Christ your Son our Lord, who lives and reigns with you and the Holy Spirit, one God, now and ever. *Amen.*

ALMIGHTY FATHER, who didst give thine only Son to die for our sins and to rise for our justification: Give us grace so to put away the leaven of malice and wickedness, that we may always serve thee in pureness of living and truth; through Jesus Christ our Lord, who liveth and reigneth with thee and the Holy Spirit, one God, now and ever. *Amen.*

The Psalms

[Entrance Psalm]	118:19-24
[Between Readings]	116:1-9

The Lessons

Acts 4:1-12
John 21:1-14

PROPER PREFACE OF EASTER

Saturday in Easter Week

The Collect

WE THANK YOU, heavenly Father, for delivering us from the power of darkness, and bringing us into the kingdom of your Son; and we pray that, as by his death he has recalled us to life, so by his presence abiding in us he may raise us to joys eternal; through Jesus Christ your Son our Lord, who lives and reigns with you in the unity of the Holy Spirit, one God, now and for ever. *Amen.*

WE THANK THEE, heavenly Father, for delivering us from the power of darkness, and bringing us into the kingdom of thy Son; and we pray that, as by his death he hath recalled us to life, so by his presence abiding in us he may raise us to joys eternal; through the same thy Son Jesus Christ our Lord, who liveth and reigneth with thee in the unity of the Holy Spirit, one God, now and for ever. *Amen.*

The Psalms

| [Entrance Psalm] | 118:19-24 |
| [Between Readings] | 118:14-18 |

The Lessons

| Acts 4:13-21 |
| Mark 16:9-15, 20 |

PROPER PREFACE OF EASTER

The Second Sunday of Easter

The Collect

ALMIGHTY AND EVERLASTING GOD, who established in the Paschal mystery the new covenant of reconciliation: Grant to all who have been reborn into the fellowship of Christ's Body, that they may show forth in their lives what they profess by their faith; through Jesus Christ our Lord, who lives and reigns in eternal glory with you and the Holy Spirit, one God, now and ever. *Amen.*

ALMIGHTY AND EVERLASTING GOD, who hast established the new covenant of reconciliation in the Paschal mystery of Christ: Grant that all who have been reborn into the fellowship of his Body, may show forth in their lives what they profess by their faith; through Jesus Christ our Lord, who liveth and reigneth in eternal glory with thee and the Holy Spirit, one God, for ever and ever. *Amen.*

The Psalms

[Entrance Psalm]	124
[Between Readings]	126

The Lessons

A	Acts 2:42-47	B	Acts 4:32-35	C	Acts 5:12-16
	1 Peter 1:3-9		1 John 5:1-6		Revelation 1:4-10a, 12-18
	John 20:19-31		John 20:19-31		John 20:19-31

PROPER PREFACE OF EASTER

The Third Sunday of Easter

The Collect

O GOD, whose blessed Son made himself known to his disciples in the breaking of bread: Open the eyes of our faith, that we may behold him in all his redeeming work; through Jesus Christ your Son our Lord, who lives and reigns with you in the unity of the Holy Spirit, one God, now and ever. *Amen.*

    O GOD, whose blessed Son did manifest himself to his disciples in the breaking of bread: Open, we pray thee, the eyes of our faith, that we may behold him in all his redeeming work; through the same thy Son Jesus Christ our Lord, who liveth and reigneth with thee in the unity of the Holy Spirit, one God, now and ever. *Amen.*

The Psalms

[Entrance Psalm]	71:18-23
[Between Readings]	116:11-16

The Lessons

A	Acts 2:22-32 1 Peter 1:17-23 Luke 24:13-35	B	Acts 3:13-15, 17-21 1 John 1:3-2:5a Luke 24:35-48	C	Acts 5:27-35 Revelation 5:6-14 John 21:1-14

PROPER PREFACE OF EASTER

The Fourth Sunday of Easter

The Collect

HEAVENLY FATHER, whose Son our Savior is the good shepherd of your people: Grant that we, who are guarded by his continual care, may daily be nourished and led by his risen presence, who lives and reigns with you and the Holy Spirit, one God, now and ever. *Amen.*

HEAVENLY FATHER, whose Son our Savior is the good shepherd of thy people: Grant that we, who are guarded by his continual care, may daily be nourished and led by his risen presence, the same thy Son Jesus Christ our Lord, who liveth and reigneth with thee and the Holy Spirit, one God, now and ever. *Amen.*

The Psalms

[Entrance Psalm]	116:1-9
[Between Readings]	23

The Lessons

A	Acts 2:14a, 36-41 1 Peter 2:19-25 John 10:1-10	B	Acts 4:5, 7-12 1 John 3:1-8 John 10:11-16	C	Acts 13:16, 26-33 Revelation 7:9-17 John 10:22-30

PROPER PREFACE OF EASTER

The Fifth Sunday of Easter

The Collect

ALMIGHTY GOD, whom truly to know is everlasting life: Grant us perfectly to know your Son Jesus Christ to be the way, the truth, and the life; that we may steadfastly follow his steps in the way that leads to eternal life; through Jesus Christ your Son our Lord, who lives and reigns with you in the unity of the Holy Spirit, one God, for ever and ever. *Amen.*

ALMIGHTY GOD, whom truly to know is everlasting life: Grant us perfectly to know thy Son Jesus Christ to be the way, the truth, and the life; that, following in his steps, we may steadfastly walk in the way that leadeth to eternal life; through the same thy Son Jesus Christ our Lord, who liveth and reigneth with thee in the unity of the Holy Spirit, one God, for ever and ever. *Amen.*

The Psalms

[Entrance Psalm]	108:1-6
[Between Readings]	67

The Lessons

	A	Acts 6:1-7a		B	Acts 9:26-31		C	Acts 13:44-52
		1 Peter 2:1-10			1 John 3:18-24			Revelation 19:1, 4-9
		John 14:1-12			John 15:1-11			John 13:31-35

PROPER PREFACE OF EASTER

The Sixth Sunday of Easter

The Collect

O GOD, who prepared for those who love you such good things as pass man's understanding: Pour into our hearts such love towards you, that we, loving you in all things and above all things, may obtain your promises; through Jesus Christ our Lord, who lives and reigns with you and the Holy Spirit, one God, for ever and ever. *Amen.*

O GOD, who hast prepared for those who love thee such good things as pass man's understanding: Pour into our hearts such love towards thee, that we, loving thee in all things and above all things, may obtain thy promises, which exceed all that we can desire; through Jesus Christ our Lord, who liveth and reigneth with thee and the Holy Spirit, one God, for ever and ever. *Amen.*

The Psalms

[Entrance Psalm]	20
[Between Readings]	144:9-15

The Lessons

A	Acts 8:5-8, 14-17	B	Acts 11:5a, 11-18	C	Acts 15:1-6, 22-29
	1 Peter 3:13-18		1 John 4:7-21		Revelation 21:2-4, 14, 22-24
	John 14:15-21		John 15:9-17		John 14:23-29

PROPER PREFACE OF EASTER

Ascension Day

The Collect

GRANT, we pray, ALMIGHTY GOD, that as we believe your only-begotten Son our Lord Jesus Christ to have ascended into heaven, so we may also in heart and mind there ascend, and with him continually dwell; through Jesus Christ our Lord, who lives and reigns with you and the Holy Spirit, one God, for ever and ever. *Amen.*

GRANT, we beseech thee, ALMIGHTY GOD, that like as we do believe thine only-begotten Son our Lord Jesus Christ to have ascended into the heavens; so we may also in heart and mind thither ascend, and with him continually dwell, who liveth and reigneth with thee and the Holy Spirit, one God, for ever and ever. *Amen.*

The Psalms

[Entrance Psalm]	110:1-4
[Between Readings]	24:7-10

The Lessons

Acts 1:1-11
Ephesians 1:16-23
Luke 24:49-53

PROPER PREFACE OF ASCENSION

The Seventh Sunday of Easter

The Collect

ALMIGHTY GOD, whose blessed Son our Savior Jesus Christ ascended far above all heavens, that he might fill all things: Mercifully give us faith to perceive that according to his promise he abides with his Church on earth, even to the end of the world; through Jesus Christ our Lord, who lives and reigns with you and the Holy Spirit, one God, for ever and ever. *Amen.*

ALMIGHTY GOD, whose blessed Son our Savior Jesus Christ ascended far above all heavens, that he might fill all things: Mercifully give us faith to perceive that according to his promise he abides with his Church on earth, even unto the end of the world; through the same Jesus Christ our Lord, who liveth and reigneth with thee and the Holy Spirit, one God, for ever and ever. *Amen.*

The Psalms

[Entrance Psalm]	48:8-13
[Between Readings]	47

The Lessons

	Acts 1:8-14		Acts 1:15-26		Acts 7:55-60
A	1 Peter 4:12-19	B	1 John 5:9-15	C	Revelation 22:12-14, 16-17, 20
	John 14:1-11a		John 17:11b-19		John 17:20-26

PROPER PREFACE OF ASCENSION

The Day of Pentecost, or Whitsunday

When there is more than one celebration of the Liturgy on this day, the following proper may be used:

The Collect

ALMIGHTY GOD, who gave us the abiding presence of the Holy Spirit: Increase in us daily, we pray, the manifold gifts of his grace, that we may know the freedom of the children of God, and bear witness boldly for the Name of our Lord Jesus Christ, who now lives and reigns with you and the Holy Spirit, one God, for ever and ever. *Amen.*

ALMIGHTY GOD, who hast given to us the abiding presence of the Holy Spirit: Increase in us, we beseech thee, the manifold gifts of his grace, that we may know the freedom of the children of God, and bear witness boldly for the Name of our Lord Jesus Christ, who now liveth and reigneth with thee and the same Holy Spirit, one God, for ever and ever. *Amen.*

The Psalms

| [Entrance Psalm] | 68:1-4, 18-20 |
| [Between Readings] | 68:32-35 |

The Lessons

| Joel 2:28-32 |
| Romans 8:14-17, 22-27 |
| Luke 11:9-13 |

PROPER PREFACE OF PENTECOST

At the principal celebration, this proper is used:

The Collect

O GOD, who taught the hearts of your faithful people by sending to them the light of your Holy Spirit: Grant us by the Spirit to have a right judgment in all things, and evermore to rejoice in his strength; through Jesus Christ your Son our Lord, who lives and reigns with you in the unity of the Spirit, one God, now and for ever. *Amen.*

O GOD, who didst teach the hearts of thy faithful people by sending to them the light of thy Holy Spirit: Grant us by the same Spirit to have a right judgment in all things, and evermore to rejoice in his holy strength; through Jesus Christ our Lord, who liveth and reigneth with thee and the same Holy Spirit, one God, now and for ever. *Amen.*

The Psalms

| [Entrance Psalm] | 122 |
| [Between Readings] | 33:12-14, 17-21 |

The Lessons

| Acts 2:1-11 |
| 1 Corinthians 12:4-13 |
| John 20:19-23 |

PROPER PREFACE OF PENTECOST

The First Sunday after Pentecost, or Trinity Sunday

The Collect

ALMIGHTY AND EVERLASTING GOD, who gave to us your servants grace, by the confession of a true faith, to acknowledge the glory of the eternal Trinity, and in the power of your divine Majesty to worship the Unity: We humbly pray you to keep us steadfast in this faith, and evermore defend us from all adversities, who live and reign, one God, for ever and ever. *Amen.*

ALMIGHTY AND EVERLASTING GOD, who hast given unto us thy servants grace, by the confession of a true faith, to acknowledge the glory of the eternal Trinity, and in the power of the Divine Majesty to worship the Unity: We beseech thee that thou wouldest keep us steadfast in this faith, and evermore defend us from all adversities, who livest and reignest, one God, for ever and ever. *Amen.*

The Psalms

| [Entrance Psalm] | 148 |
| [Between Readings] | 150 |

The Lessons

A	Isaiah 6:1-8	B	Exodus 3:1-6	C	Numbers 6:22-27
	Revelation 4:1-11		Acts 2:32-39		Romans 8:12-17
	Matthew 28:16-20		John 3:1-16		John 14:8-17

PROPER PREFACE OF TRINITY SUNDAY

The Second Sunday after Pentecost

The Collect

ALMIGHTY AND EVERLASTING GOD: Give us the increase of faith, hope, and charity; and, that we may obtain what you promise, make us love what you command; through Jesus Christ our Lord, who lives and reigns with you in the unity of the Holy Spirit, one God, now and for ever. *Amen.*

ALMIGHTY AND EVERLASTING GOD: Give unto us the increase of faith, hope, and charity; and, that we may obtain that which thou dost promise, make us to love that which thou dost command; through Jesus Christ our Lord, who liveth and reigneth with thee in the unity of the Holy Spirit, one God, now and for ever. *Amen.*

The Psalms

[Entrance Psalm]	8:1-10
[Between Readings]	15

The Lessons

A	Deuteronomy 11:18-21, 26-28	B	Deuteronomy 5:6-21; *or* verses 12-15	C	1 Kings 8:41-43
	Romans 3:21-25a, 28		2 Corinthians 4:7-11		Galatians 1:1-10
	Matthew 7:21-27		Mark 2:23-28		Luke 7:1-10

PROPER PREFACE OF THE LORD'S DAY

The Third Sunday after Pentecost

The Collect

ALMIGHTY AND EVERLASTING GOD, ever more ready to hear than we to pray, and to give more than we desire or deserve: Pour upon us the abundance of your mercy; forgiving us those things of which our conscience is afraid, and giving us those good things which we are not worthy to ask, but for the sake of our Savior Jesus Christ, who lives and reigns with you and the Holy Spirit, one God, now and for ever. *Amen.*

ALMIGHTY AND EVERLASTING GOD, who art always more ready to hear than we to pray, and art wont to give more than either we desire or deserve: Pour down upon us the abundance of thy mercy; forgiving us those things whereof our conscience is afraid, and giving us those good things which we are not worthy to ask, but through the merits and mediation of Jesus Christ thy Son our Lord, who liveth and reigneth with thee and the Holy Spirit, one God, now and for ever. *Amen.*

The Psalms

| [Entrance Psalm] | 50:7-15 |
| [Between Readings] | 30:6-13 |

The Lessons

| | A | Hosea 6:3-6
Romans 4:18-25
Matthew 9:9-13 | B | Genesis 3:9-15
2 Corinthians 4:13-5:1
Mark 3:20-35 | C | 1 Kings 17:17-24
Galatians 1:11-19
Luke 7:11-17 |

PROPER PREFACE OF THE LORD'S DAY

The Fourth Sunday after Pentecost

The Collect

KEEP, O LORD, your household the Church in your steadfast faith and love; that, by the help of your grace, we may proclaim your truth with courage, and minister your love with compassion; for the sake of our Savior Jesus Christ, your Son our Lord, who lives and reigns with you and the Holy Spirit, one God, for ever and ever. *Amen.*

KEEP, O LORD, we beseech thee, thy household the Church in thy stedfast faith and love; that, by the help of thy grace, it may proclaim thy truth with courage, and minister thy love with compassion; for the sake of our Savior Jesus Christ, thy Son our Lord, who liveth and reigneth with thee and the Holy Spirit, one God, for ever and ever. *Amen.*

The Psalms

| [Entrance Psalm] | 94:8-15 |
| [Between Readings] | 94:16-22 |

The Lessons

A	Exodus 19:2-6a	B	Ezekiel 17:22-24	C	2 Samuel 12:7-10, 13
	Romans 5:6-11		2 Corinthians 5:6-10		Galatians 2:11-21
	Matthew 9:35-10:8		Mark 4:26-34		Luke 7:36-50

PROPER PREFACE OF THE LORD'S DAY

The Fifth Sunday after Pentecost

The Collect

ALMIGHTY FATHER, whose blessed Son laid down his life for us that we might live in him: Grant us so perfectly, and without any doubt, to commit our lives to him, that our faith may never be found wanting in your sight; through Jesus Christ our Lord, who lives and reigns with you and the Holy Spirit, one God, now and evermore. *Amen.*

ALMIGHTY FATHER, whose blessed Son laid down his life for us that we might live in him: Grant us so perfectly, and without any doubt, to commit our lives to him, that our faith may never be found wanting in thy sight; through Jesus Christ our Lord, who liveth and reigneth with thee and the Holy Spirit, one God, now and evermore. *Amen.*

The Psalms

[Entrance Psalm]	69:30-37
[Between Readings]	107:23-32

The Lessons

A	Jeremiah 20:7-13	B	Job 38:1-11, 16-18	C	Zechariah 12:9-11
	Romans 5:12-15		2 Corinthians 5:14-17		Galatians 3:23-29
	Matthew 10:26-33		Mark 4:35-41		Luke 9:18-24

PROPER PREFACE OF THE LORD'S DAY

The Sixth Sunday after Pentecost

The Collect

O GOD, whose almighty power is made known chiefly in showing mercy and pity: Stir our hearts with such desire for your gracious promises, that we may become partakers of your heavenly treasure; through Jesus Christ our Lord, who lives and reigns with you and the Holy Spirit, one God, now and ever. *Amen.*

O GOD, who declarest thy almighty power chiefly in showing mercy and pity: Mercifully grant unto us such a measure of thy grace, that we, running the way of thy commandments, may obtain thy gracious promises, and be made partakers of thy heavenly treasure; through Jesus Christ our Lord, who liveth and reigneth with thee and the Holy Spirit, one God, now and ever. *Amen.*

The Psalms

[Entrance Psalm]	89:1-2, 16-19
[Between Readings]	16

The Lessons

A	Isaiah 2:10-17	B	Wisdom 1:13-15; 2:23-24	C	1 Kings 19:15-16, 19-21
	Romans 6:3-11		2 Corinthians 8:1-9, 13-15		Galatians 4:31-5:1, 13-18
	Matthew 10:34-42		Mark 5:21-24, 35b-43		Luke 9:51-62

PROPER PREFACE OF THE LORD'S DAY

The Seventh Sunday after Pentecost

The Collect

O GOD, who taught us to keep all your commandments by loving you and our neighbor: Grant us the grace of your Holy Spirit, that we may be devoted to you with our whole heart, and united to one another with pure affection; through Jesus Christ our Lord, who lives and reigns with you and the Holy Spirit, one God, for ever and ever. *Amen.*

O GOD, who hast taught us to keep all thy commandments by loving thee and our neighbor: Grant unto us the grace of thy Holy Spirit, that we may be devoted to thee with our whole heart, and united to one another with pure affection; through Jesus Christ our Lord, who liveth and reigneth with thee and the Holy Spirit, one God, for ever and ever. *Amen.*

The Psalms

[Entrance Psalm]	138
[Between Readings]	123

The Lessons

A	Zechariah 9:9-10	B	Ezekiel 2:2-5	C	Isaiah 66:10-14
	Romans 8:9-17		2 Corinthians 12:7-10		Galatians 6:14-18
	Matthew 11:25-30		Mark 6:1-6		Luke 10:1-9, 16-20

PROPER PREFACE OF THE LORD'S DAY

The Eighth Sunday after Pentecost

The Collect

LORD, we pray that your grace may always go before us and follow us, that by your continual help we may accomplish those good works which are pleasing to you; through Jesus Christ our Lord, who lives and reigns with you and the Holy Spirit, one God, now and for ever. *Amen.*

LORD, we pray thee that thy grace may always go before us and follow us, that by thy continual help we may accomplish those good works which are pleasing to thee; through Jesus Christ our Lord, who liveth and reigneth with thee and the Holy Spirit, one God, now and for ever. *Amen.*

The Psalms

[Entrance Psalm]	65:9-14
[Between Readings]	85:8-13

The Lessons

A	Isaiah 55:10-11	B	Amos 7:10-15	C	Deuteronomy 30:10-14
	Romans 8:18-23		Ephesians 1:3-14		Colossians 1:1-12
	Matthew 13:1-9, 18-23		Mark 6:7-13		Luke 10:25-37

PROPER PREFACE OF THE LORD'S DAY

The Ninth Sunday after Pentecost

The Collect

GRANT, O LORD, we pray, that the course of this world may be so peaceably ordered by your governance, that your Church may serve you in all joy and peace; through Jesus Christ our Lord, who lives and reigns with you and the Holy Spirit, one God, now and for ever. *Amen.*

GRANT, O LORD, we beseech thee, that the course of this world may be so peaceably ordered by thy governance, that thy Church may joyfully serve thee in all godly quietness; through Jesus Christ our Lord, who liveth and reigneth with thee and the Holy Spirit, one God, now and for ever. *Amen.*

The Psalms

[Entrance Psalm]	86:11-17
[Between Readings]	23

The Lessons

	Wisdom 12:13, 16-19		Jeremiah 23:1-6		Genesis 18:1-10a
A	Romans 8:26-27	B	Ephesians 2:11-18	C	Colossians 1:21-28
	Matthew 13:24-34		Mark 6:30-34		Luke 10:38-42

PROPER PREFACE OF THE LORD'S DAY

THE TENTH SUNDAY AFTER PENTECOST

The Collect

O LORD, we pray, mercifully receive the prayers of your people who call upon you, and grant that they may know and understand what things they ought to do, and may have grace and power faithfully to accomplish them; through Jesus Christ our Lord, who lives and reigns with you in the unity of the Holy Spirit, one God, now and ever. *Amen.*

O LORD, we beseech thee, mercifully to receive the prayers of thy people who call upon thee; and grant that they may both perceive and know what things they ought to do, and also may have grace and power faithfully to fulfill the same; through Jesus Christ our Lord, who liveth and reigneth with thee in the unity of the Holy Spirit, one God, now and ever. *Amen.*

The Psalms

[Entrance Psalm]	145:14-21
[Between Readings]	119:129-136

The Lessons

	1 Kings 3:5-12		2 Kings 4:42-44		Genesis 18:20-32
A	Romans 8:28-30	B	Ephesians 4:1-6	C	Colossians 2:6-15
	Matthew 3:44-49a		Mark 6:35-44		Luke 11:1-13

PROPER PREFACE OF THE LORD'S DAY

The Eleventh Sunday after Pentecost

The Collect

ALMIGHTY GOD, the fountain of all wisdom, as you know our necessities before we ask, and our ignorance in asking: Have compassion on our weakness; and mercifully give us those things which for our unworthiness we dare not, and for our blindness we cannot ask, for the sake of your Son Jesus Christ our Lord, who lives and reigns with you and the Holy Spirit, one God, now and for ever. *Amen.*

ALMIGHTY GOD, the fountain of all wisdom, who knowest our necessities before we ask, and our ignorance in asking: We beseech thee to have compassion upon our infirmities; and those things which for our unworthiness we dare not, and for our blindness cannot ask, mercifully give us, for the sake of thy Son Jesus Christ our Lord, who liveth and reigneth with thee and the Holy Spirit, one God, now and for ever. *Amen.*

The Psalms

[Entrance Psalm]	95:1-7
[Between Readings]	36:5-12

The Lessons

	Isaiah 55:1-3		Exodus 16:2-4, 12-15		Ecclesiastes 1:2, 2:18-23
A	Romans 8:35-39	B	Ephesians 4:17-24	C	Colossians 3:1-5, 9-11
	Matthew 14:13-21		John 6:24-35		Luke 12:13-21

PROPER PREFACE OF THE LORD'S DAY

The Twelfth Sunday after Pentecost

The Collect

O Lord, we pray, let your continual mercy cleanse and defend your Church; and, because it cannot continue in safety without your aid, preserve and govern it always by your help and goodness; through Jesus Christ our Lord, who lives and reigns with you and the Holy Spirit, one God, for ever and ever. *Amen.*

    O Lord, we beseech thee, let thy continual pity cleanse and defend thy Church; and, because it cannot continue in safety without thy succor, preserve it evermore by thy help and goodness; through Jesus Christ our Lord, who liveth and reigneth with thee and the Holy Spirit, one God, for ever and ever. *Amen.*

The Psalms

[Entrance Psalm]	34:1-8
[Between Readings]	27:1-7

The Lessons

	1 Kings 19:9-12		1 Kings 19:4-8		Genesis 15:1-6
A	Romans 9:1-5	B	Ephesians 4:30-5:2	C	Hebrews 11:1-2,8-16
	Matthew 14:22-23		John 6:41-51		Luke 12:32-40

PROPER PREFACE OF THE LORD'S DAY

The Thirteenth Sunday after Pentecost

The Collect

Grant to us, Lord, we pray, the spirit to think and do always such things as are right; that we, who cannot exist without you, may by your strength live according to your will; through Jesus Christ our Lord, who lives and reigns with you and the Holy Spirit, one God, now and ever. *Amen.*

    Grant to us, Lord, we beseech thee, the spirit to think and do always such things as are right; that we, who cannot exist without thee, may by thee be enabled to live according to thy will; through Jesus Christ our Lord, who liveth and reigneth with thee and the Holy Spirit, one God, now and ever. *Amen.*

The Psalms

[Entrance Psalm]	147:1-7
[Between Readings]	62:1-8

The Lessons

	Isaiah 56:1, 6-7		Proverbs 9:1-6		Jeremiah 23:23-29
A	Romans 11:13-15,29-32	B	Ephesians 5:15-20	C	Hebrews 12:1-4
	Matthew 15:21-28		John 6:53-58		Luke 12:49-56

PROPER PREFACE OF THE LORD'S DAY

The Fourteenth Sunday after Pentecost

The Collect

ALMIGHTY GOD, who built your Church upon the foundation of the apostles and prophets, Jesus Christ himself being the head corner-stone: Grant us so to be joined together in unity of spirit by their teaching, that we may be made a holy temple acceptable to you; through Jesus Christ our Lord, who lives and reigns with you and the Holy Spirit, one God, now and for ever. *Amen.*

ALMIGHTY GOD, who hast built thy Church upon the foundation of the apostles and prophets, Jesus Christ himself being the head corner-stone: Grant us so to be joined together in unity of spirit by their doctrine, that we may be made a holy temple, acceptable unto thee; through the same Jesus Christ our Lord, who liveth and reigneth with thee and the Holy Spirit, one God, now and for ever. *Amen.*

The Psalms

[Entrance Psalm]	71:1-7
[Between Readings]	125

The Lessons

	Isaiah 22:15-16, 19-23		Joshua 24:1-2a, 14-18		Isaiah 66:18b-23
A	Romans 11:33-36	B	Ephesians 5:21-32	C	Hebrews 12:5-7, 11-13
	Matthew 16:13-20		John 6:60-69		Luke 13:22-30

PROPER PREFACE OF THE LORD'S DAY

The Fifteenth Sunday after Pentecost

The Collect

ALMIGHTY GOD, who gave your only Son to be for us both a sacrifice for sin, and also an example of godly life: Give us grace always to receive thankfully his incomparable benefit, and also daily endeavor to follow the blessed steps of his most holy life; through Jesus Christ your Son our Lord, who lives and reigns with you and the Holy Spirit, one God, now and ever. *Amen.*

ALMIGHTY GOD, who hast given thine only Son to be unto us both a sacrifice for sin, and also an example of godly life: Give us grace that we may always most thankfully receive that his inestimable benefit, and also daily endeavor ourselves to follow the blessed steps of his most holy life; through the same thy Son Jesus Christ our Lord, who liveth and reigneth with thee and the Holy Spirit, one God, now and ever. *Amen.*

The Psalms

[Entrance Psalm]	112
[Between Readings]	113

The Lessons

A	Jeremiah 20:7-9	B	Deuteronomy 4:1-2, 6b-8	C	Ecclesiasticus 3:17-18, 20, 28-29
	Romans 12:1-2		James 1:17-18, 21b-22, 27		Hebrews 12:18-19, 22-24
	Matthew 16:21-26		Mark 7:1-8, 14-15, 21-23		Luke 14:1, 7-14

PROPER PREFACE OF THE LORD'S DAY

The Sixteenth Sunday after Pentecost

The Collect

GRANT, we pray, merciful God, that your Church, being gathered together in unity by your Holy Spirit, may show forth your power among all peoples, to the glory of your Name; through Jesus Christ our Lord, who lives and reigns with you and the Holy Spirit, one God, now and for ever. *Amen.*

GRANT, we beseech thee, merciful God, that thy Church, being gathered together in unity by thy Holy Spirit, may manifest thy power among all peoples, to the glory of thy Name; through Jesus Christ our Lord, who liveth and reigneth with thee and the same Spirit, one God, now and for ever. *Amen.*

The Psalms

| [Entrance Psalm] | 146 |
| [Between Readings] | 82 |

The Lessons

A	Ezekiel 33:7-9	B	Isaiah 35:4-7a	C	Wisdom 9:13-18
	Romans 13:8-10		James 2:1-5		Philemon 1, 7-17
	Matthew 18:15-20		Mark 7:31-37		Luke 14:25-33

PROPER PREFACE OF THE LORD'S DAY

The Seventeenth Sunday after Pentecost

The Collect

GRANT US, O LORD, we pray, to trust in you with all our heart; for since you always resist the proud who confide in their own strength, so you never forsake those who make their boast in your mercy; through Jesus Christ our Lord, who lives and reigns with you and the Holy Spirit, one God, now and for ever. *Amen.*

GRANT UNTO US, O LORD, we beseech thee, to trust in thee with all our heart; seeing that, as thou dost always resist the proud who confide in their own strength, so thou dost not forsake those who make their boast in thy mercy; through Jesus Christ our Lord, who liveth and reigneth with thee and the Holy Spirit, one God, now and for ever. *Amen.*

The Psalms

| [Entrance Psalm] | 103:1-12 |
| [Between Readings] | 103:13-22 |

The Lessons

	Ecclesiasticus 27:29-28:7		Isaiah 50:5-9a		Exodus 32:7-11,13-14
A	Romans 14:7-9	B	James 2:14-18	C	Timothy 1:12-17
	Matthew 18:21-35		Mark 8:27-38		Luke 15:1-10

PROPER PREFACE OF THE LORD'S DAY

The Eighteenth Sunday after Pentecost

The Collect

O GOD, since without you we are not able to please you: Mercifully grant that your Holy Spirit may in all things direct and rule our hearts; through Jesus Christ our Lord, who lives and reigns with you and the Holy Spirit, one God, now and ever. *Amen.*

O GOD, forasmuch as without thee we are not able to please thee: Mercifully grant that thy Holy Spirit may in all things direct and rule our hearts; through Jesus Christ our Lord, who liveth and reigneth with thee and the same Spirit, one God, now and ever. *Amen.*

The Psalms

[Entrance Psalm]	80:7-14
[Between Readings]	54

The Lessons

	Isaiah 55:6-9		Wisdom 2:1,12-20		Amos 8:4-7
A	Philippians 1:20c-24, 27a	B	James 3:16-4:3	C	Timothy 2:1-8
	Matthew 20:1-16		Mark 9:30-37		Luke 16:10-13

PROPER PREFACE OF THE LORD'S DAY

The Nineteenth Sunday after Pentecost

The Collect

REMEMBER, O LORD, what you have wrought in us and not what we deserve; and as you have called us to your service, make us worthy of our calling; through Jesus

Christ our Lord, who lives and reigns with you and the Holy Spirit, one God, now and for ever. *Amen.*

REMEMBER, O LORD, what thou hast wrought in us and not what we deserve; and as thou hast called us to thy service, make us worthy of our calling; through Jesus Christ our Lord, who liveth and reigneth with thee and the Holy Spirit, one God, now and for ever. *Amen.*

The Psalms

[Entrance Psalm]	18:21-29
[Between Readings]	19:7-14

The Lessons

	A	Ezekiel 18:25-28	B	Numbers 11:25-29	C	Amos 6:1, 3-7
		Philippians 2:1-11		James 5:1-6		1 Timothy 6:11-16
		Matthew 21:28-32		Mark 9:38-43, 45, 47-48		Luke 16:19-31

PROPER PREFACE OF THE LORD'S DAY

The Twentieth Sunday after Pentecost

The Collect

O GOD, the protector of all who trust in you, without whom nothing is strong, nothing is holy: Increase and multiply upon us your mercy, that we may so pass through things temporal, that we lose not the things eternal; through Jesus Christ our Lord, who lives and reigns with you and the Holy Spirit, one God, now and ever. *Amen.*

O GOD, the protector of all that trust in thee, without whom nothing is strong, nothing is holy: Increase and multiply upon us thy mercy; that, thou being our ruler and guide, we may so pass through things temporal, that we lose not the things eternal; through Jesus Christ our Lord, who liveth and reigneth with thee and the Holy Spirit, one God, now and ever. *Amen.*

The Psalms

[Entrance Psalm]	80:14-19
[Between Readings]	128

The Lessons

	Isaiah 5:1-7		Genesis 2:18-24		Habakkuk 1:2-3; 2:2-4
A	Philippians 4:4-8	B	Hebrews 2:9-18	C	2 Timothy 1:6-14
	Matthew 21:33-43		Mark 10:2-9		Luke 17:5-10

PROPER PREFACE OF THE LORD'S DAY

The Twenty-First Sunday after Pentecost

The Collect

GRANT US, O LORD, not to be anxious about earthly things, but to love things heavenly; and even now, while we are placed among things that are passing away, to cleave to those that shall abide; through Jesus Christ our Lord, who lives and reigns with you and the Holy Spirit, one God, now and for ever. *Amen.*

GRANT US, O LORD, not to mind earthly things, but to love things heavenly; and even now, while we are placed among things that are passing away, to cleave to those that shall abide; through Jesus Christ our Lord, who liveth and reigneth with thee and the Holy Spirit, one God, now and for ever. *Amen.*

The Psalms

[Entrance Psalm]	92:1-5, 11-14
[Between Readings]	84:1-7

The Lessons

	Isaiah 25:6-10a		Wisdom 7:7-11		Ruth 1:8-19a
A	Philippians 4:10-13	B	Hebrews 3:1-6	C	2 Timothy 2:8-13
	Matthew 22:1-14		Mark 10:17-27		Luke 17:11-19

PROPER PREFACE OF THE LORD'S DAY

The Twenty-Second Sunday after Pentecost

The Collect

O GOD OF HOPE, fill us with all joy and peace in believing, that we may ever abound in hope by the power of your Holy Spirit, and show forth our thankfulness to you in trustful and courageous lives; through Jesus Christ our Lord, who lives and reigns with you and the Holy Spirit, one God, now and for ever. *Amen.*

O God of Hope, fill us, we beseech thee, with all joy and peace in believing, that we may ever abound in hope by the power of thy Holy Spirit, and show forth our thankfulness to thee in trustful and courageous lives; through Jesus Christ our Lord, who liveth and reigneth with thee and the same Spirit, one God, now and for ever. *Amen.*

The Psalms

[Entrance Psalm]	96:1-8
[Between Readings]	121

The Lessons

	Isaiah 45:1,4-6		Isaiah 53:10-11		Exodus 17:8-12
A	1 Thessalonians 1:1-5b	B	Hebrews 4:12-16	C	2 Timothy 3:14-4:2
	Matthew 22:15-21		Mark 10:35-45		Luke 18:1-8a

PROPER PREFACE OF THE LORD'S DAY

The Twenty-Third Sunday after Pentecost

The Collect

Lord of all power and might, the author and giver of all good things: Graft in our hearts the love of your Name; increase in us true religion; and nourish us with all goodness; through Jesus Christ our Lord, who lives and reigns with you and the Holy Spirit, one God, now and for ever. *Amen.*

Lord of all power and might, who art the author and giver of all good things: Graft in our hearts the love of thy Name, increase in us true religion, nourish us with all goodness, and of thy great mercy keep us in the same; through Jesus Christ our Lord, who liveth and reigneth with thee and the Holy Spirit, one God, now and for ever. *Amen.*

The Psalms

[Entrance Psalm]	1
[Between Readings]	17:1-7

The Lessons

A	Exodus 22:21-27	B	Jeremiah 31:7-9	C	Ecclesiasticus 35:12-14, 16-19
	1 Thessalonians 1:5c-10		Hebrews 5:1-9		2 Timothy 4:6-8,16-18
	Matthew 22:34-40		Mark 10:46-52		Luke 18:9-14

PROPER PREFACE OF THE LORD'S DAY

The Twenty-Fourth Sunday after Pentecost

The Collect

O GOD, from whom all good things come: Grant to us your servants, that by your holy inspiration we may think those things which are good, and by your merciful guidance may bring them to good effect; through Jesus Christ our Lord, who lives and reigns with you and the Holy Spirit, one God, now and for ever. *Amen.*

O GOD, from whom all good things do come: Grant to us thy humble servants, that by thy holy inspiration we may think those things that are good, and by thy merciful guiding may perform the same; through Jesus Christ our Lord, who liveth and reigneth with thee and the Holy Spirit, one God, now and for ever. *Amen.*

The Psalms

[Entrance Psalm]	4
[Between Readings]	32:1-8

The Lessons

A	Malachi 1:14b-2:2b, 8-10	B	Deuteronomy 6:1-6	C	Wisdom 11:23-12:2
	1 Thessalonians 2:7-13		Hebrews 7:23-28		2 Thessalonians 1:1-5,11-12
	Matthew 23:1-12		Mark 12:28b-34		Luke 19:1-10

PROPER PREFACE OF THE LORD'S DAY

The Twenty-Fifth Sunday after Pentecost

The Collect

ALMIGHTY AND EVERLASTING GOD, who revealed your glory by Christ among all nations: Preserve the works of your mercy, that your Church, which is spread throughout the world, may persevere with steadfast faith in the confession of your Name; through Jesus Christ our Lord, who lives and reigns with you in the unity of the Holy Spirit, one God, now and ever. *Amen.*

ALMIGHTY AND EVERLASTING GOD, who hast revealed thy glory by Christ among the nations: Preserve the works of thy mercy, that thy Church, which is spread throughout the world, may persevere with steadfast faith in the confession of thy Name; through Jesus Christ our Lord, who liveth and reigneth with thee in the unity of the Holy Spirit, one God, now and ever. *Amen.*

The Psalms

[Entrance Psalm]	105:1-8
[Between Readings]	111

The Lessons

	Jeremiah 26:1-9		1 Kings 17:10-16		Job 19:23-27
A	1 Thessalonians 3:7-13	B	Hebrews 9:24-28	C	2 Thessalonians 2:15-3:5
	Matthew 24:4-14		Mark 12:38-44		Luke 20:27, 34-38

PROPER PREFACE OF THE LORD'S DAY

The Twenty-Sixth Sunday after Pentecost

The Collect

ALMIGHTY GOD, whose sovereign purpose none can make void: Give us faith to be steadfast amid the tumults of the world, knowing that your kingdom shall come and your will be done, to the eternal glory of your Name; through Jesus Christ our Lord, who lives and reigns with you and the Holy Spirit, one God, now and for ever. *Amen.*

ALMIGHTY GOD, whose sovereign purpose none can make void: Give us faith to be steadfast amidst the tumults of the world, knowing that thy kingdom shall come and thy will be done, to the eternal glory of thy Name; through Jesus

Christ our Lord, who liveth and reigneth with thee and the Holy Spirit, one God, now and for ever. *Amen.*

The Psalms

[Entrance Psalm]	57:8-12
[Between Readings]	40:1-7

The Lessons

A	Wisdom 6:12-16	B	Daniel 7:9-12	C	Malachi 4:1-2a
	1 Thessalonians 4:12-17		Hebrews 10:11-14, 18		2 Thessalonians 3:7-12
	Matthew 25:1-13		Mark 13:14-23		Luke 21:5-19

PROPER PREFACE OF THE LORD'S DAY

The Twenty-Seventh Sunday after Pentecost

The Collect

O GOD, whose blessed Son came into the world that he might destroy the works of the devil, and make us the sons of God, and heirs of eternal life: Grant us, we pray, that, having this hope, we may purify ourselves, even as he is pure; that, when he shall appear again with power and great glory, we may be made like him in his eternal and glorious kingdom, where he lives and reigns with you and the Holy Spirit, one God, now and for ever. *Amen.*

O GOD, whose blessed Son was manifested that he might destroy the works of the devil, and make us the sons of God, and heirs of eternal life: Grant us, we pray, that, having this hope, we may purify ourselves, even as he is pure; that, when he shall appear again with power and great glory, we may be made like unto him in his eternal and glorious kingdom, where he liveth and reigneth with thee and the Holy Spirit, one God, now and for ever. *Amen.*

The Psalms

[Entrance Psalm]	90:1-8, 12
[Between Readings]	90:13-17

The Lessons

A	Proverbs 31:10-13, 19-20, 30-31	B	Daniel 12:1-3	C	Malachi 3:1-5, 4:5-6
	Hebrews 10:31-33, 35-39		1 Thessalonians 5:1-10		1 Peter 4:17-19
	Mark 13:24-32		Matthew 25:14-15, 19-30		Luke 21:32-36

PROPER PREFACE OF SUNDAY

The Last Sunday after Pentecost, or the Sunday Before Advent

The proper for this Sunday is always to be used on the Sunday before the First Sunday in Advent, whether the Sundays after Pentecost be twenty-three or more in number.

The Collect

ALMIGHTY AND EVERLASTING GOD, whose will it is to restore all things in your well-beloved Son, the King of kings and Lord of lords: Mercifully grant that all the peoples of the earth, being set free from the captivity of sin and death, may be brought under his gracious rule, who lives and reigns with you and the Holy Spirit, one God, now and for ever. *Amen.*

ALMIGHTY AND EVERLASTING GOD, who didst will to restore all things in thy well-beloved Son, the King of kings, and Lord of lords: Mercifully grant that all the peoples of the earth, being set free from the captivity of sin and death, may be brought under his gracious rule, who liveth and reigneth with thee and the Holy Spirit, one God, now and for ever. *Amen.*

The Psalms

[Entrance Psalm]	24
[Between Readings]	46

The Lessons

	Ezekiel 34:11-17		Daniel 7:13-14		Jeremiah 23:2-6
A	1 Corinthians 15:20-26,28	B	Revelation 1:4b-8	C	Colossians 1:12-20
	Matthew 25:31-46		John 18:33b-37		Luke 23:35-43

PROPER PREFACE OF THE LORD'S DAY

Saint Andrew the Apostle
November 30

The Collect

ALMIGHTY GOD, who gave such grace to your apostle Andrew, that he readily obeyed the calling of your son Jesus Christ, and followed him without delay: Grant, we pray, that we, who are called by your holy Word, may offer ourselves in glad obedience to your service; through Jesus Christ our Lord, who lives and reigns with you and the Holy Spirit, one God, now and ever. *Amen.*

ALMIGHTY GOD, who didst give such grace to thine apostle Andrew, that he readily obeyed the calling of thy Son Jesus Christ, and followed him without delay: Grant, we beseech thee, that we, who are called by thy holy Word, may offer ourselves in glad obedience to thy service; through Jesus Christ our Lord, who liveth and reigneth with thee and the Holy Spirit, one God, now and ever. *Amen.*

The Psalms

[Entrance Psalm]	117
[Between Readings]	102:15-22

The Lessons

Deuteronomy 30:11-14
Romans 10:8-18
Matthew 4:18-22

PROPER PREFACE OF APOSTLES

Saint Thomas the Apostle
December 21

The Collect

ETERNAL GOD, who strengthened Thomas your apostle, being doubtful, with firm and certain faith in the resurrection of your Son our Lord: Grant to us your people, that we may be not faithless but believing, until we come to see our Savior in his glory face to face; through Jesus Christ your Son our Lord, who lives and reigns with you and the Holy Spirit, one God, now and for ever. *Amen.*

O ETERNAL GOD, who didst strengthen thine apostle Thomas, being doubtful, with firm and certain faith in the resurrection of thy Son our Lord: Grant unto us thy people, that we may be not faithless but believing, until we come to see our Savior in his glory face to face; through the same thy Son Jesus Christ our Lord, who liveth and reigneth with thee and the Holy Spirit, one God, now and for ever. *Amen.*

The Psalms

[Entrance Psalm]	48:1-7
[Between Readings]	126

The Lessons

Habakkuk 2:1-4
Hebrews 10:35-11:1
John 20:24-29

PROPER PREFACE OF APOSTLES

Saint Stephen, Deacon and Martyr
December 26

When this feast falls on the First Sunday after Christmas, it is transferred to the Monday following.

The Collect

GRANT, O FATHER, that in all our sufferings here on earth in witness to your truth, we may follow the example of our Lord and of his first martyr Saint

Stephen, and learn to love our enemies and forgive our persecutors; through Jesus Christ our Savior, who lives and reigns with you and the Holy Spirit, one God, in glory everlasting. *Amen.*

GRANT, O FATHER, that in all our sufferings here on earth in witness to thy truth, we may follow the example of our Lord and of his first martyr Saint Stephen, and learn to love our enemies and forgive our persecutors; through Jesus Christ our Savior, who liveth and reigneth with thee and the Holy Spirit, one God, in glory everlasting. *Amen.*

The Psalms

| [Entrance Psalm] | 30:1–5 |
| [Between Readings] | 31:1-6 |

The Lessons

| 2 Chronicles 24:17-22 |
| Acts 7:55-60 |
| Matthew 23:34-39 |

PROPER PREFACE OF CHRISTMAS

Saint John, Apostle and Evangelist
December 27

When this feast falls on the First Sunday after Christmas, it is transferred to the Monday following; but if Saint Stephen's Day has been transferred to the Monday, this feast is observed on the Tuesday following.

The Collect

MERCIFUL LORD, pour upon your Church, we pray, the brightness of your light, that we, being illumined by the teaching of your apostle and evangelist Saint John, may so live by the light of your truth that we may obtain eternal life; through our Lord Jesus Christ, who lives and reigns with you and the Holy Spirit, one God, for ever and ever. *Amen.*

MERCIFUL LORD, we beseech thee to cast thy bright beams of light upon thy Church, that we, being illumined by the doctrine of thy blessed apostle and evangelist Saint John, may so walk in the light of thy truth that we may at length attain to life everlasting; through Jesus Christ our Lord, who liveth and reigneth with thee and the Holy Spirit, one God, for ever and ever. *Amen.*

The Psalms

| [Entrance Psalm] | 92:11-14 |
| [Between Readings] | 23 |

The Lessons

| Proverbs 8:22-30 |
| John 1:1-5 |
| John 21:19-24 |

PROPER PREFACE OF CHRISTMAS

The Holy Innocents
December 28

This feast is observed on the day following the feast of Saint John; but if that day is the First Sunday after Christmas, this feast is transferred to the Monday following.

The Collect

GRANT, most merciful Father, that, as we remember the slaughter of innocent babes by the order of a tyrant, when our Lord was born in Bethlehem, so we may be firm to defend all helpless people from cruelty and oppression, for the sake of our Savior Jesus Christ, who also suffered death though he had done no wrong, and who now lives and reigns with you and the Holy Spirit, one God, for ever and ever. *Amen.*

GRANT, most merciful Father, that, as we remember the slaughter of innocent children by the order of a tyrant, when our Lord was born in Bethlehem, so we may be firm to defend all helpless people from cruelty and oppression, for the sake of our Savior Jesus Christ, who also suffered death though he had done no wrong, and who now liveth and reigneth with thee and the Holy Spirit, one God, for ever and ever. *Amen.*

The Psalms

| [Entrance Psalm] | 9:11-14 |
| [Between Readings] | 9:16-20 |

The Lessons

| Jeremiah 31:15-20 |
| Revelation 21:3-5 |
| Matthew 2:13-18 |

PROPER PREFACE OF CHRISTMAS

The Confession of Saint Peter the Apostle
January 18

The Collect

ALMIGHTY FATHER, who inspired Simon Peter, first among the apostles, to confess Jesus as the Messiah and Son of the living God: Keep your Church steadfast upon the rock of this faith, that in unity and peace it may proclaim one truth and follow one Lord, your Son our Savior Jesus Christ, who lives and reigns with you and the Holy Spirit, one God, now and for ever. *Amen.*

ALMIGHTY FATHER, who didst inspire Simon Peter, first among the apostles, to confess Jesus as the Messiah and Son of the living God: Keep thy Church steadfast upon the rock of this faith, that in unity and peace it may proclaim one truth and follow one Lord, thy Son our Savior Jesus Christ, who liveth and reigneth with thee and the Holy Spirit, one God, now and for ever. *Amen.*

The Psalms

| [Entrance Psalm] | 89:9-18 |
| [Between Readings] | 133 |

The Lessons

| Ezekiel 3:4-11 |
| Acts 4:8-13 |
| Matthew 16:13-19 |

PROPER PREFACE OF APOSTLES

The Conversion of Saint Paul the Apostle
January 25

The Collect

O GOD, who caused the light of the gospel to shine throughout the world by the preaching of your apostle Saint Paul: Grant that we may ever hold in remembrance his wonderful conversion, and show our thanksgiving by following his holy teaching; through Jesus Christ our Lord, who lives and reigns with you in the unity of the Holy Spirit, one God, now and ever. *Amen.*

O GOD, who hast caused the light of the gospel to shine throughout the world by the preaching of thy blessed apostle Saint Paul: Grant that we may ever hold in remembrance his wonderful conversion, and show our thanksgiving unto thee for the same by following the holy doctrine which he taught; through Jesus Christ our Lord, who liveth and reigneth with thee in the unity of the Holy Spirit, one God, now and ever. *Amen.*

The Psalms

| [Entrance Psalm] | 66:1-8 |
| [Between Readings] | 67 |

The Lessons

| Acts 26:9-20 |
| Galatians 1:11-24 |
| Luke 21:10-19 |

PROPER PREFACE OF APOSTLES

The Presentation of our Lord Jesus Christ in the Temple, also called
The Purification of Saint Mary the Virgin
February 2

The Collect

ALMIGHTY AND EVERLIVING GOD, we humbly pray, that, as your only Son our Savior was presented in the temple of the old covenant, so we, who are the temple of his Holy Spirit, may come before you with pure and clean hearts; through Jesus Christ our Lord, who lives and reigns with you and the Holy Spirit, one God, for ever and ever. *Amen.*

ALMIGHTY AND EVERLIVING GOD, we humbly beseech thee, that, as thine only Son our Savior was presented in the temple of the old covenant, so we, who are the temple of his Holy Spirit, may come before thee with pure and clean hearts; through Jesus Christ our Lord, who liveth and reigneth with thee and the same Spirit, one God, for ever and ever. *Amen.*

The Psalms

| [Entrance Psalm] | 84:1-5 |
| [Between Readings] | 48:8-13 |

The Lessons

| Malachi 3:1-4 |
| John 3:1-8 |
| Luke 2: 22-40 |

PROPER PREFACE OF THE INCARNATION

Saint Matthias the Apostle
February 24

The Collect

ALMIGHTY GOD, who in the place of a traitor chose your faithful servant Matthias to be counted in the number of the Twelve: Grant that your Church may ever be preserved in loyalty to your Son, and also be ordered and guided by faithful and true pastors; through Jesus Christ your Son our Lord, who lives and reigns with you in the unity of the Holy Spirit, one God, now and ever. *Amen.*

ALMIGHTY GOD, who in the place of a traitor didst choose thy faithful servant Matthias to be counted in the number of the Twelve: Grant that thy Church may ever be preserved in loyalty to thy Son, and also be ordered and guided by faithful and true pastors; through the same thy Son Jesus Christ our Lord, who liveth and reigneth with thee in the unity of the Holy Spirit, one God, now and ever. *Amen.*

The Psalms

| [Entrance Psalm] | 15 |
| [Between Readings] | 11:1-6 |

The Lessons

| Acts 1:15-26 |
| Philippians 3:13-21 |
| John 15:1,6-16 |

PROPER PREFACE OF APOSTLES

Saint Joseph
March 19

The Collect

O GOD, who called blessed Joseph to be the guardian of your only Son, and the spouse of his virgin mother: Give us grace to follow his faithfulness and obedience to your commands, that our homes may be blessed by your presence and peace; through Jesus Christ our Lord, who lives and reigns with you and the Holy Spirit, one God, now and for ever. *Amen.*

O GOD, who didst call blessed Joseph to be the guardian of thine only Son, and the spouse of his virgin mother: Give us grace to follow his faithfulness and obedience to thy commands, that our homes may be blessed by thy presence and peace; through Jesus Christ our Lord, who liveth and reigneth with thee and the Holy Spirit, one God, now and for ever. *Amen.*

The Psalms

| [Entrance Psalm] | 127:1-4 |
| [Between Readings] | 119:57-64 |

The Lessons

| Isaiah 63:7-9, 16 |
| Philippians 4:5-8, 9b |
| Luke 2:41-51a |

PROPER PREFACE OF ALL SAINTS

The Annunciation of our Lord Jesus Christ to the Blessed Virgin Mary
March 25

The Collect

O LORD, we pray, pour your grace into our hearts, that, as we have known the birth of your son Jesus Christ by the message of an angel, so by his cross and passion we may be brought to the glory of his resurrection; through Jesus Christ our Lord, who lives and reigns with you in the unity of the Holy Spirit, one God, now and for ever. *Amen.*

O LORD, we beseech thee, pour thy grace into our hearts; that, as we have known the incarnation of thy Son Jesus Christ by the message of an angel, so by his cross and passion we may be brought unto the glory of his resurrection; through the same Jesus Christ our Lord, who liveth and reigneth with thee in the unity of the Holy Spirit, one God, now and for ever. *Amen.*

The Psalms

[Entrance Psalm]	113
[Between Readings]	131

The Lessons

Isaiah 7:10-14; 8:10c
Hebrews 10:4-10
Luke 1:26-38

PROPER PREFACE OF THE INCARNATION

Saint Mark the Evangelist
April 25

The Collect

ALMIGHTY GOD, we thank you for the gospel of your Son Jesus Christ, committed to his Church by the hand of your evangelist Saint Mark; and we pray that, being firmly grounded in its truth, we may be faithful to its teaching both in word and deed; through Jesus Christ our Lord, who lives and reigns with you and the Holy Spirit, one God, now and evermore. *Amen.*

ALMIGHTY GOD, we thank thee for the gospel of thy Son Jesus Christ, committed to his Church by the hand of thine evangelist Saint Mark; and we pray that, being firmly grounded in its truth, we may be faithful to its teaching both in word and deed; through the same Jesus Christ our Lord, who liveth and reigneth with thee and the Holy Spirit, one God, now and evermore. *Amen.*

The Psalms

| [Entrance Psalm] | 19:1-6 |
| [Between Readings] | 119:9-16 |

The Lessons

| Isaiah 62:6-8, 10-12 |
| Ephesians 4:7-8, 11-16 |
| Mark 13:1-10 |

PROPER PREFACE OF ALL SAINTS

Saint Philip and Saint James, Apostles
May 1

The Collect

ALMIGHTY GOD, who gave to your apostles Saint Philip and Saint James grace and strength fearlessly to bear testimony to the truth: Grant that we, being always mindful of their victory of faith, may learn like them to overcome the world, and glorify the Name of our Lord Jesus Christ, who lives and reigns with you and the Holy Spirit, one God, now and ever. *Amen.*

ALMIGHTY GOD, who didst give to thine apostles Saint Philip and Saint James grace and strength fearlessly to bear testimony to the truth: Grant that we, being ever mindful of their victory of faith, may learn like them to overcome the world, and glorify the Name of our Lord Jesus Christ, who liveth and reigneth with thee and the Holy Spirit, one God, now and ever. *Amen.*

The Psalms

| [Entrance Psalm] | 25:1-4 |
| [Between Readings] | 119:41-48 |

The Lessons

| Isaiah 30:18-21 |
| 2 Corinthians 4:1-6 |
| John 14:6-13a |

PROPER PREFACE OF APOSTLES

The Visitation of the Blessed Virgin Mary
May 31

The Collect

FATHER IN HEAVEN, who chose in wondrous grace the blessed Virgin Mary to be the mother of your incarnate Son: Grant that, as we honor the exaltation of her lowliness, so we may follow the example of her humble obedience to your will; through Jesus Christ your Son our Lord, who now lives and reigns with you and the Holy Spirit, one God, in glory everlasting. *Amen.*

FATHER IN HEAVEN, who didst choose in wondrous grace the blessed Virgin Mary to be the mother of thine incarnate Son: Grant that, as we honor the exaltation of her lowliness, so we may follow the example, of her humble obedience to thy will; through Jesus Christ our Lord, who now liveth and reigneth with thee and the Holy Spirit, one God, in glory everlasting. *Amen.*

The Psalms

| [Entrance Psalm] | 121 |
| [Between Readings] | 23 |

The Lessons

| Zephaniah 3:14-17 |
| Ephesians 5:18b-20 |
| Luke 1:39-49 |

PROPER PREFACE OF THE INCARNATION

Saint Barnabas the Apostle
June 11

The Collect

O GOD, whose Son Jesus Christ has taught us that it is more blessed to give than to receive: Help us, by the example of your apostle and servant Barnabas, to be generous in our judgments and unselfish in our service; through Jesus Christ our Lord, who lives and reigns with you and the Holy Spirit, one God, now and for ever. *Amen.*

O GOD, whose Son Jesus Christ hath taught us that it is more blessed to give than to receive: Help us, by the example of thine apostle and servant Barnabas, to be generous in our judgments and unselfish in our service; through Jesus Christ our Lord, who liveth and reigneth with thee and the Holy Spirit, one God, now and for ever. *Amen.*

The Psalms

| [Entrance Psalm] | 112:1-6 |
| [Between Readings] | 37:23-28 |

The Lessons

| Job 29:11-16 |
| Acts 11:22-30 |
| Mark 10:23-31 |

PROPER PREFACE OF APOSTLES

The Nativity of Saint John the Baptist
June 24

The Collect

ALMIGHTY GOD, by whose providence your servant John the Baptist was wonderfully born to be the forerunner of our Savior Jesus Christ: Give us grace to repent according to his preaching, and turn to you with all our hearts, that we may be ready for that day when the glory of the Lord shall be revealed; through Jesus Christ our Lord, who lives and reigns with you in the unity of the Holy Spirit, one God, now and ever. *Amen.* ALMIGHTY GOD, by whose providence thy servant John the Baptist was wonderfully born to be the forerunner of our Savior Jesus Christ: Give us grace to repent according to his preaching, and to turn to thee with all our hearts, that we may be ready for that day when the glory of the Lord shall be revealed; through Jesus Christ our Lord, who liveth and reigneth with thee in the unity of the Holy Spirit, one God, now and ever. *Amen.*

The Psalms

| [Entrance Psalm] | 85:7-13 |
| [Between Readings] | 81:9-15 |

The Lessons

| Isaiah 40:1-1 |
| Acts 13:14b-26 |
| Luke 1:57-80 |

PROPER PREFACE OF ADVENT

Saint Peter and Saint Paul, Apostles
June 29

The Collect

ALMIGHTY GOD, who made this day holy by the martyrdom of your blessed apostles Peter and Paul: Grant that your household the Church, being instructed by their teaching and example, and knit together in unity by your Spirit, may ever stand firm upon the one foundation, which is Jesus Christ our Lord, who lives and reigns with you and the Holy Spirit, one God, for ever and ever. *Amen.*

ALMIGHTY GOD, who hast made this day holy by the martyrdom of thy blessed apostles Peter and Paul: Grant that thy household the Church, being instructed by their teaching and example, and knit together in unity by thy Spirit, may ever stand firm upon the one foundation, which is Jesus Christ our Lord, who liveth and reigneth with thee and the same Spirit, one God, for ever and ever. *Amen.*

The Psalms

| [Entrance Psalm] | 18:1-7 |
| [Between Readings] | 87 |

The Lessons

| Ezekiel 34:11-16 |
| 2 Timothy 4:1-8 |
| John 21:15-19 |

PROPER PREFACE OF APOSTLES

Independence Day
July 4

The Collect

ETERNAL GOD, through whose mighty power our fathers won their liberties of old: Grant, we pray, that we and all the people of this land may have grace to maintain these liberties in righteousness and peace; through Jesus Christ our Lord, who lives and reigns with you and the Holy Spirit, one God, in glory everlasting. *Amen.*

ETERNAL GOD, through whose mighty power our fathers won their liberties of old: Grant, we beseech thee, that we and all the people of this land may have grace to maintain these liberties in righteousness and peace; through Jesus Christ, our Lord, who liveth and reigneth with thee and the Holy Spirit, one God, in glory everlasting. *Amen.*

The Psalms

| [Entrance Psalm] | 145:1-9 |
| [Between Readings] | 145:14-21 |

The Lessons

| Micah 4:1-5 |
| Hebrews 11:8-16 |
| Matthew 5:43-48 |

PROPER PREFACE OF TRINITY SUNDAY

Saint Mary Magdalene
July 22

The Collect

ALMIGHTY GOD, whose blessed Son restored Mary Magdalene to health of body and of mind, and called her to be a witness of his resurrection: Mercifully grant that by your grace we may be healed of all our infirmities, and serve you in the power of his endless life, who with you and the Holy Spirit lives and reigns, one God, now and for ever. *Amen.*

ALMIGHTY GOD, whose blessed Son restored Mary Magdalene to health of body and of mind, and called her to be a witness of his resurrection: Mercifully grant that by thy grace we may be healed of all our infirmities, and serve thee in the power of his endless life, who with thee and the Holy Spirit liveth and reigneth, one God, now and for ever. *Amen.*

The Psalms

| [Entrance Psalm] | 138:1-5 |
| [Between Readings] | 116:5-9 |

The Lessons

| Acts 13:27-31 |
| 2 Corinthians 5:14-18 |
| John 20:11-18 |

PROPER PREFACE OF ALL SAINTS

Saint James the Apostle
July 25

The Collect

ALMIGHTY GOD, who gave to your apostle Saint James a ready will to obey the calling of your Son, and strength to suffer for his Name: Mercifully grant that no worldly affections may draw our hearts away from steadfast devotion to his service, through Jesus Christ your Son our Lord, who lives and reigns with you and the Holy Spirit, one God, now and evermore. *Amen.*

ALMIGHTY GOD, who didst give to thine apostle Saint James a ready will to obey the calling of thy Son, and strength to suffer for his Name: Mercifully grant that no worldly affections may draw our hearts away from steadfast devotion to his service, through thy Son Jesus Christ our Lord, who liveth and reigneth with thee and the Holy Spirit, one God, now and evermore. *Amen.*

The Psalms

| [Entrance Psalm] | 75:1-8 |
| [Between Readings] | 33:13-18 |

The Lessons

| Jeremiah 45 |
| Acts 11:27-12:2 |
| Matthew 20:20-28 |

PROPER PREFACE OF APOSTLES

The Transfiguration of Our Lord Jesus Christ
August 6

The Collect

O GOD, who on the holy mount revealed to chosen witnesses your well-beloved Son, wonderfully transfigured with your sublime glory: Mercifully grant that we, being delivered from the disquiet of this world, may by faith behold the King in his beauty, who with you and the Holy Spirit now lives and reigns, one God, for ever and ever. *Amen.*

O GOD, who on the holy mount didst reveal to chosen witnesses thy well-beloved Son, wonderfully transfigured with thy sublime glory: Mercifully grant that we, being delivered from the disquiet of this world, may by faith behold the King in his beauty, who with thee and the Holy Spirit now liveth and reigneth, one God for ever and ever. *Amen.*

The Psalms

| [Entrance Psalm] | 99:5-9 |
| [Between Readings] | 27:4-7 |

The Lessons

Exodus 34:29-35
2 Peter 1:13-21
Luke 9:28-26 [sic]

PROPER PREFACE OF THE INCARNATION

Saint Mary the Virgin
August 15

The Collect

O GOD, who received to yourself the blessed Virgin Mary, mother of your only Son: Grant that we, who have been redeemed by his blood, may share with her the glory of your eternal kingdom; through Jesus Christ your Son our Lord, who lives and reigns with you in the unity of the Holy Spirit, one God, for ever and ever. *Amen.*

O GOD, who hast taken to thyself the blessed Virgin Mary, mother of thine only Son: Grant that we, who have been redeemed by his blood, may share with her the glory of thine eternal kingdom; through the same thy Son Jesus Christ our Lord, who liveth and reigneth with thee in the unity of the Holy Spirit, one God, for ever and ever. *Amen.*

The Psalms

[Entrance Psalm]	34:1-4
[Between Readings]	66:14-18

The Lessons

Isaiah 61:7-11
Galatians 4:4-7
Luke 1:46-55

PROPER PREFACE OF ALL SAINTS

Saint Bartholomew the Apostle
August 24

The Collect

ALMIGHTY AND EVERLASTING GOD, who gave to your apostle Bartholomew grace truly to believe and to preach your Word: Grant, we pray, that your Church may love the Word which he believed, and both preach it and obey it; through Jesus Christ our Lord, who lives and reigns with you and the Holy Spirit, one God, now and ever. *Amen.*

ALMIGHTY AND EVERLASTING GOD, who didst give to thine apostle Bartholomew grace truly to believe and to preach thy Word: Grant, we beseech thee, that thy Church may love the Word which he believed, and both preach and obey the same; through Jesus Christ our Lord, who liveth and reigneth with thee and the Holy Spirit, one God, now and ever. *Amen.*

The Psalms

| [Entrance Psalm] | 91:1-4 |
| [Between Readings] | 119:161-168 |

The Lessons

| Deuteronomy 18:15-18 |
| 1 Corinthians 4:9-15 |
| Luke 22:24-30 |

PROPER PREFACE OF APOSTLES

Holy Cross Day
September 14

The Collect

ALMIGHTY GOD, whose Son our Savior Jesus Christ was lifted high upon the cross that he might draw all men to himself: Mercifully grant that we, who glory in his death for our salvation, may also glory in his call to take up our cross and follow him, who now lives and reigns with you and the Holy Spirit, one God, in glory everlasting. *Amen.*

ALMIGHTY GOD, whose Son our Savior Jesus Christ was lifted high upon the cross that he might draw all men unto himself: Mercifully grant that we, who glory in his death for our salvation, may also glory in his call to take up our cross and follow him, who now liveth and reigneth with thee and the Holy Spirit, one God, in glory everlasting. *Amen.*

The Psalms

| [Entrance Psalm] | 27:1-6 |
| [Between Readings] | 98:1-4 |

The Lessons

| Isaiah 45:21-25 |
| Philippians 2:5-11 *or* Galatians 6:14-18 |
| John 12:31-36 |

PROPER PREFACE OF HOLY WEEK

Saint Matthew, Apostle and Evangelist
September 21

The Collect

WE THANK YOU, heavenly Father, for the witness of your apostle and evangelist Matthew to the gospel of your Son our Savior; and we pray that, after his example, we may with ready wills and hearts obey the calling of our Lord to follow him; through Jesus Christ our Lord, who lives and reigns with you and the Holy Spirit, one God, now and ever. *Amen.*

WE THANK THEE, heavenly Father, for the witness of thine apostle and evangelist Matthew to the gospel of thy Son our Savior; and we pray that, after his example, we may with ready wills and hearts obey the calling of our Lord to follow him; through Jesus Christ our Lord, who liveth and reigneth with thee and the Holy Spirit, one God, now and ever. *Amen.*

The Psalms

| [Entrance Psalm] | 65:1-5 |
| [Between Readings] | 119:33-40 |

The Lessons

| Proverbs 3:1-6 |
| 2 Timothy 3:14-17 |
| Matthew 9:9-13 |

PROPER PREFACE OF APOSTLES

Saint Michael and all Angels
September 29

The Collect

EVERLASTING GOD, by whom the ministries of angels and men have been ordained and constituted in a wonderful order: Mercifully grant that, as your holy angels always serve and worship you in heaven, so by your appointment they may help and defend us on earth; through Jesus Christ our Lord, who lives and reigns with you and the Holy Spirit, one God, now and ever. *Amen.*

EVERLASTING GOD, who hast ordained and constituted the ministries of angels and men in a wonderful order: Mercifully grant that, as thy holy angels always serve and worship thee in heaven, so by thy appointment they may help and defend us on earth; through Jesus Christ our Lord, who liveth and reigneth with thee and the Holy Spirit, one God, now and ever. *Amen.*

The Psalms

| [Entrance Psalm] | 148:1-5 |
| [Between Readings] | 103:19-22 |

The Lessons

| Genesis 28:10-17 |
| Revelation 12:7-11 |
| John 1:47-51 |

PROPER PREFACE OF TRINITY SUNDAY

Saint Luke the Evangelist
October 18

The Collect

ALMIGHTY GOD, who inspired your servant Saint Luke, the physician, to set forth in the gospel the love and healing power of your Son: Graciously continue in your Church the like love and power to heal, to the praise and glory of your Name; through Jesus Christ our Lord, who lives and reigns with you in the unity of the Holy Spirit, one God, now and forever. *Amen.*

ALMIGHTY GOD, who didst inspire thy servant Saint Luke, the physician, to set forth in the gospel the love and healing power of thy Son: Graciously continue in thy Church the like love and power to heal, to the praise and glory of thy Name; through Jesus Christ our Lord, who liveth and reigneth with thee in the unity of the Holy Spirit, one God, now and for ever. *Amen.*

The Psalms

| [Entrance Psalm] | 68:4-6 |
| [Between Readings] | 37:38-41 |

The Lessons

| Ecclesiasticus 38:1-4, 6-10, 12-14 |
| 2 Timothy 4:5-13 |
| Luke 4:14-21 |

PROPER PREFACE OF ALL SAINTS

Saint James of Jerusalem Brother of our Lord Jesus Christ and Martyr
October 23

The Collect

GRANT, we pray, O God, that after the example of your servant James, the brother of our Lord, your Church may give itself continually to prayer, and to the reconciliation of all who are at variance and enmity; through Jesus Christ our Lord, who lives and reigns with you in the unity of the Holy Spirit, one God, now and for ever. *Amen.*

GRANT, we beseech thee, O God, that after the example of thy servant James, the brother of our Lord, thy Church may give itself continually to prayer, and to the reconciliation of all who are at variance and enmity; through Jesus Christ our Lord, who liveth and reigneth with thee in the unity of the Holy Spirit, one God, now and for ever. *Amen.*

The Psalms

| [Entrance Psalm] | 1 |
| [Between Readings] | 119:145-152 |

The Lessons

| Acts 15:12-22 |
| 1 Corinthians 15:1-11 |
| Mark 3:31-35, *or* Matthew 13:54-58 |

PROPER PREFACE OF ALL SAINTS

Saint Simon and Saint Jude, Apostles
October 28

The Collect

O GOD, we thank you for the glorious company of the apostles, and especially on this day for Saint Simon and Saint Jude; and we pray that, as they were faithful and zealous in their mission, so we may with ardent devotion make known among the nations the love and mercy of our Lord and Savior Jesus Christ, who lives and reigns with you in the unity of the Holy Spirit, one God, now and for ever. *Amen.*

O GOD, we thank thee for the glorious company of the apostles, and especially on this day for Saint Simon and Saint Jude; and we pray that, as they were faithful and zealous in their mission, so we may with ardent devotion make known among the nations the love and mercy of our Lord and Savior Jesus Christ, who liveth and reigneth with thee in the unity of the Holy Spirit, one God, now and for ever. *Amen.*

The Psalms

| [Entrance Psalm] | 62:7-12 |
| [Between Readings] | 119:137-144 |

The Lessons

| Deuteronomy 32:1-4 |
| Ephesians 2:13-22 |
| John 14:21-27 |

PROPER PREFACE OF APOSTLES

All Saints' Day
November 1

The Collect

ALMIGHTY GOD, whose elect are knit together in one communion and fellowship, in the mystical body of your Son Christ our Lord: Grant us grace so to follow your blessed saints in all virtuous and holy living, that we may come to those inexpressible joys that you have prepared for those who truly love you; through Jesus Christ our Lord, who lives and reigns with you and the Holy Spirit, one God, in glory everlasting. *Amen.*

ALMIGHTY GOD, who hast knit together thine elect in one communion and fellowship, in the mystical body of thy Son Christ our Lord: Grant us grace so to follow thy blessed saints in all virtuous and godly living, that we may come to those unspeakable joys which thou hast prepared for those who unfeignedly love thee; through Jesus Christ our Lord, who liveth and reigneth with thee and the Holy Spirit, one God, in glory everlasting. *Amen.*

The Psalms

| [Entrance Psalm] | 149 |
| [Between Readings] | 34:4-9 |

The Lessons

| Ecclesiasticus 44:1-10, 13-14 |
| Revelation 7:9-17 |
| Matthew 5:1-12 |

PROPER PREFACE OF ALL SAINTS

Thanksgiving Day

The Collect

ALMIGHTY AND GRACIOUS FATHER, we give you thanks for the fruits of the earth in their season, and for the labors of those who harvest them. Make us, we pray, faithful stewards of your great bounty, in the provision for our necessities, and the relief of all who are in need, to the glory of your Name; through Jesus Christ our Lord, who lives and reigns with you and the Holy Spirit, one God, now and for ever. *Amen.*

ALMIGHTY AND GRACIOUS FATHER, we give thee thanks for the fruits of the earth in their season, and for the labors of those who harvest them. Make us, we beseech thee, faithful stewards of thy great bounty, in the provision for our necessities, and the relief of all who are in need, to the glory of thy Name; through Jesus Christ our Lord, who liveth and reigneth with thee and the Holy Spirit, one God, now and for ever. *Amen.*

The Psalms

[Entrance Psalm]	147:7-11
[Between Readings]	65:9-14

The Lessons

Deuteronomy 8:6-11
James 1:16-21
Matthew 6:25-33

PROPER PREFACE OF TRINITY SUNDAY

At the celebration of the Holy Eucharist, the following Litany of Thanksgiving may be used in place of the Prayer of Intercession:

LET US GIVE THANKS to God our Father for all his gifts so freely bestowed upon us:
For the beauty and wonder of his creation, in earth and sky and sea,

We thank you, Lord.

For all that is gracious in the lives of men and women, revealing the image of Christ,

We thank you, Lord.

For our daily food and drink, our homes and families, and our friends,

We thank you, Lord.

For minds to think, and hearts to love, and hands to serve,

We thank you, Lord.

For health and strength to work, and leisure to rest and play,

We thank you, Lord.

For the brave and courageous who are patient in suffering, and faithful in adversity,

We thank you, Lord.

For all valiant seekers after truth, liberty, and justice.

We thank you, Lord.

For the communion of saints, in all times and places,

We thank you, Lord.

Above all, let us give thanks for the great promises and mercies given to us in Christ Jesus our Lord:

To him be praise and glory, with the Father and the Holy Spirit, now and for ever. Amen.

The Common of Saints

The festival of a saint is observed according to the rules of precedence set forth in The Calendar of the Church Year (pages 28-130). At the discretion of the Priest, and as appropriate, any of the prayers and lessons following may be used:

a) in the commemoration of a saint listed in the Calendar for which this Book provides no proper collect or lessons, or for which no other provision is made by authority of this Church. b) for the patronal festival of a saint not listed in the Calendar.

1. Of a Martyr

The Collect

ALMIGHTY GOD, by whose grace and power your holy martyr *N.* triumphed over suffering, and was faithful even to death: Grant us, who now remember him in thanksgiving, to be so faithful in our witness to you in this world, that we may receive with him the crown of everlasting life; through Jesus Christ our Lord, who lives and reigns with you and the Holy Spirit, one God, now and ever. *Amen.*

ALMIGHTY GOD, by whose grace and power thy holy martyr *N.* triumphed over suffering, and was faithful unto death: Grant us, who now remember him in thanksgiving, to be so faithful in our witness to thee in this world, that we may receive with him the crown of everlasting life; through Jesus Christ our Lord, who liveth and reigneth with thee and the Holy Spirit, one God, now and ever. *Amen.*

or this Collect:

ALMIGHTY AND ETERNAL GOD, who kindled the fire of faith and love in the heart of your blessed martyr *N.*: Grant, we pray, that as we rejoice in his triumph, we may have courage to bear with him reproach for the Name of our Lord Jesus Christ, who lives and reigns with you and the Holy Spirit, one God, now and for ever. *Amen.*

ALMIGHTY AND ETERNAL GOD, who didst enkindle the fire of faith and love in the heart of thy blessed martyr N.: Grant, we beseech thee, that as we rejoice in his triumph, so we may have courage to bear with him reproach for the Name of our Lord Jesus Christ, who liveth and reigneth with thee and the Holy Spirit, one God, now and for ever. *Amen.*

The Psalms

[Entrance Psalm]	126
[Between Readings]	121

The Lessons

2 Esdras 2:42-48		Ecclesiasticus 5:1-12
1 Peter 3:12-18	*or*	Revelation 7:13-17
Matthew 10:16-22		Luke 12:2-12

PROPER PREFACE OF ALL SAINTS

2. Of a Missionary

The Collect

ALMIGHTY AND EVERLASTING GOD, we thank you for your servant *N.*, whom you called to preach the gospel to the people of _____. Raise up, we pray, in this and every land, heralds and evangelists of your kingdom, that your Church may make known the immeasurable riches of our Savior Jesus Christ, who lives and reigns with you and the Holy Spirit, one God, now and for ever. *Amen.*

ALMIGHTY AND EVERLASTING GOD, we thank thee for thy servant *N.*, whom thou didst call to preach the gospel to the people of _____. Raise up, we pray, in this and every land, heralds and evangelists of thy kingdom, that thy Church may make known the immeasurable riches of our Savior Jesus Christ, who liveth and reigneth with thee and the Holy Spirit, one God, now and for ever. *Amen.*

The Psalms

[Entrance Psalm]	96:1-7
[Between Readings]	96:8-13

The Lessons

Isaiah 52:7-10
Acts 1:1-9
Luke 10:1-9

PROPER PREFACE OF ALL SAINTS

3. Of a Pastor

The Collect

FATHER IN HEAVEN, the good shepherd of your people, we thank you for your servant *N.*, who was faithful in the care and nurture of your flock; and we pray that we, following his example and the teaching of his holy life, may by your grace grow into the full manhood and stature of our Lord and Savior Jesus Christ, who lives and reigns with you and the Holy Spirit, one God, for ever and ever. *Amen.*

FATHER IN HEAVEN, good shepherd of thy people, we thank thee for thy servant *N.*, who was faithful in the care and nurture of thy flock; and we pray that we, following his example and the teaching of his holy life, may by thy grace grow into the full manhood and stature of our Lord and Savior Jesus Christ, who liveth and reigneth, with thee and the Holy Spirit, one God, for ever and ever. *Amen.*

The Psalms

| [Entrance Psalm] | 112:1-9 |
| [Between Readings] | 23 |

The Lessons

| Ezekiel 34:11-16 |
| 1 Peter 5:1-4 |
| John 21:15-17 |

PROPER PREFACE OF ALL SAINTS

4. Of a Theologian or Teacher

The Collect

O GOD, by whose Holy Spirit is given to one the word of wisdom, and to another the word of knowledge, and to another the word of faith: We praise your Name for the gifts of grace imparted to your servant N., and pray that by his teaching we may know you, the only true God, and Jesus Christ whom you have sent, and who now lives and reigns with you and the Holy Spirit, one God, forever more. *Amen.*

O GOD, who by thy Holy Spirit dost give to one the word of wisdom, and to another the word of knowledge, and to another the word of faith: We praise thy Name for the gifts of grace imparted to thy servant N., and we pray that by his teaching we may know thee, the only true God, and Jesus Christ whom thou hast sent, and who now liveth and reigneth with thee and the Holy Spirit, one God, for evermore. *Amen.*

The Psalms

| [Entrance Psalm] | 119:33-40 |
| [Between Readings] | 119:97-104 |

The Lessons

| Wisdom 7:7-14 |
| 1 Corinthians 2:6-10, 13-16 |
| John 17:18-23 |

PROPER PREFACE OF ALL SAINTS, OR OF TRINITY SUNDAY

5. Of a Monastic

The Collect

O GOD, whose blessed Son became poor that we through his poverty might be rich: Deliver us, we pray, from an inordinate love of this world, that, following the example of your servant N., we may serve you with singleness of heart, and attain to the riches of the world to come; through Jesus Christ our Lord, who lives and reigns with you in the unity of the Holy Spirit, one God, now and for ever. *Amen.*

O GOD, whose blessed Son became poor that we through his poverty might be rich: Deliver us, we beseech thee, from an inordinate love of this world, that, following the example of thy servant N., we may serve thee with singleness of heart, and attain to the riches of the world to come; through Jesus Christ our Lord, who liveth and reigneth with thee in the unity of the Holy Spirit, one God, now and for ever. *Amen.*

The Psalms

| [Entrance Psalm] | 134 |
| [Between Readings] | 139:13-18 |

The Lessons

| Song of Songs 8:6-7 |
| Philippians 3:7-15 |
| Luke 12:33-37 |

PROPER PREFACE OF ALL SAINTS

6. Of a Saint I

The Collect

ALMIGHTY GOD, by whose grace we are surrounded with so great a cloud of witnesses: Grant that we, encouraged by the good example of your servant N., may persevere in running the race that is set before us, until at last, through your mercy, we with them attain to your eternal joy, through him who is the author and perfecter of our faith, your Son Jesus Christ our Lord, who lives and reigns with you and the Holy Spirit, one God, now and ever. *Amen.*

ALMIGHTY GOD, who hast surrounded us with so great a cloud of witnesses: Grant that we, encouraged by the good example of thy servant N., may persevere in running the race that is set before us, until at length, through thy mercy, we with them attain to thine eternal joy; through him who is the author and finisher of our faith, thy Son Jesus Christ our Lord, who liveth and reigneth with thee and the Holy Spirit, one God, now and ever. *Amen.*

The Psalms

[Entrance Psalm]	1
[Between Readings]	15

The Lessons

Micah 6:6-8		Wisdom 3:1-9
Hebrews 12:1-2	*or*	Philippians 4:4-9
Matthew 25:31-40		Luke 6:17-23

PROPER PREFACE OF ALL SAINTS

6. Of a Saint II

The Collect

O GOD, you have brought us near to an innumerable company of angels, and to the spirits of just men made perfect: Grant us during our earthly pilgrimage to abide in their fellowship, and in our heavenly country to become partakers of their joy; through Jesus Christ our Lord, who lives and reigns in glory with you and the Holy Spirit, one God, now and for ever. *Amen.*

    O GOD, who hast brought us near to an innumerable company of angels, and to the spirits of just men made perfect: Grant us during our earthly pilgrimage to abide in their fellowship, and in our heavenly country to become partakers of their joy; through Jesus Christ our Lord, who liveth and reigneth in glory with thee and the Holy Spirit, one God, now and for ever. *Amen.*

The Psalms

[Entrance Psalm]	1
[Between Readings]	15

The Lessons

Micah 6:6-8		Wisdom 3:1-9
Hebrews 2:1-2	or	Philippians 4:4-9
Matthew 25:31-40		Luke 6:17-23

PROPER PREFACE OF ALL SAINTS

6. Of a Saint III

The Collect

ALMIGHTY AND EVERLASTING GOD, who enkindled the flame of your love in the heart of your servant *N.*: Grant to us, your humble servants, a like faith and power of love; that, as we rejoice in her triumph, we may profit by her example; through Jesus Christ our Lord, who lives and reigns with you and the Holy Spirit, one God, now and for ever. *Amen.*

ALMIGHTY AND EVERLASTING GOD, who didst enkindle the flame of thy love in the heart of thy servant *N.*: Grant to us, thy humble servants, the same faith and power of love; that, as we rejoice in her triumph, we may profit by her example; through Jesus Christ our Lord, who liveth and reigneth with thee and the Holy Spirit, one God, now and for ever. *Amen.*

The Psalms

| [Entrance Psalm] | 63:1-8 |
| [Between Readings] | 34:3-10 |

The Lessons

| Ecclesiasticus 2:7-11 |
| 1 Corinthians 1:26-31 |
| Matthew 25:1-13 |

PROPER PREFACE OF ALL SAINTS

Special Occasions

The following are provided for special celebrations of the Holy Eucharist, in accordance with the rules set forth in The Calendar of the Church Year.

1. Of the Holy Trinity

The Collect

ALMIGHTY GOD, whose eternal Being of glorious majesty and perfect love has been revealed to your Church as one God in Trinity of Persons: Give us grace to abide steadfast in the confession of this faith, and constant in our worship of you, in spirit and in truth, who live and reign, one God, Father, Son, and Holy Spirit, now and for ever. *Amen.*

ALMIGHTY GOD, who hast revealed to thy Church thine eternal Being of glorious majesty and perfect love as one God in Trinity of Persons: Give us grace to abide steadfast in the confession of this faith, and constant in our worship of thee in spirit and in truth, who livest and reignest, one God, Father, Son, and Holy Spirit, now and for ever. *Amen.*

The Psalms

| [Entrance Psalm] | 148:1-6 |
| [Between Readings] | 148:7-13 |

The Lessons

| Exodus 3:11-15 |
| Romans 11:33-36 |
| Matthew 28:18-20 |

PROPER PREFACE OF TRINITY SUNDAY

2. Of the Holy Spirit

The Collect

ALMIGHTY AND MOST MERCIFUL GOD, grant that the indwelling of your Holy Spirit in our hearts may enlighten us by your truth and strengthen us for your service; through Jesus Christ our Lord, who lives and reigns with you in the unity of the Spirit, one God, now and for ever. *Amen.*

ALMIGHTY AND MOST MERCIFUL GOD grant, we beseech thee, that by the indwelling of the Holy Spirit, we may be enlightened and strengthened for thy service; through Jesus Christ our Lord, who liveth and reigneth with thee in the unity of the same Spirit, one God, now and for ever. *Amen.*

The Psalms

[Entrance Psalm]	139:6-11
[Between Readings]	51:10-13

The Lessons

Isaiah 61:1-3
1 Corinthians 12:4-14
Luke 11:9-13

PROPER PREFACE OF PENTECOST

3. Of the Holy Angels

The Collect

EVERLASTING GOD, by whom the ministries of angels and men have been ordained and constituted in a wonderful order: Mercifully grant that, as your holy angels always serve and worship you in heaven, so by your appointment they may help and defend us on earth; through Jesus Christ our Lord, who lives and reigns with you and the Holy Spirit, one God, now and ever. *Amen.*

EVERLASTING GOD, who hast ordained and constituted the ministries of angels and men in a wonderful order: Mercifully grant that, as thy holy angels always serve and worship thee in heaven, so by thy appointment they may help and defend us on earth; through Jesus Christ our Lord, who liveth and reigneth with thee and the Holy Spirit, one God, now and ever. *Amen.*

The Psalms

[Entrance Psalm]	103:19-22
[Between Readings]	104:1-4

The Lessons

Daniel 7: 9-10a
Revelation 5:11-14
John 1:47-51

PROPER PREFACE OF TRINITY SUNDAY

4. Of the Incarnation

The Collect

ALMIGHTY FATHER, by whom the world has been filled with the new light of your beloved Son, the incarnate Word: Grant, we pray, that as he kindles the flame of faith and love in our hearts, so his light may shine forth in our lives, who now lives and reigns with you in the unity of the Holy Spirit, one God, now and for ever. *Amen.*

ALMIGHTY FATHER, who has filled the world with the new light of thy beloved Son, the incarnate Word: Grant, we beseech thee, that as he enkindles the flame of faith and love in our hearts, so his light may shine forth in our lives; the same thy Son, Jesus Christ our Lord, who liveth and reigneth with thee in the unity of the Holy Spirit, one God, now and for ever. *Amen.*

The Psalms

| [Entrance Psalm] | 113 |
| [Between Readings] | 111:1-4,8-9 |

The Lessons

| Isaiah 11:1-10 |
| 1 John 4:1-11 |
| Luke 1:26-38 |

PROPER PREFACE OF THE INCARNATION

5. Of the Holy Eucharist

Especially suitable for Thursdays.

The Collect

GOD OUR FATHER, whose Son our Lord Jesus Christ gave us in this wonderful sacrament the memorial of his passion: Grant us so to reverence the sacred mysteries of his Body and Blood, that we may always discern within ourselves the fruit of his redemption, who now lives and reigns with you in the unity of the Holy Spirit, one God, for ever and ever. *Amen.*

O GOD OUR FATHER, whose Son our Lord Jesus Christ hath given us in this wonderful sacrament the memorial of his passion: Grant us so to reverence the sacred mysteries of his Body and Blood, that we may ever perceive within ourselves the fruit of his redemption, who now liveth and reigneth with thee in the unity of the Holy Spirit, one God, for ever and ever. *Amen.*

The Psalms

| [Entrance Psalm] | 145:14-18 |
| [Between Readings] | 116:11-16 |

The Lessons

| Deuteronomy 8:2-3 |
| Revelation 19:1-2a, 4-9 |
| John 6:47-59 |

PROPER PREFACE OF THE INCARNATION

6. Of the Holy Cross

Especially suitable for Fridays.

The Collect

ALMIGHTY GOD, whose beloved Son for our sake willingly endured the agony and shame of the Cross: Give us courage and patience to take up our cross and follow him, who lives and reigns with you and the Holy Spirit, one God, now and for ever. *Amen.*

ALMIGHTY GOD, whose beloved Son for our sake willingly endured the agony and shame of the Cross: Give us courage and patience to take up our cross and follow him, who liveth and reigneth with thee and the Holy Spirit, one God, now and for ever. *Amen.*

The Psalms

| [Entrance Psalm] | 56:1-4 |
| [Between Readings] | 40:5-10 |

The Lessons

| Isaiah 52:12-15; 53:10-12 |
| 1 Corinthians 1:18-24 |
| John 12:23-33 |

PROPER PREFACE OF HOLY WEEK

7. For all Baptized Christians

Especially suited for Saturdays.

The Collect

GRANT, LORD GOD, to all who have been baptized into the death and resurrection of your Son our Savior Jesus Christ, that, as we have put away the old life of sin, so we may be renewed in the spirit of our minds, and live in righteousness and true holiness; through Jesus Christ our Lord, who now lives and reigns with you in the unity of the Holy Spirit, one God, for ever and ever. *Amen.*

GRANT, O LORD GOD, to all who have been baptized into the death and resurrection of thy Son our Savior Jesus Christ, that, as we have put away the old life of sin, so we may be renewed in the spirit of our minds, and live in righteousness and true holiness; through Jesus Christ our Lord, who now liveth and reigneth with thee in the unity of the Holy Spirit, one God, for ever and ever. *Amen.*

The Psalms

[Entrance Psalm]	18:1-7
[Between Readings]	16:9-12

The Lessons

Jeremiah 17:7-8
Roman 6:3-11
Mark 10:35-45

PROPER PREFACE OF LENT, OR OF BAPTISM

8. The Commemoration of all Faithful Departed

The Collect

ETERNAL LORD GOD, by whom all souls are held in life: Give, we pray, to your whole Church in paradise and on earth, your light and your peace; and grant that we, following the good examples of those who have served you here and are now at rest, may at the last enter with them into your unending joy; through Jesus Christ our Lord, who lives and reigns with you in the unity of the Holy Spirit, one God, now and ever. *Amen.*

O ETERNAL LORD GOD, who holdest all souls in life: Give, we beseech thee, to thy whole Church in paradise and on earth, thy light and thy peace; and grant that we, following the good examples of those who have served thee here and are now at rest, may at the last enter with them into thine unending joy; through Jesus Christ our Lord, who liveth and reigneth with thee in the unity of the Holy Spirit, one God, now and ever. *Amen.*

The Psalms

| [Entrance Psalm] | 36:5-10 |
| [Between Readings] | 103:15-22 |

The Lessons

| Isaiah 25:6-9, *or* Wisdom 3:1-9 |
| 1 Corinthians 15:50-58 |
| John 11:21-27 |

PROPER PREFACE OF THE COMMEMORATION OF THE DEAD

At the discretion of the Priest, and when appropriate, any of the Collects, Psalms, and Lessons appointed in the office for the Burial of the Dead may be used in place of those given above.

9. Of the Reign of Christ

The Collect

ALMIGHTY AND EVERLASTING GOD, whose will it is to restore all things in your well-beloved Son, the King of kings and Lord of lords: Mercifully grant that the peoples of the earth, divided and enslaved by sin, may be freed and brought together under his most gracious rule, who lives and reigns with you and the Holy Spirit, one God, now and for ever. *Amen.*

ALMIGHTY AND EVERLASTING GOD, who didst will to restore all things in thy well-beloved Son, the King of kings, and Lord of lords: Mercifully grant that the peoples of the earth, divided and enslaved by sin, may be freed and brought together under his most gracious rule, who liveth and reigneth with thee and the Holy Spirit, one God, now and for ever. *Amen.*

The Psalms

| [Entrance Psalm] | 99:1-5 |
| [Between Readings] | 21:1-6 |

The Lessons

| Daniel 7:13-14 |
| Colossians 1:12-20 |
| John 18:33-37 |

PROPER PREFACE OF ASCENSION

10. On the Anniversary of the Dedication of a Church

The Collect

ALMIGHTY GOD, to whose glory we celebrate the dedication of this house of prayer: We give you thanks for the fellowship of those who have used it; and we pray that all who seek you here may find you, and be filled with your joy and peace; through Jesus Christ our Lord, who lives and reigns with you in the unity of the Holy Spirit, one God, now and for ever. *Amen.*

ALMIGHTY GOD, to whose glory we celebrate the dedication of this house of prayer: We give thee thanks for the fellowship of those who have used it; and we pray that all who seek thee here may find thee, and be filled with thy joy and peace; through Jesus Christ our Lord, who liveth and reigneth with thee in the unity of the Holy Spirit, one God, now and for ever. *Amen.*

The Psalms

| [Entrance Psalm] | 122 |
| [Between Readings] | 84:1-7 |

The Lessons

| 1 Kings 8:22-30 |
| 1 Peter 2:1-9 |
| Matthew 21:12-16 |

PROPER PREFACE OF TRINITY SUNDAY

11. For a Church Convention

The Collect

ALMIGHTY AND EVERLASTING FATHER, who gave us the Holy Spirit to abide with us for ever: Bless, we pray, with his grace and presence the Bishops and other

Clergy, and the Laity here assembled in your Name; that your Church, being preserved in true faith and godly discipline, may fulfill all the mind of him who loves it and gave himself for it, your Son our Savior Jesus Christ, who lives and reigns with you and the Holy Spirit, one God, now and ever. *Amen.*

Almighty and Everlasting Father, who hast given us the Holy Spirit to abide with us for ever: Bless, we beseech thee, with his grace and presence the Bishops and other Clergy, and the Laity here assembled in thy Name; that thy Church, being preserved in true faith and godly discipline, may fulfill all the mind of him who loves it and gave himself for it, thy Son our Savior Jesus Christ, who liveth and reigneth with thee and the same Spirit, one God, now and ever. *Amen.*

The Psalms

[Entrance Psalm]	146
[Between Readings]	125

The Lessons

Isaiah 55
2 Corinthians 4:1-10
John 15:1-8

PROPER PREFACE OF PENTECOST, OR OF THE SEASON

12. For Education

The Collect

Almighty God, the fountain of all wisdom: Enlighten by your Holy Spirit those who teach and those who learn, that, rejoicing in the knowledge of your truth, they may worship and serve you from generation to generation; through Jesus Christ our Lord, who lives and reigns with you in the unity of the Holy Spirit, one God, now and for ever. *Amen.*

Almighty God, the fountain of all wisdom: Enlighten by thy Holy Spirit those who teach and those who learn, that, rejoicing in the knowledge of thy truth, they may worship and serve thee from generation to generation; through Jesus Christ our Lord, who liveth and reigneth with thee in the unity of the same Spirit, one God, now and for ever. *Amen.*

The Psalms

| [Entrance Psalm] | 78:1-8 |
| [Between Readings] | 25:3-9 |

The Lessons

| Deuteronomy 6:4-9, 20-25 |
| 2 Timothy 3:14-4:5 |
| Matthew 11:25-30 |

PROPER PREFACE OF THE SEASON

13. For the Ministry

Ember Days

The following propers are used as appropriate to times and occasions.

The traditional days of Ordination, or Ember Days, are the Wednesdays, Fridays, and Saturdays after the Third Sunday in Advent, the First Sunday in Lent, the Day of Pentecost, and Holy Cross Day.

I

Especially suitable at the time of Ordination.

The Collect

ALMIGHTY GOD, the giver of all good gifts, who of your divine providence appointed various Orders in your Church: Give your grace, we humbly pray, to all who are now called to any office and ministration for your people; and so replenish them with the truth of your doctrine, and endue them with holiness of life, that they may faithfully serve before you to the glory of your great Name, and to the benefit of your holy Church; through Jesus Christ our Lord, who lives and reigns with you in the unity of the Holy Spirit, one God, now and ever. *Amen.*

ALMIGHTY GOD, the giver of all good gifts, who of thy divine providence hast appointed various Orders in thy Church: Give thy grace, we humbly beseech thee, to all who are now called to any office and ministration for thy people; and so replenish them with the truth of thy doctrine, and endue them with holiness of life, that they may faithfully serve before thee to the glory of thy great Name, and to the benefit of thy holy Church; through Jesus Christ our Lord, who liveth and reigneth with thee in the unity of the Holy Spirit, one God, now and ever. *Amen.*

The Psalms

[Entrance Psalm]	132:8-18
[Between Readings]	27:1-7

The Lessons

Numbers 11:16-17, 24-29
1 Corinthians 3:5-11
John 4:31-38

PROPER PREFACE OF APOSTLES

13. For the Ministry II

Especially suitable at times of prayer for the increase of ministries in the Church.

The Collect

ALMIGHTY GOD, whose Son entrusted to the hands of men the ministry of reconciliation: Inspire by your Holy Spirit the hearts and minds of many to give themselves to this ministry, that all mankind may be drawn to your blessed kingdom; through Jesus Christ your Son our Lord, who lives and reigns with you and the Holy Spirit, one God, now and for ever. *Amen.*

ALMIGHTY GOD, whose Son hath entrusted to the hands of men and ministry of reconciliation: Inspire by thy Holy Spirit the hearts and minds of many to give themselves to this ministry, that all mankind may be drawn to thy blessed kingdom; through Jesus Christ thy Son our Lord, who liveth and reigneth with thee and the same Spirit, one God, now and for ever. *Amen.*

The Psalms

[Entrance Psalm]	61
[Between Readings]	63:1-9

The Lessons

1 Samuel 3:1-10
Ephesians 4:11-16
Matthew 9:35-38

PROPER PREFACE OF THE SEASON

13. For the Ministry III

Especially suitable for all Christians in their vocation and ministry.

The Collect

ALMIGHTY AND EVERLASTING GOD, by whose Spirit the whole company of your faithful people is governed and sanctified: Receive our prayers which we now offer before you for all members of your holy Church, that in their vocation and ministry they may truly and devoutly serve you, to the glory of your Name; through our Lord and Savior Jesus Christ, who lives and reigns with you in the unity of the Holy Spirit, one God, now and ever. *Amen.*

ALMIGHTY AND EVERLASTING GOD, by whose Spirit the whole body of the Church is governed and sanctified: Receive our supplications and prayers, which we offer before thee for all members of thy holy Church, that every member of the same, in his vocation and ministry, may truly and godly serve thee; through our Lord and Savior Jesus Christ, who liveth and reigneth with thee in the unity of the Holy Spirit, one God, now and ever. *Amen.*

The Psalms

| [Entrance Psalm] | 15 |
| [Between Readings] | 112:1-9 |

The Lessons

| Exodus 19:3-8 |
| 1 Peter 4:7-11 |
| Matthew 16:24-27 |

PROPER PREFACE OF BAPTISM, OR THE SEASON

14. For the Mission of the Church I

The Collect

O GOD, who made of one blood all nations of men to dwell on the face of the whole earth, and sent your blessed Son to preach peace to those who are far and to those who are near: Grant that all men everywhere may seek after you and find you; bring the nations into your fold, pour out your Spirit upon all mankind, and hasten your kingdom; through Jesus Christ your Son our Lord, who lives and reigns with you and the Holy Spirit, one God, now and for ever. *Amen.*

O GOD, who hast made of one blood all nations of men to dwell on the face of the whole earth, and didst send thy blessed Son to preach peace to those who are far off and to those who are nigh: Grant that all men everywhere may seek after thee and find thee; bring the nations into thy fold, pour out thy Spirit upon all mankind, and hasten thy kingdom; through Jesus Christ thy Son our Lord, who liveth and reigneth with thee and the Holy Spirit, one God, now and for ever. *Amen.*

The Psalms

[Entrance Psalm]	96
[Between Readings]	66:1-7

The Lessons

Isaiah 2:2-4		Isaiah 49:5-13
Ephesians 2:13-22	*or*	Ephesians 3:1-12
Luke 10:1-9		Matthew 28:16-20

PROPER PREFACE OF THE SEASON, OR OF APOSTLES

14. For the Mission of the Church II

The Collect

O GOD of all nations of the earth: Remember the multitudes who have been created in your image, but have not known the redeeming work of our Savior Jesus Christ; and grant that, by the prayers and labors of your holy Church, they may be delivered from unbelief, and brought to worship you, through him who is the resurrection and the life of all men, your Son Jesus Christ our Lord, who lives and reigns with you and the Holy Spirit, one God, now and ever. *Amen.*

O GOD of all the nations of the earth: Remember the multitudes who have been created in thine image, but have not known the redeeming work of our Savior Jesus Christ; and grant that, by the prayers and labors of thy holy Church, they may be delivered from unbelief, and brought to worship thee, through him who is the resurrection and the life of all men, the same thy Son Jesus Christ our Lord, who liveth and reigneth with thee and the Holy Spirit, one God, now and ever. *Amen.*

The Psalms

[Entrance Psalm]	96
[Between Readings]	66:1-7

The Lessons

Isaiah 2:2-4		Isaiah 49:5-13
Ephesians 2:13-22	*or*	Ephesians 3:1-12
Luke 10:1-9		Matthew 28:16-20

PROPER PREFACE OF THE SEASON, OR OF APOSTLES

15. For the Nation

The proper for Independence Day (page 230) may be used in place of the following:

The Collect

LORD GOD ALMIGHTY, who made all the peoples of the earth for your glory, and summon all nations to serve in freedom and peace: Grant to the people of our country a zeal for righteousness, and the strength of self-control, that we may exercise our liberty in justice and compassion; through Jesus Christ our Lord, who lives and reigns with you and the Holy Spirit, one God, in glory everlasting. *Amen.*

LORD GOD ALMIGHTY, who hast made all nations of the earth for thy glory, to serve thee in freedom and peace: Grant to the people of our country a zeal for righteousness, and the strength of self-control, that we may exercise our liberty in accordance with thy gracious will; through Jesus Christ our Lord, who liveth and reigneth with thee and the Holy Spirit, one God, in glory everlasting. *Amen.*

The Psalms

[Entrance Psalm]	67
[Between Readings]	47

The Lessons

Isaiah 26:1-8
Romans 13:1-10
Mark 12:13-17

PROPER PREFACE OF TRINITY SUNDAY

16. For Peace

The Collect

ALMIGHTY GOD, from whom all thoughts of truth and peace proceed: Kindle in the hearts of all men the true love of peace; and guide with your pure and peaceable wisdom those who take counsel for the nations of the earth, that in tranquillity your kingdom may go forward, until the earth is filled with the knowledge of your love; through Jesus Christ our Lord, who lives and reigns with you in the unity of the Holy Spirit, one God, now and ever. *Amen.*

ALMIGHTY GOD, from whom all thoughts of truth and peace proceed: Kindle, we pray thee, in the hearts of all men the true love of peace; and guide with thy pure and peaceable wisdom those who take counsel for the nations of the earth, that in tranquillity thy kingdom may go forward, until the earth is filled with the knowledge of thy love; through Jesus Christ our Lord, who liveth and reigneth with thee in the unity of the Holy Spirit, one God, now and ever. *Amen.*

The Psalms

| [Entrance Psalm] | 85:7-13 |
| [Between Readings] | 119:161-168 |

The Lessons

| Micah 4:1-5 |
| Ephesians 2:13-18 |
| John 16:23-33 |

17. For Rogation Days

The following propers may be used at any time, as appropriate.

The traditional Rogation Days occur on the Monday, Tuesday, and Wednesday before Ascension Day.

I

For fruitful seasons

The Collect

ALMIGHTY GOD, Lord of heaven and earth: We humbly pray that your gracious providence may give and preserve to our use the harvests of the land and sea, and may prosper all who labor to gather them; that we, who are constantly receiving your bounty, may always give thanks to you, the giver of all good things; through Jesus Christ our Lord. *Amen.*

ALMIGHTY GOD, Lord of heaven and earth: We humbly pray that thy gracious providence may give and preserve to our use the harvests of the land and sea, and may prosper all who labor to gather them; that we, who constantly receive from thy bounty, may always give thanks to thee, the giver of all good things; through Jesus Christ our Lord. *Amen.*

The Psalms

| [Entrance Psalm] | 147:5-11 |
| [Between Readings] | 144:9-15 |

The Lessons

| Ezekiel 34:25-31 |
| 1 Corinthians 3:6-9 |
| Luke 11:5-13 |

PROPER PREFACE OF THE SEASON

17. Rogation Days II

For commerce and industry

The Collect

O GOD, our Creator, from whom all men receive their appointed work on earth: Give your blessing, we pray, to those who are engaged in commerce and industry, that, receiving the due reward of their labors, they may supply the needs of men in humble and unselfish service; through Jesus Christ our Lord. *Amen.*

O GOD, our Creator, from whom all men receive their appointed work on earth: Give thy blessing, we beseech thee, to those who are engaged in commerce and industry, that, receiving the due reward of their labors, they may supply the needs of men in humble and unselfish service; through Jesus Christ our Lord. *Amen.*

The Psalms

| [Entrance Psalm] | 107:1-9 |
| [Between Readings] | 107:21-32 |

The Lessons

| Acts 20:32-35 |
| Romans 12:9-18 |
| Matthew 6:19-24 |

PROPER PREFACE OF THE SEASON

17. Rogation Days III

For stewardship of creation

The Collect

ALMIGHTY FATHER, whose hand is open to fill all things living with plenteousness: Make us ever thankful for your great goodness; and grant that we, remembering the account which we must one day give, may be faithful stewards of your bounty; through Jesus Christ our Lord. *Amen.*

ALMIGHTY FATHER, whose hand is open to fill all things living with plenteousness: Make us ever thankful for thy great goodness; and grant that we, remembering the account which we must one day give, may be faithful stewards of thy bounty; through Jesus Christ our Lord. *Amen.*

The Psalms

| [Entrance Psalm] | 24:1-6 |
| [Between Readings] | 104:1, 13-15, 23-31 |

The Lessons

| Job 38:1-18 |
| 1 Timothy 6:7-10, 17-19 |
| Luke 12:16-31 |

PROPER PREFACE OF THE SEASON

18. For the Sick

The Collect

HEAVENLY FATHER, Giver of all life and health: Comfort and strengthen by your healing power your sick servants for whom our prayers are offered, and bless those who minister to them; that they may have confidence and peace in your loving care; through Jesus Christ our Lord. *Amen.*

HEAVENLY FATHER, Giver of all life and health: Comfort and strengthen by thy healing power thy sick servants for whom our prayers are offered, and bless those who minister to them; that they may have confidence and peace in thy loving care; through Jesus Christ our Lord. *Amen.*

The Psalms

| [Entrance Psalm] | 3 |
| [Between Readings] | 13 |

The Lessons

| 2 Kings 20:1-5 |
| James 5:13-16 |
| Mark 2:1-12 |

PROPER PREFACE OF THE SEASON

The Minister may at his discretion select other collects, psalms, and lessons from the Ministration to the Sick.

19. For Social Justice

The Collect

ALMIGHTY GOD, who created man in your own image: Grant us grace fearlessly to contend against evil, and to make no peace with oppression; and, that we may reverently use our freedom, help us to employ it in the maintenance of justice among men and nations, to the glory of your holy Name; through Jesus Christ our Lord, who lives and reigns with you and the Holy Spirit, one God, now and for ever. *Amen.*

ALMIGHTY GOD, who hast created man in thine own image: Grant us grace fearlessly to contend against evil, and to make no peace with oppression; and, that we may reverently use our freedom, help us to employ it in the maintenance of justice among men and nations, to the glory of thy holy Name; through Jesus Christ our Lord, who liveth and reigneth with thee and the Holy Spirit, one God, now and for ever. *Amen.*

The Psalms

| [Entrance Psalm] | 72:1-4, 12-14 |
| [Between Readings] | 75 |

The Lessons

| Isaiah 42:1-8 |
| James 2:5-9, 12-17 |
| Matthew 10:32-42 |

PROPER PREFACE OF THE SEASON

20. For Social Service

The Collect

HEAVENLY FATHER, whose blessed Son came not to be served but to serve: Bless all, we pray, who, following in his steps, give themselves to the service of their fellow men; that with wisdom, patience, and courage, they may minister in his Name to the suffering, the friendless, and the needy; for the love of him who laid down his life for us, your Son our Savior Jesus Christ. *Amen.*

HEAVENLY FATHER, whose blessed Son came not to be ministered unto but to minister: Bless all, we pray thee, who, following in his steps, give themselves to the service of their fellow men; that with wisdom, patience, and courage, they may minister in his Name to the suffering, the friendless, and the needy; for the love of him who laid down his life for us, thy Son our Savior Jesus Christ. *Amen.*

The Psalms

| [Entrance Psalm] | 146 |
| [Between Readings] | 22:23-28 |

The Lessons

| Zechariah 8:3-12, 16-17 |
| 1 Peter 4:7-11 |
| Mark 10:42-52 |

PROPER PREFACE OF THE SEASON

21. For the Unity of the Church

The Collect

ALMIGHTY FATHER, whose blessed Son before his passion prayed for his disciples that they might be one, even as you and he are one: Grant that, bound together in love and obedience to you, your Church may be united in one body by the one Spirit; that the world may believe in him whom you have sent, your Son our Lord Jesus Christ, who lives and reigns with you in the unity of the Holy Spirit, one God, now and ever. *Amen.*

ALMIGHTY FATHER, whose blessed Son before his passion prayed for his disciples that they might be one, even as thou and he are one: Grant that, bound together in love and in obedience to thee, thy Church may be united in one body by the one Spirit; that the world may believe in him whom thou hast sent, thy Son our Lord Jesus Christ, who liveth and reigneth with thee in the unity of the Holy Spirit, one God, now and ever. *Amen.*

The Psalms

[Entrance Psalm]	122
[Between Readings]	87

The Lessons

Isaiah 35
Ephesians 4:1-6
John 17:15-23

PROPER PREFACE OF BAPTISM, OR OF TRINITY SUNDAY

22. For Vocation in Daily Work

The Collect

ALMIGHTY GOD, heavenly Father, whose glory and handiwork are shown forth in the heavens and in the earth: Deliver us, we pray, in our several occupations from selfish love of riches, that we may do the work which you give us, with singleness of heart as your servants, and to the benefit of our fellow men; for the sake of him who came among us as one that serves, your Son Jesus Christ our Lord. *Amen.*

ALMIGHTY GOD, heavenly Father, who showest forth thy glory and handiwork in the heavens and in the earth: Deliver us, we beseech thee, in our several occupations from selfish love of riches, that we may do the work which thou givest us, with singleness of heart as thy servants, and to the benefit of our fellow men; for the sake of him who came among us as one that serveth, thy Son Jesus Christ our Lord. *Amen.*

The Psalms

| [Entrance Psalm] | 1 |
| [Between Readings] | 8 |

The Lessons

| Ecclesiastes 3:1, 9-13 |
| 1 Peter 2:11-17 |
| Matthew 6:19-24 |

PROPER PREFACE OF THE SEASON

PRAYER BOOK STUDIES 20: THE ORDINATION OF BISHOPS, PRIESTS, AND DEACONS

1970

PREFACE

The ordained ministry of the Church has been under intensive consideration during recent years. The rites of ordination, therefore, have been an important subject for the Standing Liturgical Commission. The forms of ordination here proposed are being put forward for the serious consideration of all churchmen. It is hoped that these forms will provide a clearer and better understanding of the orders of Bishops, Priests, and Deacons, and of their mission to serve God and man.

The Standing Liturgical Commission proposed in 1957 a very modest revision of the rites of ordination.* Since then, the revision of such rites in other parts of the Christian world has gone much further in restoring a clearer and more ancient pattern of solemn prayer and ceremonial action. The pace of revision has been further accelerated by the demand for a more contemporary liturgical language, and by the revision of eucharistic liturgies into which the ordination rites are fitted. The restoration, in many parts of the Christian World of the classic liturgical pattern of the Proclamation of the Word, followed by the Offertory, the Consecration, the Breaking of the Bread, and Communion, has unavoidably affected the rites of ordination.

Following the General Convention of 1967, when the Standing Liturgical Commission was directed to proceed with the preparation of a revised Book of Common Prayer, a Drafting Committee was appointed to frame new rites of ordination. The Committee was constituted as follows:

The Reverend H. Boone Porter, Jr., member of the Standing Liturgical Commission and Chairman of the Drafting Committee;
The Reverend Canon Frederick H. Belden,
The Right Reverend Harvey D. Butterfield,
The Reverend E. Otis Charles,
The Right Reverend John S. Higgins,†
The Reverend Harry H. Jones,
Mrs. William M. Sloan.

---

* The Standing Liturgical Commission: The Ordinal; *Prayer Book Studies VIII*, New York: The Church Pension Fund; 1957.

† Bishop Higgins was able to serve only during the first half of the triennium.

The Committee alternated its meetings between the Berkeley Divinity School at New Haven, Conn., and the home of Mr. and Mrs. William Sloan in Providence, R.I. In the course of its work the Committee produced no fewer than twelve separate reports. In accordance with the Plan of Revision approved by the General Convention, the Committee's drafts, as they proceeded through successive stages, were distributed to the 260 Consultants of the Standing Liturgical Commission. Many others throughout the country also read and criticized the Committee's work as it developed. Contacts and collaboration were also possible with some of those who are engaged in similar undertakings in other parts of the world. Through their comments, criticisms and suggestions, the Consultants and other experts have made a large and invaluable contribution to the final result.

Indeed, the use of qualified Consultants, representative of a cross-section of the whole Church, is one of the distinctive characteristics of the present process of Prayer Book Revision. The Consultants included Bishops and Priests, men and women, teachers, doctors, writers, housewives and students. Their function was not only to read the successive texts and comment on them; they were invited to make suggestions and proposals, and many of them did.

Their number was expanded towards the end of the triennium, by the inclusion among them of Chairmen of diocesan liturgical commissions or committees. During the trial use of *The Liturgy of the Lord's Supper*, these diocesan bodies had acted as focal points for the distribution of Questionnaires to parishes and to priests within their dioceses, and subsequently they collated them and evaluated the results. In the course of this work, the members of the diocesan liturgical organs demonstrated a fine perception and understanding of the tasks assigned by the General Convention to the Standing Liturgical Commission, and the practical comments and observations they made on the work-in-progress have greatly enriched the resources available to the Commission. It is for this reason, among others, that a special role for members of these Commissions is suggested on page 293 of the Introduction.

The Standing Liturgical Commission repeatedly studied the work of the Drafting Committee, and at the end of 1969, the Commission adopted the forms for the ordination of Bishops, Priests and Deacons.

In offering this work to the Church, the Commission hopes that the rites of ordination here presented will receive careful study and reflection, and that they may commend themselves for trial use, under such conditions as the General Convention may set down. The Introduction is intended to provide the historical background and rationale of the rites. The Introduction also has the added value of providing a brief general survey of the recent revision of ordination rites, and a commentary on the subject as a whole. It is hoped that those who desire to pursue more detailed studies will find the Bibliography helpful.**

** The listing of secondary works is limited to those published since World War II, and attention is mainly given to works in English. Within the books cited, references can be found to earlier works and to publications in other languages.

The Commission desires to place on record its sincere appreciation to all who have contributed in various ways to make this publication possible: to the members of the Drafting Committee; to the Commission's Consultants and other experts who gave generously of their time and attention; to the Dean and Faculty of Berkeley Divinity School and to Mr. and Mrs. William Sloan for their gracious hospitality to the Drafting Committee; to the Drafting Committee on Occasional Prayers and Thanksgivings, under the. Chairmanship of the Reverend Charles P. Price, for preparing the Litany for the Ministry of the Church; to the Reverend Norman C. Mealy, of the Joint Commission on Church Music, who noted the Litany for chant; to the Librarians of the George F. Mercer Jr. School of Theology for checking the Bibliography prepared by the Drafting Committee; to Mr. Alston Purvis, for the layout and typographical design of this Study; and finally to the Editorial Committee of the Standing Liturgical Commission, under the Chairmanship of the Reverend Robert Estill, for their careful and thorough review of the final text.††

The Commission invites all who see this Study, whatever may be their background or point of view, to contribute to the process of liturgical revision by sending their comments and suggestions to the Standing Liturgical Commission, 815 Second Avenue, New York 10017. All correspondence will be acknowledged, and all comments will be given serious consideration. To all who may assist in this way, the Commission offers its sincere thanks.

The Standing Liturgical Commission

Chilton Powell, *Chairman*
John W. Ashton
Dupuy Bateman, Jr.
James D. Dunning
Robert W. Estill
William C. Frey
Charles M. Guilbert, *Secretary*
Mrs. Richard Harbour
Joseph M. Harte
Louis B. Keiter
H. Boone Porter, Jr.
Charles P. Price

---

†† The Editorial Committee is constituted as follows: The Reverend Robert W. Estill, Chairman; the Reverend Donald L. Garfield, the Reverend Canon Charles M. Guilbert, the Reverend H. Boone Porter, Jr., and the Reverend Massey H. Shepherd, Jr., members; and Captain Howard Galley, C.A. and the Reverend Leo Malania, Co-ordinator for Prayer Book Revision, members *ex officio*.

Massey H. Shepherd, Jr., *Vice Chairman*
Jonathan G. Sherman
Charles W. F. Smith
Bonnell Spencer, O.H.C.
Albert R. Stuart
Leo Malania, *Co-ordinator*

Introduction to the Proposed Rites

The Christian Church has always proclaimed that Jesus Christ is our "great high priest," the only authentic mediator between God and man. All Christians, as members of Christ's Body, participate in his royal priesthood; we are a priestly people, a living temple consecrated by the Holy Spirit.[1]

The priesthood of Jesus Christ and the derivative priesthood of his baptized people do not eliminate the need for special priestly offices in the Christian community. The first followers of our Lord were called to be preachers of his Gospel, shepherds of souls, and ministers of the sacramental rites he left to his Church. In every succeeding generation, some Christians have been called and ordained to discharge these same responsibilities. In ordination they are given grace to perform their functions, and a solemn and authoritative expression of the burdens and the privileges which are entrusted to them both by God and by their fellow-Christians. At the same time, the ordained minister is, in certain respects being charged to fulfill in more specific ways the duties to which all Christians are called. The Christian clergyman is not being assigned to witness to the Gospel, to care for the poor, or to pray, so that other members of the Church can be dispensed from these activities. Rather, the pastor is to help his people in the fulfillment of what is their vocation as well as his. Seen in this light, the mission of the ordained minister is related organically to the mission of all the baptized. The ordained ministry finds its fulfillment in the enabling of the entire Christian community to exercise its ministry in the service of God and man.

It is the distinguishing mark of man that his life must be guided by goals, values, and a sense of meaning. It is the function of true religion to express, articulate, and celebrate the values and beliefs which make life worth living for human persons. The ordained minister is consecrated to this function. It is a uniquely holy and God-centered work; it is also a uniquely human and manly work. In the present period of history, when the nature and purpose of human existence are so widely questioned, the Church owes it to God and to humanity to interpret clearly the work of its chosen leaders.

1. The Three Sacred Orders

Leadership requires within itself certain differentiations of function and rank. First of all, by its very nature, leadership is a focus for unity. In the Christian Church, this is the distinctive responsibility of the Bishop. The word "bishop" derives from a Greek term meaning overseer or supervisor. The Bishop is the

---

1. Hebrews 3:1, 4:14, 7:17, *et passim*.

1 Peter 2:5, 9, Revelation 1:6, 5:10 (Cf. Exodus 19:6, Isaiah 61:6).

1 Corinthians 3:16-17, Ephesians 2:20-22.

living sign of the unity of the Church and the unity of the Gospel. Accordingly, there is entrusted to him the fullness and totality of ministerial authority and responsibility. To phrase this differently, the episcopate represents the total ministry which the Risen Lord entrusted to his Apostles. Because Baptism and the Eucharist are the pre-eminent sacraments of the unity of the Church, Bishops have a special responsibility for them. Collectively, the Bishops are the chief custodians and interpreters of the Church's faith. They are, in a unique sense, the priestly order of the Church.

Yet one individual cannot in fact do everything, and even if he could, he ought not to. The Christian Church, even at the local level, should never appear to be the projection of one personality. The Body of Christ, by its very nature, has different members performing different functions, and leadership itself calls for differentiation of functions. Although the New Testament does not clearly describe each order of ministry, it repeatedly speaks of the principle of differentiation.[2] Hence, since the first century of Christian history, the Bishop has been surrounded by a circle of other ministers who help him, while exercising their own genuine but subordinate leadership.[3]

There are essentially two ways of helping a leader. First, he can be helped by *assistants* who carry out his decisions in the performance of subordinate tasks. Secondly, the leader can be helped by *associates* who join with him in making decisions and in carrying out some of his tasks. These are basic principles in the functioning of leadership. The channels through which these functions are carried out in the Church are the orders of the ministry which God has provided.

Within the Church's ordained leadership, the assistants or subordinate ministers, are the Deacons. This word "deacon" comes from the Greek term for servant, attendant, or waiter.[4] The Deacon serves God by serving the Bishop and the people. His classic duties have been to help the Bishop as an attendant, secretary, and messenger; to carry out administrative duties in Church charities and welfare institutions; and literally, to be a waiter at the Lord's table.[5] Because of his subordination and his role as the servant of the poor, the Deacon in a special way stands for Jesus Christ, who came among us not to be served, but to serve, and to give his life for many.

---

2. Romans 12:4-8, 1 Corinthians 12:4-30, Ephesians 4:11-16.

3. It is not the purpose of this Introduction to trace every step of development from the New Testament to later, times, as there is already an extensive literature on this topic (See the Bibliography). The emphasis of the present discussion is simply on the functional differentiation of the orders.

4. The same Greek word is often used in the New Testament to mean a minister in a more general sense (*e.g.*, 2 Corinthians 3:6, 6:4). The two formal references to the order of Deacons are Philippians 1:1 and 1 Timothy 3:8-13. St. Stephen and his companions, Acts 6 and following, have often been assumed to be Deacons, although the text does not actually state this and many modern critics question the assumption. The narrative does provide, however, a rationale for the existence of a subordinate ministry.

5. See especially the chapter by E. R. Hardy in *The Diaconate Now*, edited by R. T. Nolan, 1968.

The associate ministers are the Priests. The term "priest" is an abbreviation of the Greek word *presbyteros*, which means elder, councilor, or board member.[6] The Priests constitute the presbytery, which is the council or senate of the Church in a particular region.[7] The Bishop is, of course, chairman of this council. Priests sit with the Bishop in making plans and decisions, and they stand with him as fellow-ministers in many of the rites and sacraments of the Church. In the absence of the Bishop, they preside in his place in the usual services of public worship and they lead the local congregations in their life and work.

In the earliest centuries of Christian history, pastoral, liturgical, and sacerdotal duties seem to have been largely in the Bishop's hands. Hence, he was frequently called the Christian High Priest, or Pontiff. From the fourth and fifth centuries onward, however, Bishops delegated many of these duties to Presbyters assigned to local congregations.[8] The Bishops devoted more of their own attention to administrative and governmental duties. Thus, the Priest, rather than the Bishop, came to be viewed as the sacerdotal person. Accordingly, the meaning of the word underwent a change. The Latin word *presbyter* originally meant councilor or Church-elder, but centuries later when English (and other modern European languages) had shortened Presbyter to Priest, it had come to carry new connotations, emphasizing the sacerdotal aspect of the ministry.

This led to serious misunderstandings and confusions. In the Greek and Latin Bibles and in early Christian writings, a single word (*sacerdos* in Latin, *hiereus* in Greek) is used to designate Christ as our great high Priest, the Bishop, and the general priesthood of baptized people. An entirely different word (*presbyter*) was used for the second order of the ordained ministry. English and other modern European languages have only one word—priest—to designate both the sacerdotal and the presbyteral aspects of the ministry.

At the time of the Reformation, some reformers wished to resolve this ambiguity by abolishing the word, priest; and replacing it by pastor, minister, elder, or by the ancient word, presbyter. The Counter-reformation sought, instead, to insist on the Latin word *sacerdos*, emphasizing the sacerdotality of the priesthood. Theological writings continue to reflect the possible ambiguity of the English

---

6. In the Bible this term, or its Hebrew equivalent, is used to designate the "aldermen" of towns in Palestine (e.g., Deuteronomy 21:2-6, Ruth 4:2) and the "senators" who sat in the Sanhedrin at Jerusalem (e.g., Matthew 21:23, Acts 4:5-8). In Jewish thought the Sanhedrin was prefigured in Numbers 11:16-30. *Presbyter* is later used in the New Testament to designate leaders in the Christian community (e.g., Acts 14:23, 15:2-6, James 5:14, etc.). Our English versions consistently translate it "elder" which is often misunderstood to mean merely an older man.

7. In the polity of The Episcopal Church, this is primarily embodied in the clerical order of the Diocesan Convention; but also, by representation, in the Standing Committee, the Ecclesiastical Courts, and other such bodies.

8. Among other summaries of this development, see *The Apostolic Ministry*, edited by K. E. Kirk (1946), especially pages 216-233 and 314-340, and D. N. Power, O.M.I., *Ministers of Christ and His Church* (1969).

word, priest. Thus, it can be said that Christ is our Priest (*sacerdos*), and that all baptized people are priests (*sacerdotes*); but it could hardly be said that Christ, or all Christians, are presbyters. Anglican tradition has sought to retain a hold on both horns of the dilemma. As presbyteral Priests, clergymen are called to work under the leadership of their Bishop and with one another in the second order of the ordained ministry. As sacerdotal Priests, they are to pronounce absolution and blessing, and officiate at the altar, doing so, not merely as the licensed deputies of the Bishop, but as the ordained representatives of Christ. In Anglican tradition, members of the second order of the ministry are also called to be pastors and teachers as well as priests, but the English word, priest, has come to contain all these meanings.

2. An Historical Survey

The Classical Rites of Ordination

Since New Testament times, ordination has essentially consisted of solemn prayer with the laying on of hands by those who already possess the authority to confer it.[9] It is preceded by the act of choosing or electing the candidates, an act which is also associated with fervent prayer as, in later times, on the Ember Days.[10] Ordination is followed by the introduction of the newly ordained into his new ministerial duties.

The oldest known text of the rites of ordination occurs in the *Apostolic Tradition*,[11] a book believed to have been written at Rome by a St. Hippolytus during the early years of the third century. Hippolytus' services are of special interest, for they strongly influenced ordination rites in almost all parts of the ancient Church, and they illustrate many of the principles we are considering.

In the order of Hippolytus, a Bishop is first elected by the people of the local Church. He is ordained on Sunday—the day our Lord rose from the dead, commissioned his Apostles, and bestowed on them his Holy Spirit. After silent prayer for the descent of the Spirit upon the Bishop-elect, an assembly of Bishops lay their hands on his head. This is both the scriptural gesture of blessing and a visible expression of their acceptance of the new Bishop into the episcopate. Then one of the Bishops says an extended prayer for the gift of the Holy Spirit to the ordinand. The prayer speaks of God the Father and Creator, of Abraham, and the leaders of the Old Testament. All of these allusions typify in some way the kind of ministry which the Bishop is to exercise as spiritual father of the people. The

---

9. Acts 6:3-8, 1 Timothy 4:14, 2 Timothy 1:6.

10. Cf. Luke 6:12-13 and Acts 1:24-25. The first of these passages appears to have influenced the custom of having ordinations on Ember Days, which, in the ancient Roman Church, were times when most of the night was spent in prayer.

11. See the Bibliography.

prayer goes on to petition that the new Bishop may have power to remit sins and to exercise the responsibilities entrusted to the Apostles by our Lord. The Bishop is to be the heir and witness to the whole history of salvation: his ministry is to embody here and now, within the Church, the biblical ministry which has continued in various forms down through the centuries. After the laying on of hands and prayer, comes the Kiss of Peace. The other Bishops at this time embrace their new colleague, and the clergy and people of the diocese greet and receive him as their new pastor—a very human but appropriate and meaningful act within the service. The eucharistic liturgy then proceeds with the Offertory. The new Bishop, now Father-in-God of his diocese, presides at the altar as chief celebrant.

The ordinations of Priests and Deacons follow much the same lines. They too were first elected or approved by the people. As leaders of the Church it was deemed important that they be the men whom their fellow-Christians knew, admired, and desired to have as ministers. They were not necessarily Church employees, for in many cases it was assumed that they would continue to earn their living by secular work, as St. Paul had encouraged his followers to do.[12] When a Deacon was ordained, his Bishop alone laid on hands since the Deacon was directly responsible to the Bishop for the performance of his duties. The Bishop recited a prayer alluding to Christ's obedience and service to God the Father, and petitioning for the Holy Spirit to give the Deacon care and diligence in his duties. The Priest, or Presbyter, on the other hand, was not ordained as a personal assistant to the Bishop. Rather, he was admitted to a corporate body, the presbytery, over which the Bishop presided. Accordingly, the other members of the presbytery joined the Bishop in laying hands on the new Presbyter's head. The Bishop recited a prayer referring to the Jewish elders who were associated with Moses,[13] and petitioning for the Holy Spirit to bestow wisdom and ability, to govern. As in the ordination of a Bishop, the Peace evidently followed and the new ministers were greeted and embraced. The Eucharist likewise continued, with the newly ordained, no doubt, joining the others of his order in carrying out his new liturgical duties. The Deacon, with other Deacons, would place the bread and wine on the altar at the Offertory. The Presbyter would join the semi-circle of concelebrating Presbyters who stood with the Bishop around the altar and who presumably then, as in later centuries,[14] solemnly broke the consecrated Bread, which is the Food of Life to Christ's people and the sacrament of their unity in him.

---

12. Acts 20:33-35, 2 Thessalonians 3:7-12.

13. Numbers 11:16-30.

14. J. M. McGowan, R.S.C. J., *Concelebration* (1964), page 34; and A. A. King, *Concelebration in the Christian Church* (1966), page 24-25. King's further discussion, pages 23-31, is clouded by his deference to the official Roman view that participation in the Words of Institution alone constitutes "sacramental concelebration".

The arrangement prescribed by Hippolytus was widely imitated in ancient times, and some of his directions have remained in force to the present. His book enables us to see, for instance, why a Deacon is ordained by the Bishop alone, whereas a Priest receives the laying on of hands from the Bishop and a group of Priests. Likewise, we see the relation between the act of ordination and the initiation into new liturgical duties in the celebration of the Eucharist. Most dramatic of all is the direct correlation between the liturgical role and the responsibilities of authentic leadership in the Christian community. The totality of spiritual leadership is committed to the Bishop as Father-in-God to his people. The Priest is the Bishop's associate, colleague, and councilor. The Deacon is the assisting subordinate minister, who by this very fact has a place of honor. Precisely because of Hippolytus' clear and forceful presentation both of Biblical values and of the basic structures of leadership, modern theologians and liturgical scholars have given very serious attention to his work.

The Medieval Rites of Ordination

During the subsequent centuries, the laying on of hands remained as the characteristic sacramental action of ordination. The ordination itself generally continued to be preceded by some vestige of election, or at least a symbolic expression of popular assent. Likewise, ordination has continued to be related to the celebration of the Eucharist. In other respects there have been many changes. The earliest ordination prayers were translated into other languages, altered, and in most cases ultimately replaced by later compositions. In the Eastern Orthodox Churches the fundamental simplicity of the ancient ordination rites has remained. In the Latin West, the rites became progressively more complicated. In place of one solemn ordination prayer accompanying the laying on of hands, there came to be a series of such prayers for each order. During the eighth century, the Roman ordination rites were combined with the Gallican ones, and so the service came to include two complete sets of prayers.[15] A Deacon or a Priest was virtually ordained twice to the same order! A variety of other acts also acquired a place in the ordination liturgy. The candidate was required to vow obedience to his ecclesiastical superiors and to the canons of the Church, and to express his faith and commitment. He was ceremonially clothed with the vestments of his order and given the implements and symbols of his new duties. In imitation of the Old Testament, Priests and Bishops were anointed with oil. These different ceremonies were duly embellished with versicles and responses, prayers and blessings. The anointing of the hands of a new Priest, and the ceremonial giving to him of the vessels to be used in the Eucharist, had such dramatic impact that even informed theologians believed

---

15. For texts, see H. B. Porter, Jr., *Ordination Prayers of the Ancient Western Church* (1967), chapters II, III, and VI.

that these ceremonies, rather than the laying on of hands, were the essential outward acts of ordination.[16] By the end of the middle ages, the Latin rites of ordination, as they appeared in the Roman Pontifical, were not only very long and complicated, but they had incorporated so many heterogeneous elements that their essential meaning was confused. This remained the case until these rites were drastically reformed in the years following Vatican Council II.

The Medieval Concept of Ordination

Although the three orders of Bishop, Priest, and Deacon form an integral unity, other persons have also shared in ecclesiastical and liturgical responsibilities. In every period of history, lay persons have performed some tasks associated with the ordained ministry. This is to be expected, because all Christians are called to serve God in ways not unrelated to the special vocations of Bishops, Priests, and Deacons. From an early period, moreover, certain persons, while not actually ordained, were given distinctive ecclesiastical tasks. For men, the most ancient of these unordained offices was that of Readers, who read the Scriptures in the liturgy, and Sub-deacons, who helped the Deacons. These continue to be the two "minor orders" of the Eastern Orthodox Church.

Among the women were the Virgins, who devoted themselves primarily to prayer, and the Widows,[17] who, as older and more influential persons, sometimes performed certain pastoral functions. In the third and fourth centuries, the order of Deaconesses tended to absorb the women officials. Later, with the rise of monasticism, the ministry of women was entirely taken over by nuns, and the order of Deaconesses gradually died out. It was revived in the nineteenth century, with great success, among German Lutherans. It has subsequently been revived on a smaller scale among Anglicans and in several other Communions.[18]

In the medieval West, we encounter a considerable increase in the number of lesser ecclesiastical offices. These were arranged in an ascending series. The boy who was studying for the ministry was admitted, over a period of years, first as Doorkeeper, then as Exorcist, then as Reader, and then as Acolyte. These offices constituted the four "minor orders". Some men remained for life as "minor clerics", and served in various capacities as subordinate employees of the Church. The more ambitious (and those who felt called to accept celibacy) went on to the three "major orders" as Subdeacons, then Deacons, and finally as Priests. Thus, the ministry consisted of seven steps, and seven expressed a sacred totality in the symbolic thinking of the medieval Churchman. Such has continued to be the

---

16. E.g., St. Thomas Aquinas, *Summa Theologica*, Supplement, Question 37, article 5.

17. Virgin and Widow already appear as formal ranks in the New Testament, as in Acts 21:9, 1 Corinthians 7:25, and 1 Timothy 5:2-10. "*Deaconess*" may be an official title in Romans 16:1, although it is usually translated in that verse by the vaguer term "servant".

18. See chapter on Deaconesses by M. P. Truesdell in Nolan's *The Diaconate Now*.

system within Roman Catholicism until the present era, when the effort is again being made to speak of Deacons, Priests, and Bishops (rather than Subdeacons, Deacons, and Priests), as the three principal orders.

How did Bishops fit into the medieval scheme? Not too conveniently. Since priesthood was defined as the highest order, the Bishop was seen not as belonging to another order, but simply as a superior and more powerful sort of priest. Hence St. Thomas Aquinas and many other thoughtful medieval writers, hesitated to speak of the ordination of a Bishop.[19] Instead, he was "consecrated"—an honorific but vague term. In an earlier period, consecration, ordination, or blessing were used indiscriminately of all orders, or the term "consecration" was used for the principal ordination prayer for Bishops, Priests, and Deacons. Later on, for the reasons indicated, the term tended to be restricted to Bishops.[20]

Because the medieval rites were so lengthy, reference to almost any doctrinal or practical aspect of Christian ministry can be found somewhere within them. The over-all impression which they provide, however, is that of a vast series of sacred acts and sacred words whereby a minister becomes increasingly a sacralized person who is himself empowered to perform sacred rites.

Ordination in The Book of Common Prayer

Any effort to translate the Latin Pontifical into a modern vernacular had to move toward simplification and abbreviation. The basic simplification adopted by the English Reformers was to define the ordained ministry in terms of Bishops, Priests, and Deacons alone. Minor clerics continued to exist in the Church of England,[21] but their admission to office ceased to be thought of in any respect as an ordination. Concentration on the "three-fold ministry" of Bishops, Priests, and Deacons, committed the Anglican Church to the position held by the ancient Church Fathers, and to the position still held, in substance, by the Eastern Churches. It effectually separated Anglican teaching from the medieval Latin view outlined above, and from Protestant Churches which in most cases abandoned the episcopate, reduced the diaconate to a lay office, and defined their ordained ministry in terms of pastors or presbyters.

---

19. E.g., *Summa Theologica*, Supplement, Question 40, articles 4 and 5.

20. Similarly Abbots and Abbesses are "consecrated" in a rite of great solemnity, but without the character of a sacrament.

21. The modern English "parish clerk" usually takes care of the church building, and may carry the cross in processions, supervise the altar boys, or attend to other similar duties. Cathedrals also have clerks who are singers in the choir.

The ordination rites for the three orders as finally formulated by Archbishop Cranmer for the English Book of Common Prayer,[22] retain the eucharistic liturgy as the frame for ordination. They also rightly concentrate on the laying on of hands and prayer as the essential matter of ordination. The laying on of hands, however, is somewhat separated from the principal ordination prayer. It is accompanied by words addressed to the candidate, rather than by prayer addressed to God. In the case of the Deacon, the relevant prayers come at widely separated points of the rite.[23] The clothing with liturgical vesture is much reduced, and the Bible, or a portion of it, is the only implement of office given to the newly ordained.[24] The ordinands are to receive Holy Communion, but their active participation at the altar in the celebration of the sacrament is no longer clearly specified. Doctrinally, Cranmer emphasized the pastoral and teaching responsibilities of the clergy, and their power to pronounce forgiveness of sins, all of which was most fully expressed at the ordination of Priests. The scriptural character of Cranmer's views is weakened by the curious fact that it is not clearly indicated to the congregation that Priests belong to that order of ministers referred to in the New Testament as Christian "Elders". The details of Cranmer's ordination rites are discussed in many commentaries on the Prayer Book.

3. Recent Revisions

Revisions of the Prayer Book in the seventeenth, eighteenth, and nineteenth centuries made various small changes in Anglican ordination rites. A more substantial alteration occurred in the Scottish Prayer Book of 1929, and the Proposed English Book of 1928. In these, a solemn prayer preceding the laying on of hands was inserted into the rite for Deacons. This was also proposed for the American Episcopal Church in 1957 in *Prayer Book Studies VIII*.[25]

More thorough-going revisions of material originally Anglican, appeared in the rites of the Church of South India in the 1950's. The South Indian Ordinal

---

22. Before the Reformation, ordination rites were contained in a separate volume called a *Pontifical*. The first English rites were likewise issued separately, in 1550, for use with the Prayer Book of 1549. They were revised in 1552. In the 17th Century the word "Ordinal", which had been formerly used for a book of ceremonial directions, began to be used as a collective title for the ordination rites and it entered the Book of Common Prayer with the revision of 1662.

23. I.e., the Collect near the beginning and the Collect before the Benediction at the end of the rite.

24. In 1550, in addition to the Bible, a new Priest received "the Chalice or cuppe with the breade" and a Bishop received "the pastorall staffe". These ceremonial presentations were eliminated in 1552.

25. In accord with a trend among Anglican liturgiologists of the past generation, it was also proposed that the great Ordination Prayer for each order be introduced by the *Sursum corda*, as in the Latin Pontificals. This was intended to give greater solemnity to the principal prayer. Today, scholars usually interpret the *Sursum corda* as meaning "Let us lift up our hearts and perform The Thanksgiving, i.e., the Eucharist." Hence it does not seem appropriate to other rites and blessings. The *Sursum corda* before the Ordination Prayers has also now been eliminated from the Roman Pontifical.

has been justly admired. For all three orders of the ministry the same pattern is followed. The candidate is presented at the beginning; and the people may not only object to an unworthy candidate, but, if they approve, are required to voice their approval. Then follows the Ministry of the Word, the examination of the candidate, the invoking of the Holy Spirit in the *Veni Creator*, and the solemn ordination prayer. The English 1928 prayer for Deacons is strengthened by an introductory reference to Christ as servant, based on the second chapter of Philippians. The prayers for Presbyters and Bishops, respectively, are strengthened by references to their liturgical and sacramental roles, in phrases apparently adapted from the ancient prayers of Hippolytus. Most notable is the fact that the laying on of hands takes place during the prayer itself at the point where the gift of the Spirit is asked for.

During the 1960's, the South Indian Ordinal was revised for the Anglican-Methodist Unity Commission by Professor E. C. Ratcliff of Cambridge. After his death it was brought to a final form and published officially as an Ordinal which could be acceptable in the future to the Church of England the Methodist Church, and perhaps also to some other Churches. It is a notable achievement, but in a number of respects it would not be entirely suitable for American use. As in South India, there is the same format in the conferring of all three orders, but nothing takes place before the Ministry of the Word which is rather meager. Unlike the South Indian, it provides no Old Testament Lessons or Psalms; unlike the existing versions of the Prayer Book, it gives no alternative Epistles or Gospels. After the Sermon and Creed, the candidates are presented and acclaimed by the people as worthy. The examination follows, with a relatively brief set of questions and answers. There is then silent prayer and the hymn *Veni Creator*. The great Ordination Prayer for each order resembles that of South India, and the imposition of hands takes place during the prayer itself. The Bible is then given, and the Eucharist resumes with the Offertory. The rubrics encourage the new minister, together with the other clergymen who are present, to take an active role in the performance of the liturgy.

Materials from South India, from the Anglican-Methodist English revision, and from the rites of this present publication, have been taken in 1970 by the Consultation on Church Union in the United States for its proposed Ordinal. The forms in the Consultation Ordinal resemble the others in their general structure, although the doctrinal emphasis is, of course, not identical.

Meanwhile revision of the Roman Pontifical has at last been undertaken, and new simplified rites have appeared in the vernacular. The very title of the published text, The Ordination of Deacons, Priests, and Bishops, proclaims a new emphasis on the "three-fold ministry". The rubrics are much simplified, and many options are allowed, including a wide choice of biblical passages for Old Testament Lessons, Epistles, and Gospels. As in the newly proposed English order, all the special material for ordination takes place after the Liturgy of the Word. The candidates are presented and the "consent of the people" is asked for. After an allocution by the Bishop on the duties of the ministry, the candidates are briefly examined. The Litany of the Saints follows. In recent centuries, it has been the custom in the Latin rite for the Bishop to rise to his feet during the Litany and, with his crozier in hand, to recite the suffrage for the Ordinands. This practice is now abrogated. Instead, there is now the more classic arrangement of the Bishop rising at the end of the Litany to recite a summary collect.

In accordance with a unique custom of the Roman rite, the laying on of hands takes place in total silence, after which the ordination prayer, or "Prayer of Consecration", is said by the Bishop. In the ordination of Deacons and Priests, these prayers of consecration are modified versions of the traditional ordination prayers of the Roman Church. In the ordination of Bishops, the traditional prayer has been boldly discarded, and in its place appears the older, briefer, and more evangelical prayer which Hippolytus had provided for the episcopate — a change of striking ecumenical significance. In an arrangement not unlike that of the new English forms, the central petition for the gift of the Spirit to the new Bishop is said by all the co-consecrating Bishops in unison. After the prayer, the newly ordained are vested, anointed (in the case of Priests and Bishops), and given implements of office. The newly ordained are greeted with the Peace, and Mass proceeds with the Offertory, the new ministers actively participating according to their own order.

It would exceed the scope of this Introduction to describe the ordination rites of every major Christian Church, but many of them have interesting and significant features. Very briefly, it may be said that Methodist forms continue to resemble those in the English Prayer Book from which they are derived. Presbyterian ordination typically includes a long and solemn summary of the faith, followed by questions and answers and a long Ordination Prayer during which the laying on of hands occurs. The Lord's Prayer, declaration of ordination, and right-hand-of-fellowship follow. The characteristic Lutheran rite includes a series of exhortations taken from the New Testament, a short set of questions and answers, the laying on of hands with a declaratory formula, followed by the Lord's Prayer and other prayers. As has been said before, Eastern Orthodox ordinations follow a simple and ancient pattern, and of course occur during the eucharistic liturgy. For Deacons and for Priests, the Bishop lays on his hand and says a short declaratory formula, and then, in a low voice, says two prayers, with his hands still on the head of the ordinand. A litany is sung during the second prayer. A Bishop-elect must first recite the Nicene Creed and other long declarations of faith. Then an open Gospel book is imposed on his head while a declaratory formula is said. Finally, while several Bishops lay on hands, a prayer, a litany; and another prayer are said.

4. The Present Proposed Rites

The rites for the Ordination of Bishops, Priests, and Deacons, as these are now being proposed for trial use, are based in many respects on the other recently revised rites which have just been described. In the present section we will survey these proposed rites, the structure being the same for all three orders. The special features of each of the three rites will then be examined.

In order to indicate the centrality of the episcopate, the arrangement of the liturgical books of the early Church has been followed in placing the Ordination of a Bishop first. The rites for Priests and Deacons follow. Each order is presented as a distinctive vocation, having its own characteristics. This avoids the misleading impression that the three orders are simply three steps in an ascending scale of promotions.

The medieval custom of ordaining a large number of candidates together in the cathedral has not established itself in most parts of America. For many reasons it seems preferable to ordain a candidate in a local church where he is known, or where he is to minister. Thus the titles and phraseology of the ordination rites assume a single ordinand; where there are two or more, adjustments are easily made. It should also be noted that for purposes of trial use these rites may be used either with the eucharistic liturgy of 1928 or with a proposed revised liturgy. The technical details are outlined in rubrics at the end of each rite.

In all these orders, the service begins, after an opening Doxology and invocation of the Holy Spirit, with the presentation of the person to be ordained. For a Deacon or Priest, the presentation takes the form of an election, with the congregation acclaiming the candidate as one they desire to have ordained. In the ordination of a Bishop, it is explained that an actual election has in fact already taken place. It is made clear that ordination is not an act for which the individual is to put himself forward. Rather, it is the responsibility of the Church, through its canonical procedures, to select persons who are meet to fulfill its spiritual needs. This word "meet" presents difficulties. It translates the Latin term *dignus* which, in many of the older liturgies, designates the duly chosen candidate. Modern translators agree that "worthy" is the most direct rendering. It does not mean that the person possesses such individual merit that he has earned ordination. It does mean that he is a person whom the Church regards as suitable for ordination and believes to have been called by God. The cry, "He is worthy", is intended to be an acclamation, or shout, which can be repeated easily and loudly, as many times as desired, without an attempt to speak in unison. Other words of approval, if they seem more natural, can be shouted at the same time. The Presentation of the Candidate has been put first, before the Ministry of the Word, in the belief that it is dramatically misleading to read Bible passages and hear a sermon about ordination unless it has first been made clear that an ordination really is to take place. It will be noted that the questions and answers in the Presentation all have to do with the choice of the candidate, and his canonical and legal eligibility for ordination. Hence, the promise of conformity and obedience comes here, rather than in the later examination.

The Litany has also been placed near the beginning of the service to avoid overloading the later portions. It not only provides the intercessions for the liturgy, but also expresses the humility and repentance with which ordination is to be approached. Since new litanies are now being given trial use, it seems good to permit some choice here.

A litany should be chosen which will allow the insertion of suitable petitions for the ordinand and for his family (if he has one). In accordance with ancient and very reasonable custom, a Collect is said by the presiding minister (the Bishop) to sum up and conclude the Litany. If the litany chosen ends with a summary Collect of its own, such Collect is to be superseded. Accordingly, there will be the suffrages of the Litany, the Kyries, the Salutation by the Bishop, and the Collect, without any of these items being duplicated.

The Ministry of the Word for ordinations always includes an Old Testament Lesson as well as an Epistle and Gospel. The Prayer Book Ordinal has always allowed some choice of passages; such choice seems even more desirable in an era of trial use.[26] Similarly, if the sermon is to be based on passages that are read, some freedom of choice is essential. It will be noted that for each order, one Epistle refers directly to the order being conferred. Since ordinations frequently are scheduled on a Saint's day, it is anticipated that the option of using the propers of the day will be particularly welcome. At ordinations, as on other occasions, lay persons should read the Old Testament Lesson and the Epistle, and Deacons the Gospel. (Visiting Priests and Bishops should not usurp these duties, but should rather function in accordance with their own order at the altar, as the proposed rubrics provide.) The proposed Psalms can be used for Introit, Gradual, Offertory, or Communion chants, as may be desired. A Psalm is especially desirable between the Old Testament Lesson and the Epistle.

The Examination is briefer than that in the Prayer Book. An effort has been made to provide a clear characterization of the ministry being conferred, without attempting (as the proposed English Anglican-Methodist Ordinal does) to enumerate every duty that each order might perform. During the present period of change, both in the Church and in society at large, it does not seem, realistic to prescribe exactly what a man may do in the exercise of his ministry, or to predict what aspects of it may prove most important in his ministry. Since a number of our clergymen already earn their living by secular work, and that number will increase in the future, care has been taken to avoid any promises which suggest that it is unworthy or ungodly for an ordained man to have and to use secular skill and knowledge.[27]

---

26. Some of the new selections are already in the Prayer Book, in the lectionary for Morning or Evening Prayer "Before Ordinations" or "At the Institution of a Minister".

27. This accords with Resolution 33, "A Wider Ordained Ministry", adopted by the Lambeth Conference of 1968.

The actual ordination, the part of the service technically designated The Consecration, begins with the hymn invoking the Holy Spirit. The Prayer Book has long allowed a choice of translations for this hymn, and *The Hymnal 1940* provides several versions.[28] In the hope of encouraging new translations and new musical compositions, the door has been opened to any version that may be approved by those responsible for planning the service. Silent prayer follows, until the Bishop begins the Consecration Prayer. This is the most solemn text of the ordination rite. Revision of the Ordinal provides the opportunity to restore a complete and distinctive prayer for each order. The laying on of hands accompanies the specific petition for the gift of the Holy Spirit to the ordinand. This petition is, in each case, in strictly trinitarian form, being addressed to the Father, through the Son, for the gift of the Holy Spirit. It is to be repeated over each ordinand, if more than one is being ordained.

Following the Consecration, appropriate vestments and other symbols of office are conferred on the new minister. Up to this time he has been attired in simple but conspicuous white vesture, without any insignia of office or rank. Now he is vested according to his order. The Bible and, if desired, liturgical instruments of his office are conferred as symbols of the authority already given to him by the act of ordination.

The Peace is properly one of the high points of an ordination, for here (as also in Baptism and Matrimony), a normal part of the eucharistic liturgy acquires a special dramatic significance. It expresses not only the peace with one another which Christians should always have before offering their gifts at the altar,[29] but also the accolade of the newly ordained and the recognition of him in his new rank. Such a greeting comes at this point in the new Roman Ordination rites, as does the right-hand-of-fellowship in Protestant ordinations.

After the long and emotionally intense steps that have led to the actual ordination, it seems proper at this point to have a less formal interval in the rite. Since the rubrics indicate that ordination is to take place close to the people, and since the family of the ordinand will normally be in the very front of the church, there appears to be every reason to permit them to congratulate him at this happy moment.

For the Offertory, the ministers move to the altar, and the rubrics indicate that the newly ordained will fulfill the liturgical duties of his order, in co-operation with his new colleagues. The precise manner of his doing this will depend on the number of other clergymen participating, the size and shape of the sanctuary, and other factors. It is intended, however, that his participation in the eucharistic rite be clear and visible.

---

28. *The Hymnal 1940*, numbers 108, 217, 218, and 371. The *Veni Sancte Spiritus* (Hymnal number 109), known as the "Golden Sequence", is a similar text and is one of the most famous and beloved of medieval hymns. See *The Hymnal 1940 Companion* (1949), pages 79-80.

29. Matthew 5:23-24.

It is still necessary to point out that Anglican principles require reasonable and adequate opportunity for the faithful to receive Holy Communion at ordinations. To refuse the congregation opportunity to communicate is to deny to the laity their means of sacramental participation in the service. In view of the large number of clergymen who usually attend ordinations, arrangements can be made to have many ministers distributing Holy Communion at several places within the church building.

The rites here proposed permit options and variations at several places. As has been said, this appears to be consonant with the purposes of trial use. It will also be noted that at most of the points where variation is permitted, our present Prayer Book already admits of some options. Thus, the Bishop is already allowed to phrase his own bidding before the Litany (in the case of Priests and Deacons). Likewise, our Prayer Book already allows a choice of Litanies, a choice of Lessons, and a choice of versions of the *Veni Creator*.

The Ordination of a Bishop

The reasons for using the term Ordination in the title of this rite have, been indicated in the foregoing pages. Since the term consecration is in common use, it too has been employed at several points within the rite. During the Presentation, the fact of the election of the candidate is recalled, and the congregation assents to the election by acclaiming the Bishop-elect. The term Chief Pastor is used as an explanatory synonym of Bishop. Although the Diocesan Bishop alone is *the* Chief Pastor, it is fitting and desirable to describe a Suffragan or Coadjutor as *a* Chief Pastor. It would not be proper to consecrate a Bishop who was to exercise no pastoral oversight of any kind.

In the Ministry of the Word, in addition to some of the familiar passages and familiar themes, Hebrews 5 introduces the theme of the biblical high priesthood. As has been said before, such terms were often used in Christian antiquity to speak of the episcopate,[30] and the same terminology occasionally occurs in Anglican sources.[31] The concept of the Bishop as Christian High Priest continues to be highly valued in large portions of the Christian Church. The Commission feels that it is a matter of serious ecumenical importance to restore this theme to a more explicit place in our rite. The same theme occurs in Psalm 99. (Our present Prayer Book associates this Psalm with the priesthood,[32] but it is sounder to relate it to the episcopate.) Psalm 100 (The *Jubilate*) is suggested not only because of its reference to the shepherd theme, but also because its familiarity will facilitate its being sung. The prerogative of a Deacon to read the Gospel is emphasized, to

---

30. E.g., Porter, *Ordination Prayers*, pages 9, 21, 43, 75.

31. The Answer (1897) of the Archbishops of England to Leo XIII, *Anglican Orders* (English), S.P.C.K., London (1943), page 42.

32. In the lectionary for Morning or Evening Prayer "At the Institution of a Minister".

ensure to the diaconate (together with other orders) an audible role in the service. Since the whole clergy of the Diocese attends episcopal ordinations, it should not be difficult to find Deacons to officiate. It has seemed desirable to require a hymn after the Sermon to break the extended period of listening during the Gospel, Sermon, and Examination.

For the Examination of the Bishop-elect, different Bishops participating in the service may be assigned different questions. This not only gives them a vocal role, but expresses the principle that the Bishop-elect has a responsibility to the entire college of Bishops. The questions and answers are intended to suggest to those present the Bishop's responsibility to God and men, to those inside and outside the Church. His relationship to other ministers is specifically indicated. Other Bishops are to be his brothers. The Priests of his Diocese are his colleagues and fellow-Presbyters in the councils of the Church. Deacons, Deaconesses, Lay Readers, Church Army workers and other ministers are co-workers for whom he must show loving concern. The Examination culminates in the recitation of the Nicene Creed led by the Bishop-elect, an adaptation of a tradition in the Eastern Churches. It will be recalled that this Creed was formulated at Nicea, and revised at Constantinople, specifically by Bishops, as an expression of the faith the Bishops held and taught.

The Consecration Prayer is the principal formula of ordination. It will be noted that the Book of Common Prayer does not provide an entirely unique prayer at this point for Bishops, but has an adapted form of its prayer for Priests. It appears much more desirable to have a full and entirely distinct prayer for each order. Accordingly, the ancient prayer of Hippolytus for ordaining a Bishop has been adopted in a rather free contemporary translation.[33] The fact that the Roman Catholic Church has already made the same decision is of considerable ecumenical importance. As in the new Roman order, the participating Bishops say aloud the essential petition for the gift of the Spirit to the ordinand. The vesting of the new Bishop and the giving of insignia of office are carried out in whatever way is desired, since a variety of vestments is legitimate, and many symbols of office are quite suitable.

After the new Bishop has been ordained and vested, it is appropriate that popular recognition and applause be given; and this fits in well with the Peace on this occasion. It is assumed that the Presiding Bishop and other Bishops will wish to embrace their new colleague.

The new Bishop takes the leading role in celebrating the Eucharist from the Offertory on. It is suggested that, as at all Eucharists, Deacons and other servers prepare the Holy Table at the Offertory, placing the bread and wine upon it. Then the new Bishop, other Bishops, and a few representative Priests of the

---

33. See page 278 above for a discussion of this prayer.

Diocese gather at the altar for the Consecration, Fraction, and Communion.[34] The rubrics relating to the celebration of the Eucharist intentionally leave much to the choice of those planning the service.

In accord with ancient custom, the *Te Deum* is sung as a solemn thanksgiving at the end.

The Ordination of a Priest

For Priests, as also for Deacons, the form of the service is somewhat simpler than that for Bishops. At the Presentation, it is made clear that the candidate is called by God in and through the Church, not by himself. In the Ministry of the Word, among the appointed passages, one from the Old Testament and one from the New provide explicit references to the biblical presbyterate, thus remedying a notable lack in the present Prayer Book.

A major change is the curtailment of the lengthy allocution by which Cranmer introduced the Examination. The placing of the sermon after the Gospel makes an allocution a few moments later structurally unsuitable. Beautiful as this address may be, its view of the laity as a passive and helpless body has raised severe doubts as to the desirability of retaining it. New matter emphasizes the liturgical and sacramental rites which the Priest must lead, and also his role, as a Presbyter, in the councils and government of the Church. In a constitutionally governed Church, this aspect of his office is in fact highly important.

The Ordination Prayer, or Consecration, is obviously derived from that in the Prayer Book. The words from Ephesians 4 have a well-deserved place in Anglican ordinations. The remainder of the proposed prayer has been much influenced by the South Indian and proposed new English rites. It gives a fuller view of the office and work of a Priest than the prayer in our present Ordinal. Following the giving of the Bible, the new Priest may be given instruments and symbols of his office.[35]

In the remaining parts of the eucharistic liturgy, provision is made for the active participation of the newly ordained. In the detailed rubrics at the end of the rite, the new Priest is directed to break some of the Consecrated Bread so that his role as a concelebrant may be quite explicit.[36] On this occasion, the Bishop

---

34. Con-celebration has recently been discussed in some detail (see works by King, Minchin, and McGowan in the bibliography), but because the word is used in such differing senses it has not been employed in the rubrics of these services. The rubrics are simply intended to secure sufficient public and visible participation so that the corporate character of the priestly action can be recognized by the worshiping community. The rubrics take for granted that all communicants have an interior and spiritual participation in the Liturgy.

35. These may include chalice and paten, an altar service book, stoles, a vessel for taking Holy Communion to the sick and shut-in, a container for oil to anoint the sick.

36. The rubrics actually require no more than a token breaking. Where wafer bread is used, the provision on the paten of an additional large host for each Ordinand may be found helpful. See also note 14 and 34 above.

accords to the new Priest the privilege of saying the final blessing—an arrangement the Prayer Book has long had at the Institution of Ministers.

The Ordination of a Deacon

The effort has been made to provide a more positive view of the diaconate in terms of service, since "Deacon" literally means one who serves. It is not suggested that the Deacon is the only person called to serve, but rather that his formally designated and ordained service is to provide leadership and focus for the entire Church as a serving people. It is recognized that Deacons may be full-time or part-time church workers; they may or may not be preparing for the priesthood; they may or may not be licensed to preach. In any case, whether by word or deed, by life or by teaching, they are to proclaim Christ and his Gospel. The view of the diaconate here presented adheres closely to the recommendations of the last Lambeth Conference.[37]

The *Veni Creator* has been added, as in other recent Anglican revisions, together with a substantial Ordination Prayer or Consecration, generally similar to that in the South Indian and proposed English Ordinal. It will be noted that the second half of the prayer incorporates phrases which in the Prayer Book appear in the final Prayer for the ordering of Deacons. This material was taken by Cranmer from the second half of the Roman Ordination Prayer for Deacons. Thus, it is here restored to its original place. As in the new Roman revision, reference to "this inferior office" is replaced by phrases referring to our Lord's service.

In the arrangement followed here, again as in other recent revisions, there was no way to retain the reading of the Gospel by the newly ordained Deacon. He has been given, however, a role at the Offertory and at the Dismissal. As a new member of the order of Deacons, it is appropriate that he serve together with other Deacons, if any are present. Since the administration of the Chalice is now sometimes carried out by lay persons, attention is called to the propriety and legality of Deacons ministering the consecrated Bread.[38] In accord with ancient tradition, the Deacon pronounces the Dismissal. He may also perform the ablutions, but confusion may result if one newly ordained Deacon has to do too much during the last few moments of the service. When there are two or more present, these duties may conveniently be divided among them.

---

37. Resolution 32, *The Lambeth Conference 1968, Resolutions and Reports*, pages 38-39. See also pages 104-105.

38. *Special Meeting of the House of Bishops*, Wheeling, 1966. *Journal of the General Convention, 1967, Supplement B*, pages 10 and 18. The latter includes reference to the Sacrament being carried to the sick by a Deacon.

5. Trial Use of These Rites of Ordination

The rites here presented are published in the hope that they may commend themselves sufficiently to be authorized for trial use throughout the Episcopal Church. It is understood that trial use of ordination rites is somewhat different from that of more frequently used services. In some jurisdictions a year or more may pass without any opportunity to use these Services. In order to familiarize themselves with these forms, and to try the different possible variations, Bishops will need to take advantage of every opportunity to use them. So that the results of trial use may be evaluated, it is urged that the Chairmen and the members of diocesan Liturgical Committees be given opportunity to share in the planning and carrying out of every ordination in their jurisdiction using these proposed forms. It is also urged that a detailed record of every such ordination be kept, with information as to what Litany was used, what choices of Scripture were read, how the Eucharist was celebrated, and so forth, with criticism and evaluation of these different elements. If these rites are tried, they should be improved and revised in due course on the basis of experience.

It should be clearly understood, however, that trial use and further change would not have the slightest bearing on the validity and legitimacy of the ministry of those so ordained. These rites indisputably contain all that The Episcopal Church has ever taught as theologically necessary for ordination. In certain respects, it may be that these proposed forms give a clearer expression to the Church's teachings than those used hitherto.

Rooted in the Book of Common Prayer, these are Anglican rites. At the same time, it is hoped that they will be recognized primarily as Christian rites, intended to confer the episcopate, priesthood, and diaconate of Christ's One, Holy, Catholic, and Apostolic. Church. As the foregoing pages have indicated, there is now a convergence of views, from different ecclesiastical perspectives, as to what ordination should be. The South Indian Ordinal is an excellent piece of liturgical craftsmanship, combining the labors of Anglicans, Presbyterians, Methodists, and Congregationalists. The newly proposed English Ordinal is another excellent achievement resulting from further collaboration of Anglicans and Methodists. The new Roman Catholic ordination rites, and others, move in much the same direction. It is the Commission's hope that the forms here submitted may represent a further milestone on the same road.

Select Bibliography of Works on Ordination Rites and Related Topics

1. Translations into English of Ancient Rites of Ordination

Cooper, J., and Maclean, A. J.: *The Testament of Our Lord*. Edinburgh, T. & T. Clark: 1902 [pp. 64-8, 90-2, 104-5]

Dix, G., *The Treatise of the Apostolic Tradition of St. Hippolytus of Rome*. London and New York, 1937. Re-edited by Chadwick, H., London: Dacre, 1968 [pp. 2-18]

Donaldson, J., *Constitutions of the Holy Apostles*. Ante-Nicene Fathers, V. VII ; New York, Christian Literature Company, 1896. [pp. 481-94]

Easton, B. S., *The Apostolic Tradition of Hippolytus*. Cambridge and New York, 1934; reprinted Hamden, Conn. Archon, Shoe String Press, 1962.

Hapgood, I. F., *Service Book of the Holy Orthodox-Catholic Apostolic Church*. Boston and New York, 1906. Reprinted New York, Association Press 1922 [1956] [pp. 311-330]

Homer, G., *The Statutes of the Apostles*. London, Williams and Norgate, 1904 [pp. 138-45]

Porter, H. B., Jr., *The Ordination Prayers of the Ancient Western Churches*. London, S.P.C.K. 1967.

Wordsworth, J., *Bishop Sarapion's Prayer Book*. London, 1928 reprinted Hamden, Conn., Archon, Shoe String Press, 1964. [pp. 72-4]

2. Recently Compiled or Revised Rites of Ordination

Anglican-Methodist Unity, I, The Ordinal. Report of the Anglican Methodist Unity Commission, London, S.P.C.K. and Epworth, 1968.

The Book of Common Worship. The Church of South India, London, New York and Madras, Oxford University Press, 1963.

The Order for Ordination to the Ministry, Division of Publication, Board for Homeland Ministries, United Churches of Christ, 1969.

Ordinal and Service Book for use in the Courts of the Church. Second edition. The Church of Scotland, London, Glasgow and New York, Oxford University Press, 1954.

The Ordination of Deacons, Priests, and Bishops. Provisional Text. National Conference of Catholic Bishops, Bishops' Committee on the Liturgy, Washington, 1969.

"Ordination of a Pastor". Reformed Church of France, *Studia Liturgica*, Vol. IV, no 4 (Winter 1965), [pp. 111-b-1/21]

Prayer Book Studies VIII, The Ordinal. The Standing Liturgical Commission of the Episcopal Church, New York, Church Pension Fund, 1957.

Proposed Rites for Holy Baptism, The Ordination of a Minister, and The Burial of the Dead. Produced by The Commission on Worship, Liturgics and Hymnology of the Synodical Conference (The Lutheran Church-Missouri Synod and the Synod of Evangelical Lutheran Churches) St. Louis, Concordia Publication, n.d.

Service Book and Hymnal. Authorized by the Lutheran Churches co-operating in the Commission on the Liturgy and Hymnal, Text edition, Philadelphia, Board of Publication, Lutheran Church in America, 1967.

Towards Reconciliation. The Anglican-Methodist Unity Commission London, S.P.C.K. and Epworth, 1967 (contains earlier draft of *The Ordinal* referred to above)

3. Critical and Historical Studies

Addleshaw, G. W. O., *The Beginnings of the Parochial System*. St. Anthony's Hall Publications 3; London, 1953

_____. *The Development of the Parochial System from Charlemagne to Urban II*. St. Anthony's Hall Publications 6; London, 1954

Beck, H. G. J., *The Pastoral Care of Souls in South-East France*. Rome, Analecta Gregoriana, 1950.

Botte, B., and others, *The Sacrament of Holy Orders*. London, Alcuin Press, 1962.

Bouëssé, H., Benoit, P., and others. *L'Evêque dans l'Eglise du Christ*. Paris; Desclée de Brouwer, 1963.

Carey, K., ed. *The Historic Episcopate in the Fullness of the Church: Six Essays by Priests of the Church of England*. London, Dacre, 1954.

Clarke, W. K. L., and Harris, C., *Liturgy and Worship*. London, S.P.C.K. 1932.

Colson, J., *La Fonction Diaconale aux Origines de l'Eglise*. Paris, Desclée de Brouwer, 1960.

Congar, Y., and Dupuy, B. D., ed. *L'Episcopat et l'Eglise Universelle*. Paris, Cerf, 1964.

Consultation on Church Union, *Principles of Church Union*. Cincinnati, Forward Movement Publications, 1966.

Crumb, L. N., "Presbyteral Ordination and the See of Rome", *Church Quarterly Review*, CLXIV (January 1963)

Danielou, J., *The Ministry of Women in the Early Church*. translated by Glen Simon, London, Faith Press 1961.

Davis, J. G., "Deacons, Deaconesses, and the Minor Orders", *Journal of Ecclesiastical History*, XIV, no. 1 (April 1963) [pp. 7-15]

Dunstan, G. R. (ed.), *The Sacred Ministry*. London, S.P.C.K., 1970.

Eichlin, E. P., "The Deacon in the Secular Age", *Worship* V. 43, no 3 (March 1969) [pp. 154-8]

Ellard, G., *Ordination Anointings in the Western Church* ... New York, Kraus, 1932.

Fairweather, E. R., *Episcopacy Reasserted*. New York and London, Morehouse Barlow, and Mowbray, 1965.

Fairweather, E. R., and Hettlinger, R. F., *Episcopacy and Reunion*. London, Mowbray, 1965.

Ferguson-Davie, P., *The Bishop in the Church*. London, S.P.C.K., 1961.

Green, M., *Called to Serve*. Philadelphia, Westminster Press, 1964.

Guerra y Gomez, M., *Episcopos y Presbyteros*. Burgos, Publicaciones del Seminario Metropolitano de Burgos, 1962.

Hanson, A. T., *The Pioneer Ministry*. London, S.C.M. Press, 1961.

Heidt, J. T., "The Sacramental Character of Ministerial Priesthood" in *American Church Quarterly*, V. VI, no 13 (1969) [pp. 139-45]

Hebert, A. G., *Apostle and Bishop*. London, Faber & Faber, 1963.

James, E. O., *The Nature and Function of Priesthood*. New York, Vanguard, 1955.

Johnson, R. C., *The Church and its Changing Ministry*. Philadelphia, Westminster Press, 1961.

King, A. A., *Concelebration in the Christian Church*. London, Mowbray, 1966.

Kirk, K. E. (ed), *The Apostolic Ministry*. London, Hodder & Stoughton, 1946.

Kleinheyer, B, *Die Priesterweihe im Romischen Ritus*. Trier, 1962.

Macquarrie, J., "The Ministry and the Proposed New Anglican-Methodist Ordinal" in *The Anglican*, XXV no. 4 (Winter 1969-70) [pp. 7-18].

McGowan, J. C., *Concelebration*. New York, Herder & Herder, 1964.

Minchin, B., *Every Man in His Ministry*. London, Darton, Longman & Todd, 1960.

Moberly, R. C., *Ministerial Priesthood*. London, S. P. C. K., 1969 (reissue).

Nolan, R. T., (ed.) and others, *The Diaconate Now*. Washington, Corpus Books, 1968.

Paton, D. M. (ed.) *New Forms of Ministry* C.W.M.E. [Research. Pamphlets, 12] London, Edinburgh House, 1965.
Porter, H. B., *The Ministers of the Distribution of Holy Communion* (printed by the General Convention of the Episcopal Church) New York, 1964.
Power, D. N., O.M.I., *Ministers of Christ and His Church*. London, Geoffrey Chapman, 1969.
de Puniet, P., *The Roman Pontifical*. London and New York, Longmans, Green, 1932.
Ratcliff, E. C., "The Ordinal of the Church of South India" in *Theology*, LXIII (January 1960) [pp. 7-15]
Sheets, J. R., "The One Priesthood: The Union of Bishop and Priest" in *Worship*, V. 43, no 6 (June-July 1969) [pp. 339-352]
Shepherd, M. H., *The Oxford American Prayer Book Commentary*. New York, Oxford University Press, 1950.
Telfer, W., *The Office of a Bishop*. London, Darton, Longman & Todd, 1962.
Williams, D. D., and Niebuhr, H. R., (ed.) *The Ministry in Historical Perspectives*, New York, Harper, 1956.
Winninger, P., *Les Diacres, Histoire et Avenir du Diaconat*. Paris, Cerf, 1967.

THE ORDINATION OF BISHOPS, PRIESTS, AND DEACONS

At the Ordination of a Bishop

When a Bishop is to be ordained, the Presiding Bishop of the Church, or a Bishop appointed by him, shall preside and serve as Chief Consecrator. At least two other Bishops shall serve as Co.consecrators. Representatives of the Presbyterate, Diaconate, and Laity of the Diocese for which the new Bishop is to be consecrated, are to be assigned appropriate duties in the service.

From the beginning of the service until the Offertory, it is desirable that the Presiding Bishop's chair be placed close to the People, so that all may see and hear what is done. The other Bishops, or a convenient number of them, should sit to his right and left.

The Bishop-elect is to be vested in a rochet or alb, without stole, tippet, or other vesture distinctive of ecclesiastical or academic rank or order.

When the Bishop-elect is presented, his full name (designated by the symbol N.N.) shall be used. Thereafter, it is appropriate to refer to him only by the Christian name by which he wishes to be known.

Additional Directions and Suggestions are on pages 316-317.

The Ordination of a Bishop

A Psalm, or Hymn, or Anthem may be sung during the entrance of the Bishops and other Ministers.

The People being assembled, and all standing, a Bishop appointed says

Blessed be God: Father, Son, and Holy Spirit.

People

And blessed be his Kingdom, now and for ever. Amen.

From Easter Day through the Day of Pentecost, he says instead

Alleluia! Christ is risen.

People

The Lord is risen indeed. Alleluia!

Bishop

Almighty God, to you all hearts are open, all desires known, and from you no secrets are hid; cleanse the thoughts of our hearts by the inspiration of your Holy Spirit, that we may perfectly love you, and worthily magnify your holy Name; through Christ our Lord. *Amen.*

The Bishops and the People sit.

The Presentation

A Priest and a Lay Person, as representatives of the Diocese, present the man for whom they seek Consecration to the Presiding Bishop, saying

Reverend Father in God, the Clergy and People of the Diocese of *N.*, trusting in the guidance of the Holy Spirit, have chosen *N.N.* to be a Bishop and Chief Pastor. We therefore ask you to lay your hands upon him and in the power of the Holy Spirit to consecrate him a Bishop in the One, Holy, Catholic, and Apostolic Church.

The Presiding Bishop then directs that testimonials of the election be read.

When the reading of the testimonials is ended, the Presiding Bishop requires the following promise from the Bishop-elect:

In the Name of the Father, and of the Son, and of the Holy Spirit, I, *N.N.*, chosen Bishop of the Church in *N.*, do promise conformity and obedience to the Doctrine, Discipline, and Worship of The Episcopal Church.

All stand.

The Presiding Bishop then says the following, or similar words, and asks the response of the People.

Dear friends in Christ, you have heard testimony given that *N.N.* has been duly and lawfully elected to be a Bishop of the Church of God to serve in the Diocese of *N.* You have been assured of his suitability for this office, and that the Church has, through its authorized representatives, approved him for this sacred responsibility. We therefore present him to you as Bishop-elect. We ask you to voice your assent, and to express the loyalty which you will give to him as Bishop. Is he worthy?

The People respond with a loud voice saying these or other words, several times:

He is worthy.

The Presiding Bishop then says

The Scriptures tell us that our Savior Christ spent the whole night in prayer before he chose and sent forth his twelve Apostles. Likewise, the Apostles prayed before they appointed Matthias to be one of their number. Let us, therefore, follow their examples, and offer our prayers to Almighty God before we ordain this person for the work to which we trust the Holy Spirit has called him.

All kneel, and the Person appointed leads the Litany for the Ministry of the Church, or some other approved Litany. At the end of the Litany, after the Kyries, the Presiding Bishop stands and reads the Collect for the Day, or the following Collect, or both, first saying

	The Lord be with you.
Answer	And also with you.
Presiding Bishop	Let us pray.

The Collect

Almighty God, by whose Holy Spirit your people are provided with true and faithful pastors: By the same Spirit kindle in this your servant such love toward you, that he may witness to you in holiness of life, zealously proclaim the Gospel, and gather a people reconciled in your Son, Jesus Christ our Lord; who lives and reigns with you and the Holy Spirit, one God, now and ever. *Amen.*

At the Ministry of the Word

Three Lessons are to be read. Lay persons read the Old Testament Lesson and the Epistle. A Deacon reads the Gospel. The readings are ordinarily selected from the following list, except that on a major Feast, or on a Sunday, the Presiding Bishop may select readings from the Proper of the Day if they are appropriate.

Old Testament	Isaiah 61:1-8, or Isaiah 42:1-9
Suggested Psalms	99, or 40:1-14, or 100
Epistle	Hebrews 5:1-10, or 1 Timothy 3:1-7, or 2 Corinthians 3:4-9
Gospel	John 20:19-23, or John 17:1-9, 18-21, or Luke 24:44-49a

The Sermon

After the Sermon, the Congregation sings a Hymn.

The Examination

All now sit, except the Bishop-elect, who stands facing the Bishops. The Bishop-elect is questioned by one or more of the participating Bishops.

Bishop   My brother, the People have affirmed their trust in you by acclaiming your election. Will you fulfill this trust, in obedience to Christ?

Answer   I will obey Christ, and will serve in his Name.

Bishop   Will you be faithful in prayer, and in the study of Holy Scripture, that you may have the mind of Christ?

Answer   I will, for he is my help.

Bishop   Will you boldly proclaim and interpret the Gospel of Christ, enlightening the minds and stirring up the consciences of men?

Answer   I will, in the power of the Spirit.

Bishop   As a Chief Priest and Pastor, will you nourish your people from the riches of God's grace, pray for them without ceasing, and celebrate with them the Sacraments of our redemption?

Answer   I will, in the Name of Christ, the Shepherd and Bishop of our souls.

Bishop   Will you guard the faith, unity, and discipline of the Church?

Answer   I will, for the love of God.

Bishop	Will you join with your brother Bishops in the government of the whole Church? Will you sustain your fellow Presbyters and take counsel with them? Will you guide and strengthen the Deacons and all others who minister in the Church?
Answer	I will, by the grace given me.
Bishop	Will you defend, and show compassion to the poor and strangers and those who have no helper? And will you be merciful to all men?
Answer	I will for the sake of Christ Jesus.

All stand.

The Presiding Bishop then says

N., through these promises you have committed yourself to God, to serve his Church in the Office of Bishop. We therefore call upon you, chosen to be a guardian of the Church's faith, to lead us in confessing that faith.

[The version of the Creed which follows is recommended by the International Consultation on English Texts.]

Bishop-elect

We believe in one God.

Then all say together

We believe in one God,
the Father, the Almighty,
maker of heaven and earth,
of all that is seen and unseen.

We believe in one Lord, Jesus Christ,
the only Son of God,
eternally begotten of the Father,
God from God, Light from Light,
true God from true God,
begotten, not made, one in Being with the Father.
Through him all things were made.
For us men and for our salvation
he came down from heaven:
by the power of the Holy Spirit
he was born of the Virgin Mary, and became man.
For our sake he was crucified under Pontius Pilate;

he suffered, died, and was buried.
On the third day he rose again
in fulfillment of the Scriptures;
he ascended into heaven
and is seated at the right hand of the Father.
He will come again in glory to judge the living and the dead,
and his kingdom will have no end.

We believe in the Holy Spirit, the Lord, the Giver of Life,
who proceeds from the Father,
With the Father and Son he is worshiped and glorified.
He has spoken through the Prophets.
We believe in one holy catholic and apostolic Church.
We acknowledge one baptism
for the forgiveness of sins.
We look for the resurrection of the dead,
and the life of the world to come. Amen.

The Consecration of the Bishop

All continue to stand, except the Bishop-elect, who kneels before the Presiding Bishop. The other Bishops stand to the right and left of the Presiding Bishop.

The Hymn Veni Creator Spiritus, *or the Hymn* Veni Sancte Spiritus, *is sung.*

A period of silent prayer follows, the People still standing.

The Presiding Bishop then begins this Prayer of Consecration:

God and Father of our Lord Jesus Christ, Father of mercies and God of all comfort dwelling on high but having regard for the lowly, knowing all things before they come to pass: We give you thanks that from the beginning you have gathered and prepared a people to be heirs of the covenant of Abraham, and have raised up prophet, kings, and priests, never leaving your temple untended. We praise you also that from the creation you have graciously accepted the ministry of those whom you have chosen.

The Presiding Bishop and other Bishops now lay their hands upon the head of the Bishop-elect, and say together

Pour out now upon N. the power of that princely Spirit whom you bestowed upon your beloved Son Jesus Christ, with whom he endowed the Apostles, and by whom your Church is built up in every place, to the glory and unceasing praise of your Name.

The Presiding Bishop continues

To you, O Father, all hearts are open; fill, we pray, the heart of this your servant whom you have chosen to be a Bishop in your Church, with such love of you and of all the people, that he may feed and tend the flock of Christ, and exercise without reproach the high priesthood to which you have called him: serving before you day and night in the ministry of reconciliation, offering the holy gifts, and wisely overseeing the life and work of the Church. In all things may he present before you the acceptable offering of a pure, and gentle, and holy life; through Jesus Christ your Son, to whom with you and the Holy Spirit be honor and power and glory in the Church, now and for ever.

> *The People in a loud voice respond AMEN.*
> *The new Bishop now stands, and the rest of the vestments of his office are put upon him.*
> *The Bible is then presented; after which he may be given other symbols of office.*

The Peace

> *The Presiding Bishop turns the new Bishop toward the Congregation and presents him to his People.*
> *The Clergy and People offer their applause.*
> *The new Bishop then says*

The Peace of the Lord be always with you.

> *Answer*   And also with you.

The Presiding Bishop, and other Bishops, now greet the new Bishop. He may then greet other members of the Clergy, and his family, as convenient. Meanwhile, the People may greet one another.

At the Celebration of the Eucharist

> *The new Bishop says the Offertory Sentence.*
> *Then, standing at the Lord's Table as chief celebrant, and joined by Bishops and other ministers, he proceeds with the celebration of the Eucharist.*

After Communion

> *In place of the usual post-communion Prayer, one of the Bishops leads the People in the following Prayer:*

Almighty Father, we thank you for feeding us with the holy food of the Body and Blood of your Son, and for uniting us through him in the fellowship of your Holy Spirit. We thank you for raising up among us faithful servants for the ministry of your Word and Sacraments. We pray that *N.* may be to us an effective example in word and action, in love and patience, and in holiness of life. Grant that we, with him, may serve you now, and always rejoice in your glory ; through Jesus Christ your Son our Lord, who lives and reigns with you and the Holy Spirit, one God, now and for ever. Amen.

The new Bishop dismisses the People with this Blessing, first saying

	Our help is in the Name of the Lord:
Answer	The Maker of heaven and earth.
New Bishop	Blessed be the Name of the Lord.
Answer	From this time forth for evermore.
New Bishop	The blessing, mercy, and grace of God Almighty, the Father, the Son, and the Holy Spirit, be upon you, and remain with you for ever. *Amen.*

The Hymn Te Deum laudamus *is then sung as an act of thanksgiving.*

Additional Directions and Suggestions

The celebration of the Holy Eucharist at an Ordination may be according to the 1928 Liturgy, or any other Liturgy of this Church authorized for public worship. In the former case, the Prayer for the Whole State of Christ's Church and the General Confession are to be omitted, the service proceeding at once from the Offertory to "Lift up your hearts," and what follows. If another Liturgy is used, the Penitential Order and the Prayer of Intercession are omitted. In all cases, the Summary of the Law, the Gloria in excelsis, and the usual post-communion Prayer are not to be used with this service of Ordination.

After the Old Testament Lesson, and after the Epistle, a Psalm, Hymn, or Canticle is sung or said.

The Hymn to the Holy Spirit before the Prayer of Consecration of the Bishop may be sung responsively between a Bishop and the Congregation, or in some other convenient manner.

Immediately after the People's *Amen* to the Consecration Prayer, and while the new Bishop is being clothed with the vesture and insignia of the Episcopate, organ or other instrumental music may be used.

In addition to the Bible, he may be presented with a Pectoral Cross, Pastoral Staff, or other suitable symbols. It is appropriate that Church bells be rung when he is presented to the People.

At the Offertory, the Deacons and other assisting ministers prepare the Lord's Table, placing the Bread and Wine upon it. For the Eucharistic Prayer, it is appropriate that some of the consecrating Bishops, and representative Presbyters of the Diocese, stand with the new Bishop at the altar as fellow-ministers of the Sacrament.

The newly-ordained Bishop, assisted by other Ministers, shall distribute Holy Communion to the People, who shall always be allowed opportunity to communicate. Since there are normally many communicants at such a service, advantage should be taken of the presence of a large number of Bishops, Priests, and Deacons to arrange for the orderly and expeditious administration of Communion ; and, when necessary, at several different places in the Church.

When two or more Bishops are to be ordained at the same time, each shall have his own Presenters; and the Presentation, including the Promise of Conformity and the Acclamation of the People, shall take place separately for each Bishop-elect. Thereafter, in the Litany and subsequent parts of the service, references to the Bishop-elect in the singular shall be changed to the plural where necessary. All the Bishops-elect are to be examined together and shall lead the Creed in unison. During the Prayer of Consecration, the sentence, "Pour out now, etc.," is to be repeated in full over each Candidate while the Presiding Bishop and other Bishops lay their hands on his head. The new Bishops shall all join in the Peace and in the celebration of the Eucharist, one of them being designated to preside as chief celebrant.

The Bishops who are present shall not depart without signing the Letters of Consecration.

At the Ordination of a Priest

When the Bishop is to confer Holy Orders, at least two Presbyters shall be present.

From the beginning of the service until the Offertory, it is desirable that a seat for the Bishop be placed close to the People, and facing them, so that all may see and hear what is done in the Ordination.

The Ordinand is to be vested in a surplice or alb, without stole, tippet, or other vesture distinctive of ecclesiastical or academic rank or order.

When the Candidate is presented, his full name (designated by the symbol *N.N.*) shall be used. Thereafter, it is appropriate to refer to him only by the Christian name by which he wishes to be known.

The family of the newly Ordained may receive Communion before other members of the Congregation. And opportunity shall be given to the People to communicate.

Additional Directions and Suggestions are on pages 310-311.

The Ordination of a Priest

A Psalm, or Hymn, or Anthem may be sung during the entrance of the Ministers. The People being assembled, and all standing, the Bishop says

Blessed be God: Father, Son, and Holy Spirit.

People

And blessed be his Kingdom, now and for ever. Amen.

From Easter Day through the Day of Pentecost, he says instead
Alleluia! Christ is risen.
People
The Lord is risen indeed. Alleluia!
Bishop

Almighty God, to you all hearts are open, all desires known, and from you no secrets are hid; cleanse the thoughts of our hearts by the inspiration of your Holy Spirit, that we may perfectly love you, and worthily magnify your holy Name; through Christ our Lord. *Amen.*

The Presentation

The Bishop sits. A Priest and a Lay Person, standing before the Bishop, present to him the one proposed for ordination, saying

Reverend Father in God, on behalf of the Clergy and People of the Diocese of *N.*, we present to you *N.N.* to be ordained a Priest in Christ's Holy Catholic Church.

Bishop

Has he been selected in accordance with the Canons of this Church? And do you believe his manner of life to be suitable to the exercise of this Ministry?

Presenters

We certify to you that he has satisfied the requirements of the Canons, and we believe him qualified for this Order.

The Bishop says to the Person presented

Will you be loyal to the Doctrine, Discipline, and Worship of Christ as this Church has received them? And will you, in accordance with the Canons of this

Church, obey your Bishop and other Ministers who may have authority over you and your work?

> *Answer*   I am willing and ready to do so.
> *The Bishop stands and says to the People*

Dear friends in Christ, you know the importance of this Ministry, and the weight of your responsibility in presenting *N.N.* for ordination to the sacred Priesthood. Therefore, if any of you knows any impediment or crime because of which we should not proceed, let him come forward and make it known.

> *If no objection is made, the Bishop continues*

I ask you then to declare your will that this Ministry be conferred on him. Is he worthy?

> *The People respond with a loud voice saying these or other words, several times:*

He is worthy.

> *The Bishop then calls the People to prayer with these or similar words:*

Let us pray to Almighty God for his blessing upon us and all men, and for the gift of his grace to those who are called to the ordained Ministry of his Church.

> *All kneel, and the Person appointed leads the Litany for the Ministry of the Church, or some other approved Litany. At the end of the Litany, after the Kyries, the Bishop stands and reads the Collect for the Day, or the following Collect, or both, first saying*

	The Lord be with you.
Answer	And also with you.
Bishop	Let us pray.

The Collect

Almighty God, the giver of all good gifts, who of your divine providence appointed various Orders in your Church: Give your grace, we humbly pray, to this person now called to the Order of Priests: and so replenish him with the truth of your doctrine, and endue him with holiness of life, that he may faithfully serve before you to the glory of your great Name, and to the benefit of your holy Church; through Jesus Christ our Lord, who lives and reigns with you in the unity of the Holy Spirit, one God, now and ever. *Amen.*

At the Ministry of the Word

Three Lessons are to be read. Lay persons read the Old Testament Lesson and the Epistle. A Deacon or Priest reads the Gospel. The readings are ordinarily selected from the following list, except that on a major Feast, or on a Sunday, the Bishop may select readings from the Proper of the Day if they are appropriate.

Old Testament	Isaiah 6:1-8, or Numbers 11:16—17, 24-25 (omitting the final clause)
Suggested Psalms	43, or 132:8-19
Epistle	1 Peter 5:1-4***, or Ephesians 4:11-16, or Philippians 4:4-9
Gospel	Matthew 9:35-38, or John 10:11-18, or John 6:35-38

The Sermon

The Congregation then says or sings the Nicene Creed.

The Examination

All are seated except the Ordinand, who stands before the Bishop. The Bishop addresses him as follows:

My brother, the Church is the family of God, the body of Christ, and the temple of the Holy Spirit. All baptized people are called to make Christ known to men as Savior and Lord, and to share in the renewing of his world. Now you are being called to work, together with your Bishop and fellow-Presbyters, as a pastor, priest, and teacher in this ministry, and to take your share in the councils of the Church.

As Priest, it will be your task to proclaim the Gospel and to apply it, by your words and in your life. You are to love and serve the people among whom you work, caring alike for young and old, strong and weak, rich and poor. You are to preach, to declare God's forgiveness to penitent sinners, to baptize, to preside at the celebration of the mysteries of Christ's Body and Blood, and to perform the other ministrations entrusted to you.

In all that you do, you are to nourish Christ's people and strengthen them to glorify God in this life and in the life to come.

My brother, do you believe that you are truly called by God and his Church to this Priesthood?

*** It is to be noted that where the word *elder*, *elders*, and *fellow-elder* appear in translations of 1 Peter 5:1, the original Greek terms *presbyter, presbyters*, and *fellow-presbyter* are to be substituted.

Answer	I believe I am so called.
Bishop	Do you now in the presence of the Church commit yourself to this trust and responsibility?
Answer	I do.
Bishop	Will you be faithful in prayer, and in the reading and study of the Holy Scriptures?
Answer	I will, for in God's Word is my trust.
Bishop	Will you look for Christ, and serve him, in your fellow men?
Answer	I will.
Bishop	Will you do your best to pattern your life [and that of your family* in accordance with the teachings of Christ, so that you may be a wholesome example to your people?
Answer	I will, God being my helper.
Bishop	May the Lord who has given you the will to do these things, give you the grace and power to perform them.

The Consecration of the Priest

All now stand except the Ordinand, who kneels facing the Bishop and the Presbyters who stand to the right and left of the Bishop.

The Hymn Veni Creator Spiritus, *or the Hymn* Veni Sancte Spiritus, *is sung.*

A Period Of Silent Prayer Follows, The People Still Standing. The Bishop Then Says This Prayer Of Consecration:

God and Father of all, we praise you for your infinite love in calling us to be a holy people in the kingdom of your Son Jesus our Lord, who is the image of your eternal and invisible glory, the firstborn among many brethren, and the head of the Church. We thank you that by his death he has overcome death, and having ascended into heaven, has poured his gifts abundantly upon your people, making some Apostles, some Prophets, some Evangelists, some Pastors and Teachers, to equip the saints for the work of ministry and the building up of his body.

Here the Bishop lays his hands upon the head of the one being ordained, the Priests who are present also laying on their right hands. At the same time the Bishop prays

Therefore, O Father, through Jesus Christ your Son, give your Holy Spirit to *N.*; fill him with grace and power, and make him a Priest in your Church.

---

* *or,* household; *or* community.

The Bishop then continues

May he glorify you in the midst of your people, and offer spiritual sacrifices acceptable to you. May he boldly proclaim the Gospel of salvation, and rightly administer the Sacraments of the new covenant. Make him a faithful pastor, a patient teacher, and a wise councilor. Grant that in all things he may serve without reproach, so that your people may be strengthened and your Name glorified; through Jesus Christ our Lord, who with you and the Holy Spirit lives and reigns, one God, for ever and ever.

The People in a loud voice respond AMEN.

The new Priest is then vested according to his Order. The Bishop then gives him a Bible, saying

Receive this Bible as a sign of the authority given you to preach the Word of God and to administer his holy Sacraments. Forget not the trust committed to you as a Priest of the Church of God.

The Peace

The Bishop and the other Clergy present now greet the newly Ordained.
The new Priest then says to the Congregation

The Peace of the Lord be always with you.

Answer   And also with you.

He may then greet his family, or others, as may be convenient. Meanwhile the People may greet one another.

At the Celebration of the Eucharist

The Liturgy continues with the Offertory. Standing at the Lord's Table with the Bishop and other Clergy, the newly Ordained joins in the celebration of the Holy Eucharist.

After Communion

In place of the usual post-communion Prayer, the following Prayer is said:

Almighty Father, we thank you for feeding us with the holy food of the Body and Blood of your Son, and for uniting us through him in the fellowship of your Holy Spirit. We thank you for raising up among us faithful servants for the ministry of your Word and Sacraments. We pray that *N.* may be to us an effective example in word and action, in love and patience, and in holiness of life. Grant that we, with him, may serve you now, and always rejoice in your glory; through Jesus Christ your Son our Lord, who lives and reigns with you and the Holy Spirit, one God, now and for ever. *Amen.*

> *The Bishop then asks the new Priest to bless the People.*
> *The People kneel; and the new Priest says*

The Peace of God, which passes all understanding, keep your hearts and minds in the knowledge and love of God, and of his Son Jesus Christ our Lord: And the Blessing of God Almighty, the Father, the Son, and the Holy Spirit, be among you, and remain with you always. *Amen.*

> *A Deacon (or a Priest) dismisses the assembly.*

Additional Directions and Suggestions

The celebration of the Holy Eucharist at an Ordination may be according to the 1928 Liturgy, or any other Liturgy of this Church authorized for public worship. In the former case, the Prayer for the Whole State of Christ's Church and the General Confession are to be omitted, the service proceeding at once from the Offertory to "Lift up your hearts," and what follows. If another Liturgy is used, the Penitential Order and the Prayer of Intercession are omitted. In all cases, the Summary of the Law, the Gloria in excelsis, and the usual post-communion Prayer are not to be used with this service of Ordination.

Provision is made herein for two Presenters; more may be appropriate on occasion, with the permission of the Bishop.

After the Old Testament Lesson, and after the Epistle, a Psalm, Hymn, or Canticle is sung or said.

The Hymn to the Holy Spirit before the Prayer of Consecration of the Priest may be sung responsively between the Bishop and the Congregation, or in some other convenient manner.

The stole worn about the neck, or other insignia of the Office of Priest, shall be placed upon the new Priest after the Ordination Prayer is completed, immediately before the Bible is presented.

After the Presentation of the Bible, other instruments and symbols of his office may be given him.

At the Offertory, it is appropriate that the bread and wine be brought to the Altar by the family or friends of the newly Ordained.

At the Eucharistic Consecration, the new Priest and other Priests shall stand at the Altar with the Bishop as associates and fellow-ministers of the Sacrament, and shall communicate with him. After the Lord's Prayer, the new Priest shall, and other Priests may, join the Bishop in breaking the consecrated Bread.

If two or more Candidates are to be ordained together, each shall have his own Presenters. They may be presented together, or in succession, as the Bishop may direct. Thereafter, references to the Ordinand in the singular shall be changed to the plural where necessary. The Ordinands are to be examined together. During the Ordination Prayer, the Bishop is to say over each Ordinand separately the words,

> O Father, through Jesus Christ your Son, give your Holy Spirit to *N.*; fill him with grace and power, and make him a Priest in your Church.

Likewise the Bishop and Priests are to lay their hands on each Ordinand's head when these words are said. A Bible shall be given, and the words, "Receive this Bible", etc., shall also be said to each. All those newly ordained shall take part in the Peace, and shall join the Bishop and other Priests at the altar for the Consecration. Similarly, all the new Priests shall break the consecrated Bread and receive Holy Communion.

At the Ordination of a Deacon

When the Bishop is to confer Holy Orders, at least two Presbyters shall be present.

From the beginning of the service until the Offertory, it is desirable that a seat for the Bishop be placed close to the People, and facing them, so that all may see and hear what is done in the Ordination.

The Ordinand is to be vested in a surplice or alb, without tippet or other vesture distinctive of ecclesiastical or academic rank or office.

When the Candidate is presented, his full name (designated by the symbol *N.N.*) shall be used. Thereafter, it is appropriate to refer to him only by the Christian name by which he wishes to be known.

After receiving Holy Communion, the new Deacon shall assist in the distribution of the Sacrament, ministering either the consecrated Bread or Wine, or both.

The family of the newly Ordained may receive Communion before other members of the Congregation. And opportunity shall be given to the People to communicate.

Additional Directions and Suggestions are on pages 316-317.

The Ordination of a Deacon

A Psalm, or Hymn, or Anthem may be sung during the entrance of the Ministers. The People being assembled, and all standing, the Bishop says

Blessed be God : Father, Son, and Holy Spirit.

> *People*

And blessed be his Kingdom, now and for ever. Amen.

> *From Easter Day through the Day of Pentecost, he says instead*

Alleluia! Christ is risen.

> *People*

The Lord is risen indeed. Alleluia!

> *Bishop*

Almighty God, to you all hearts are open, all desires known, and from you no secrets are hid; cleanse the thoughts of our hearts by the inspiration of your Holy Spirit, that we may perfectly love you, and worthily magnify your holy Name; through Christ our Lord. *Amen.*

The Presentation

> *The Bishop sits. A Priest and a Lay Person, standing before the Bishop, present to him the one proposed for ordination, saying*

Reverend Father in God, on behalf of the Clergy and People of the Diocese of *N.*, we present to you *N.N.* to be ordained a Deacon in Christ's Holy Catholic Church.

> *Bishop*

Has he been selected in accordance with the Canons of this Church? And do you believe his manner of life to be suitable to the exercise of this Ministry?

> *Presenters*

We certify to you that he has satisfied the requirements of the Canons, and we believe him qualified for this Order.

> *The Bishop says to the Person presented*

Will you be loyal to the Doctrine, Discipline, and Worship of Christ as this Church has received them? And will you, in accordance with the Canons of this Church, obey your Bishop and other Ministers who may have authority over you and your work?

Answer I am willing and ready to do so.
The Bishop stands and says to the People

Dear friends in Christ, you know the importance of this Ministry, and the weight of your responsibility in presenting *N.N.* for ordination to the sacred Order of Deacons. Therefore, if any of you knows any impediment or crime because of which we should not proceed, let him come forward and make it known.

If no objection is made, the Bishop continues

I ask you then to declare your will that this Ministry be conferred on him. Is he worthy?

The People respond with a loud voice saying these or other words, several times:

He is worthy.

The Bishop then calls the People to prayer with these or similar words:

Let us pray to Almighty God for his blessing upon us and all men, and for the gift of his grace to those who are called to the ordained Ministry of his Church.

All kneel, and the Person appointed leads the Litany for the Ministry of the Church, or some other approved Litany. At the end of the Litany, after the Kyries, the Bishop stands and reads the Collect for the Day, or the following Collect, or both, first saying

	The Lord be with you.
Answer	And also with you.
Bishop	Let us pray.

The Collect

Almighty God, the giver of all good gifts, who of your divine providence appointed various Orders in your Church: Give your grace, we humbly pray, to this person now called to the Order of Deacons: and so replenish him with the truth of your doctrine, and endue him with holiness of life, that he may faithfully serve before you to the glory of your great Name, and to the benefit of your holy Church; through Jesus Christ our Lord, who lives and reigns with you in the unity of the Holy Spirit, one God, now and ever. *Amen.*

At the Ministry of the Word

Three Lessons are to be read. Lay persons read the Old Testament Lesson and the Epistle. A Deacon or Priest reads the Gospel. The readings are ordinarily selected from the following list, except that on a major Feast, or on a Sunday, the Bishop may select readings from the Proper of the Day if they are appropriate.

Old Testament	Jeremiah 1:4-9, or Ecclesiasticus (Sirach) 39:1-8.
Suggested Psalms	84, or 119:33-40
Epistle	2 Corinthians 4:1-2, or 1 Timothy 3:8-13, or Acts 6:2-7
Gospel	Luke 12:35-38, or Luke 22:24-27

The Sermon

The Congregation then says or sings the Nicene Creed.

The Examination

All are seated except the Ordinand, who stands before the Bishop. The Bishop addresses him as follows:

My brother, every Christian is called to follow Jesus Christ, serving God the Father in his world, through the power of the Holy Spirit. God now calls you to a special ministry of servanthood directly under your Bishop. You are to serve all people, particularly the poor, the weak, the sick, and the lonely.

As Deacon in the Church, you are to study the Holy Scriptures and to model your life upon God's Word. You are to be ready to make him known to those among whom you live, and work, and worship. You are to interpret to the Church the needs, concerns, and hopes of the world. You are to assist the Bishop and Priests in public worship and in the ministration of the Sacraments. By your teaching and your life, you are to show Christ's people that in serving the helpless they are serving Christ himself.

My brother, do you believe that you are truly called by God and his Church to the life and work of a Deacon?

Answer	I believe I am so called.
Bishop	Do you now in the presence of the Church commit yourself to this trust and responsibility?
Answer	I do.
Bishop	Will you be faithful in prayer, and in the reading and study of the Holy Scriptures?
Answer	I will, for in God's Word is my trust.
Bishop	Will you look for Christ, and serve him, in your fellow men?
Answer	I will.

Bishop	Will you do your best to pattern your life [and that of your *family*†] in accordance with the teachings of Christ, so that you may be a wholesome example to your people?
Answer	I will, God being my helper.
Bishop	May the Lord by his grace uphold you in the service he lays upon you.

The Consecration of the Deacon

All now stand except the Ordinand, who kneels facing the Bishop.

The Hymn Veni Creator Spiritus, *or the Hymn* Veni Sancte Spiritus, *is sung.*

A period of silent prayer follows, the People still standing. The Bishop then says this Prayer of Consecration:

O God, most merciful Father, we praise you for sending your Son, Jesus Christ, who took on himself the form of a servant, and humbled himself, becoming obedient even to death on the Cross. We praise you that you have highly exalted him, and made him Lord of all; and that through him we know that he who would be great must be servant of all. We praise you for the many ministries in your Church, and for calling this your servant to the Order of Deacon.

Here the Bishop lays his hands upon the head of the one being ordained, and prays

Therefore, O Father, through Jesus Christ your Son, give your Holy Spirit to *N.*; fill him with grace and power, and make him a Deacon in your Church.

The Bishop then continues

Make him, O Lord, modest and humble, strong and constant to observe the discipline of Christ. Let his life and teaching so reflect your commandments, that through him many may come to know you and love you. As your Son came not to be served but to serve, may this Deacon share in his service, and come to the unending glory of him who, with you and the Holy Spirit, lives and reigns, one God, for ever and ever.

The People in a loud voice respond AMEN.

The new Deacon is then vested according to his Order. The Bishop then gives him a Bible, saying

Receive this Bible as the sign of your authority to proclaim God's Word and to assist in the ministration of his holy Sacraments.

---

† *or,* household; *or* community.

The Peace

The Bishop and the other Clergy present now greet the newly Ordained. The Bishop then says to the Congregation

The Peace of the Lord be always with you.

Answer   And also with you.

The new Deacon may then greet his family, or others, as may be convenient. Meanwhile the People may greet one another.

At the Celebration of the Eucharist

The Liturgy continues with the Offertory; the newly-ordained Deacon prepares the Bread, pours sufficient Wine (and a little water) into the Chalice, and places the vessels on the Holy Table. The Bishop, at the Table, proceeds to the Consecration and Communion, which the newly Ordained shall receive with him.

After Communion

In place of the usual post-communion Prayer, the following Prayer is said:

Almighty Father, we thank you for feeding us with the holy food of the Body and Blood of your Son, and for uniting us through him in the fellowship of your Holy Spirit. We thank you for raising up among us faithful servants for the ministry of your Word and Sacraments. We pray that N. may be to us an effective example in word and action, in love and patience, and in holiness of life. Grant that we, with him, may serve you now, and always rejoice in your glory; through Jesus Christ your Son our Lord, who lives and reigns with you and the Holy Spirit, one God, now and for ever. *Amen.*

The Bishop then blesses the People, after which the new Deacon dismisses them.

Deacon   Go forth into the world rejoicing in the power of the Spirit.

Thanks be to God.

Additional Directions and Suggestions

The celebration of the Holy Eucharist at an Ordination may be according to the 1928 Liturgy, or any other Liturgy of this Church authorized for public worship. In the former case, the Prayer of the Whole State of Christ's Church and the

General Confession are to be omitted, the service proceeding at once from the Offertory to "Lift up your hearts," and what follows. If another Liturgy is used, the Penitential Order and the Prayer of Intercession are omitted. In all cases, the Summary of the Law, the Gloria in excelsis, and the usual post-communion Prayer are not to be used with this service of Ordination.

Provision is made herein for two Presenters; more may be appropriate on occasion, with the permission of the Bishop.

After the Old Testament Lesson, and after the Epistle, a Psalm, Hymn, or Canticle is sung or said.

The Hymn to the Holy Spirit before the Prayer of Consecration of the Deacon may be sung responsively between the Bishop and the Congregation, or in some other convenient manner.

The stole worn over the left shoulder, or other insignia of the Office of Deacon, shall be placed upon the new Deacon after the Ordination Prayer is completed, immediately before the Bible is given.

At the Offertory, it is appropriate that the bread and wine be brought to the Altar by the family or friends of the newly Ordained.

If other Deacons are present, it is appropriate that they assist the new Deacon at the Offertory.

If two or more candidates are to be ordained together, each may have his own Presenters. They may be presented together, or in succession, as the Bishop may direct. Thereafter, references to the Ordinand in the singular shall be changed to the plural where necessary. The Ordinands are to be examined together. During the Ordination Prayer, the Bishop is to say over each Ordinand separately the words,

> O Father, through Jesus Christ your Son, give your Holy Spirit to *N.*;
> fill him with grace and power, and make him a Deacon in your Church.

Likewise, he is to lay his hands on the head of each one while saying these words. A Bible shall be given, and the words "Receive this Bible", etc., shall also be said to each.

After participating in the Peace, the Deacons go to the altar for the Offertory. If there are many Deacons, some can assist in the Offertory, and others can administer Holy Communion. One appointed by the Bishop is to say the Dismissal.

It is appropriate for Deacons to consume the remaining Elements of the Sacrament and to cleanse the vessels. Also, when desired, Deacons may be appointed to carry the Sacrament and minister Holy Communion to communicants who, because of sickness or other grave cause, could not be present at the celebration.

A Litany for the Ministry

To be used at Ordinations as directed; or after the Collects at Morning or Evening Prayer; or separately.

God the Father,
Have mercy on us.
God the Son,
Have mercy on us.
God the Holy Spirit,
Have mercy on us.
Holy Trinity, one God,
Have mercy on us.

We humbly pray that you will hear us, O Lord; and that you will send peace to the whole world, which you have reconciled to yourself by the ministry of your Son, Jesus,
Lord, hear our prayer.
That you will guide all in civil authority to establish justice and maintain it for all men,
Lord, hear our prayer.
That you will heal the divisions of your visible Church, that all may be one,
Lord, hear our prayer.
That you will grant to your People the forgiveness of sins, and give us grace to amend our lives,
Lord, hear our prayer.
That you will lead every member of your Church in his particular vocation and ministry to serve you in a true and godly life,
Lord, hear our prayer.
That you will raise up able ministers for your Church, that the Gospel may be made known to all people,
Lord, hear our prayer.
That you will inspire all Bishops, Priests, and Deacons with your love, that they may hunger for truth, and thirst after righteousness,
Lord, hear our prayer.
That you will fill them with compassion, and move them to care for all your people,
Lord, hear our prayer.

At the ordination of a bishop the following is said:

That you will bless our brother *N.*, elected bishop in your Church, and pour your grace upon him, that he may faithfully fulfill the duties of this Ministry, build up your Church, and glorify your Name, Lord, hear our prayer.

At the ordination of deacons or of priests is said:

That you will bless your servant(s), *N. (N.)*, now to be admitted to the Order of Deacons (*or* Priests), and pour your grace upon *him*, that *he* may faithfully fulfill the duties of this Ministry, build up your Church, and glorify your Name,
Lord, hear our prayer.

As appropriate, the following suffrage is added, adapted when necessary.

That you will bless his *family* [the members of his household *or* community], and adorn them with all Christian virtues,
Lord, hear our prayer.

That by the indwelling of your Holy Spirit you will sustain those who have been called to the ministry of your Church, and encourage them to persevere to the end,
Lord, hear our prayer.
That we with [your blessed servant, St. ————, and] all your saints who have served you in the past, may be gathered into your unending kingdom,
Lord, hear our prayer.
Lord, have mercy.
Christ, have mercy.
Lord, have mercy.

The Bishop stands and says

	The Lord be with you.
Answer	And also with you.
Bishop	Let us pray.

The Bishop says the appointed Collect.

The Litany Noted for Chant

God the Fa-ther, *Have mer-cy on us.*

God the Son, *Have mer-cy on us.*

God the Ho-ly Spir-it, *Have mer-cy on us.*

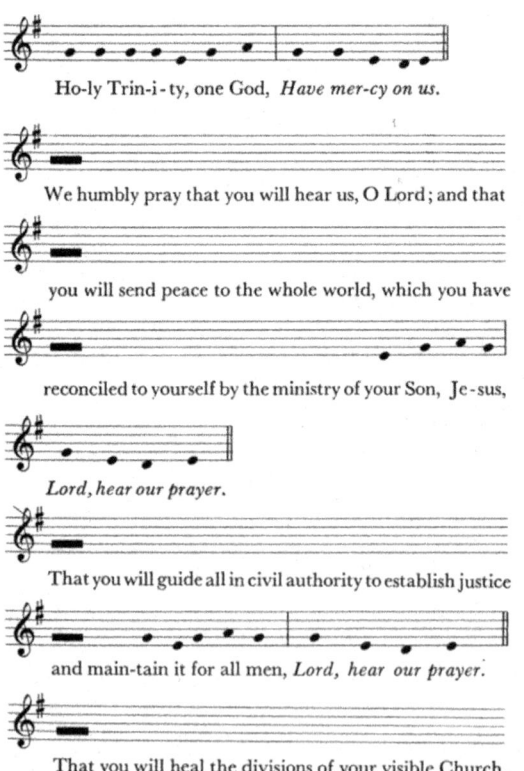

Ho-ly Trin-i-ty, one God, *Have mer-cy on us.*

We humbly pray that you will hear us, O Lord; and that

you will send peace to the whole world, which you have

reconciled to yourself by the ministry of your Son, Je-sus,

Lord, hear our prayer.

That you will guide all in civil authority to establish justice

and main-tain it for all men, *Lord, hear our prayer.*

That you will heal the divisions of your visible Church,

The Ordination of Bishops, Priests, and Deacons 321

that all may be one, *Lord, hear our prayer.*

That you will grant to your People the forgiveness of sins,

and give us grace to a-mend our lives, *Lord, hear our prayer*

That you will lead every member of your Church in his

particular vocation and ministry to serve you in a true and

god-ly life, *Lord, hear our prayer.*

That you will raise up able ministers for your Church,

that the Gospel may be made known to all peo-ple.

Lord, hear our prayer. That you will inspire all Bishops, Priests, and Deacons with your love, that they may hunger for truth, and thirst af-ter right-eous-ness.

Lord, hear our prayer.

That you will fill them with compassion, and move them to care for all your peo-ple, *Lord, hear our prayer.*

At the ordination of a bishop the following is sung:

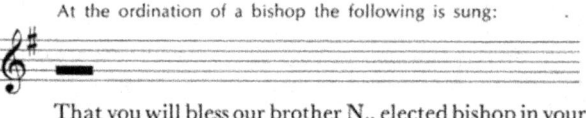

That you will bless our brother N., elected bishop in your

The Ordination of Bishops, Priests, and Deacons 323

Church, and pour your grace upon him, that he may faith-

fully fulfill the duties of this Ministry, build up your

Church, and glo-ri-fy your Name, *Lord, hear our prayer.*

At the ordination of deacons or of priests is sung:

That you will bless your servant(s), N. (N.), now to be

admitted to Order of Deacons (or Priests), and pour

your grace upon him, that he may faithfully fulfill the

duties of this Ministry, build up your Church, and

glo - ri - fy your Name, *Lord, hear our prayer.*

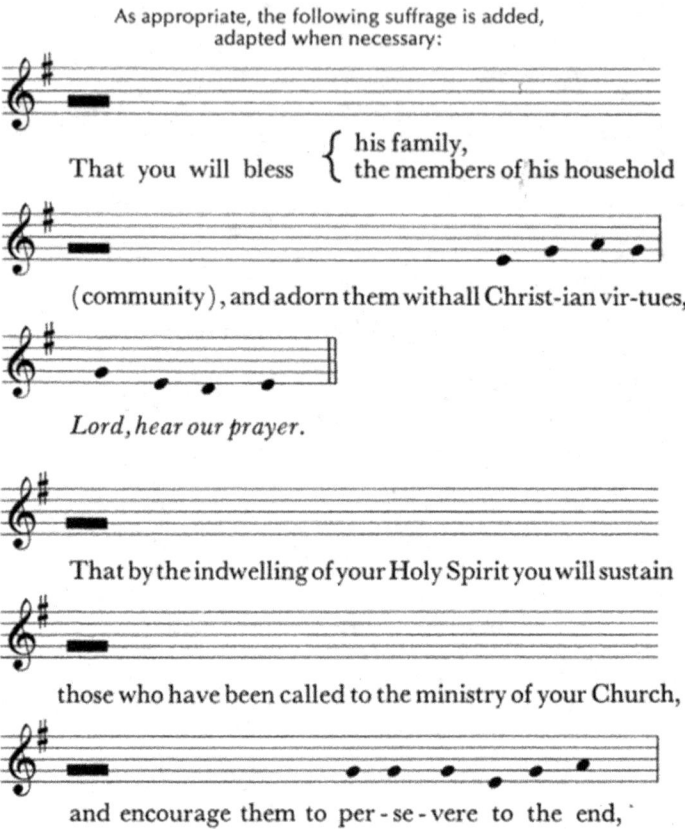

As appropriate, the following suffrage is added, adapted when necessary:

That you will bless { his family, / the members of his household (community), and adorn them with all Christian virtues,

Lord, hear our prayer.

That by the indwelling of your Holy Spirit you will sustain those who have been called to the ministry of your Church, and encourage them to persevere to the end,

The Ordination of Bishops, Priests, and Deacons 325

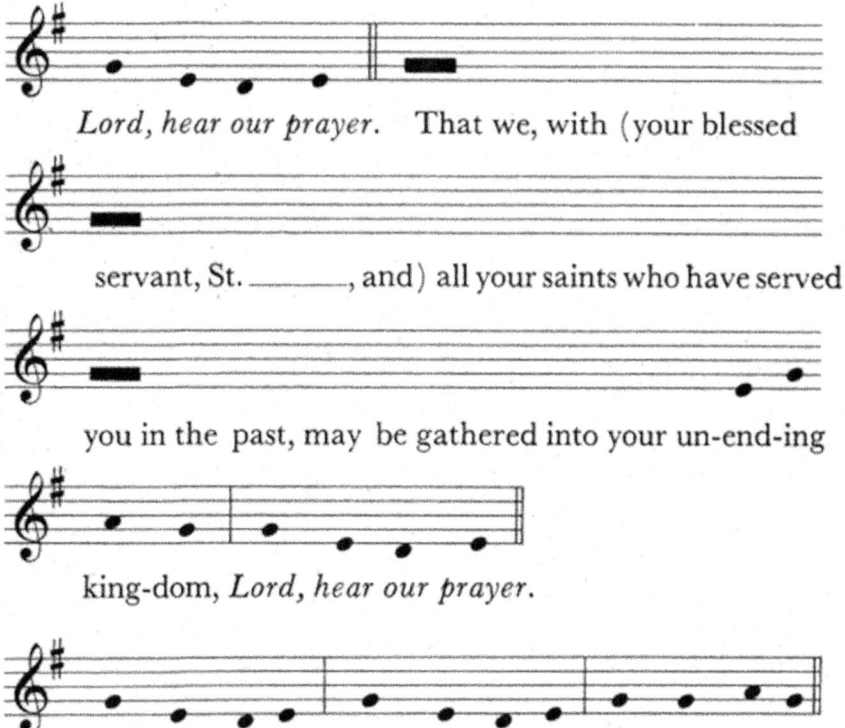

Lord, hear our prayer. That we, with (your blessed servant, St. _____, and) all your saints who have served you in the past, may be gathered into your un-end-ing king-dom, *Lord, hear our prayer.*

Lord, have mer-cy, *Christ, have mer-cy.* Lord, have mer-cy.

The Bishop stands and says:

The Lord be with you. *And also with you.* Let us pray.

The Bishop says the appointed Collect.

If he sings the Collect to the usual tone, the Conclusion is as follows:

... the Ho-ly Spir-it, one God, now and ever. *A-men.*

www.ingramcontent.com/pod-product-compliance
Lightning Source LLC
Chambersburg PA
CBHW070746020526
44116CB00032B/1985